What
Makes
Women
Happy

Also by Fay Weldon

FAY WELDON

What Makes Women Happy

CHICAGO
REVIEW
PRESS

Published by arrangement with HarperCollins Publishers Ltd.

© 2006 by Fay Weldon

All rights reserved

This U.S. edition published in 2007 by

Chicago Review Press, Incorporated

814 North Franklin Street

Chicago, Illinois 60610

ISBN-13: 978-1-55652-681-7

ISBN-10: 1-55652-681-4

Printed in the United States of America

5 4 3 2 1

Contents

ONE

Sources of Happiness

Women can be wonderfully happy. When they're in love, when someone gives them flowers, when they've finally found the right pair of shoes and they even fit. I remember once, in love and properly loved, dancing round a room singing, *'They can't take this away from me.'* I remember holding the green shoes with the green satin ribbon (it was the sixties) to my bosom and rejoicing. I remember my joy when the midwife said, *'But this is the most beautiful baby I've ever seen. Look at him, he's golden!'*

The wonderful happiness lasts for ten minutes or so. After that little niggles begin to arise. *'Will he think I'm too fat?'* *'Are the flowers his way of saying goodbye?'* *'Do the shoes pinch?'* *'Will his allegedly separated wife take this away from me?'* *'Is solitary dancing a sign of insanity?'* *'How come I've produced so wonderful a baby – did they get the name tags wrong?'*

Anxiety and guilt come hot on the heels of happiness. So the brutal answer to what makes women happy is *'Nothing, not for more than ten minutes at a time.*' But the perfect ten minutes are worth living for, and the almost perfect hours that circle them are worth fighting for, and examining, the better to prolong them.

Ask women what makes them happy and they think for a minute and come up with a tentative list. It tends to run like this, and in this order:

Sex

Food

Friends

Family

Shopping

Chocolate

'Love' tends not to get a look in. Too unfashionable, or else taken for granted. 'Being in love' sometimes makes an appearance. 'Men' seem to surface as a source of aggravation, and surveys keep throwing up the notion that most women prefer chocolate to sex. But personally I suspect this response is given to entertain the pollsters. The only thing you can truly know about what people think, feel, do and consume, some theorize, is to examine the contents of their dustbins. Otherwise it's pretty much guesswork.

There are more subtle pleasures too, of course, which the polls never throw up. The sense of virtue when you *don't* have an éclair can be more satisfactory than the flavour and texture of cream, chocolate and pastry against the tongue. Rejecting a lover can give you more gratification than the physical pleasures of love-making. Being right when others are wrong can make you very happy indeed. We're not necessarily nice people.

Some women I know always bring chocolates when they're invited to dinner – and then sneer when the hostess actually eats one. That's what I mean by 'not nice'.

Sources of Unhappiness

We are all still creatures of the cave, although we live in loft apartments. Nature is in conflict with nurture. Anxiety and guilt cut in to spoil the fun as one instinct wars with another and with the way we are socialized. Women are born to be mothers, though many of us prefer to not take up the option. *The baby cries; we go. The man calls; 'Take me!' we cry.* Unless we are very strong indeed, physiology wins. We bleed monthly and the phases of the moon dictate our moods. We are hardwired to pick and choose amongst men when we are young, aiming for the best genetic material available. The 'love' of a woman for a man is nature's way of keeping her docile and at home. The 'love' of a man for a woman is protective and keeps him at home as long as she stays helpless. (If high-flying women, so amply able to look after themselves, are so often single, it can be no surprise.)

Or that is one way of looking at it. The other is to recognize that we are moral creatures too, long for justice, and civilized ourselves out of our gross species instincts long ago. We like to think correctly and behave in an orderly and socially aware manner. If sometimes we revert, stuff our mouths with goodies, grab what we can so our neighbour doesn't get it (*'Been to the sales lately?'*) or fall upon our best friend's boyfriend when left alone in the room with him, we feel ashamed of ourselves. Doing what comes naturally does not sit well with modern woman.

And so it is that in everyday female life, doubts, dilemmas and anxieties cut in, not grandiose whither-mankind stuff, just simple things such as:

Sex: *'Should I have done it?'*

Food: *'Should I have eaten it?'*

Friends/family: *'Why didn't I call her?'*

Shopping: *'Should I have bought it?'*

Chocolate: *'My God, did I actually eat all that?'*

But you can't lie awake at night worrying about these things. You have to get up in the morning and work, so you do.

But the voice of conscience, otherwise known as the voice of guilt, keeps up its nagging undercurrent. It drives some women to therapists in their attempt to silence it. But it's better to drive into a skid than try to steer out of it. If you don't want to feel guilty, don't do it. If you want to be happy, try being good.

What Makes Men Happy

Men have their own list when it comes to sources of happiness. 'The love of a good woman' is high in the ratings. Shopping and chocolate don't get much of a look in. Watching porn and looking at pretty girls in the street, if men are honest, feature large. These fondnesses of theirs (dismissed by women as 'addictions') can make women unhappy, break up marriages and make men wretched and secretive because the women they love get upset by them.

Women should not be upset. They should not expect men to behave like women. Men are creatures of the cave too. Porn is sex in theory, not in practice. It just helps a man get through the day. And many a woman too, come to that.

Porn excites to sex, sure. Sex incited by porn is not bad, just different. Tomorrow's sex is always going to be different from today's. In a long-term partnership there is room and time for all kinds. Sex can be tender, loving, companionable, a token of closeness and respect, the kind women claim to like.

Then it's romantic, intimate, and smacks of permanence. Sometimes sex is a matter of lust, release, excitement, anger, and the sense is that any woman could inspire it. It's macho, anti-domestic. Exciting. Don't resist the mood – try and match it. Tomorrow something else will surface more to your liking. Each sexual act will have a different feel to it, the two instincts in both of you being in variable proportions from night to night, week to week, year to year. It's rare for a couple's sexual energies to be exactly matched. But lucky old you if they are.

I have friends so anxious that they can't let the man in their life out of their sight in case he runs off with someone else. It's counter-productive. Some girls just do stop traffic in the street. So it's not you – so what? Men like looking at pretty girls in the street not because they long to sleep with them, or because given a choice between them and you they'd choose them, but because it's the instinct of the cave asserting itself. Pretty girls are there to be looked at speculatively by men and, if they have any sense, with generous appreciation by women. It's bad manners in men, I grant you, to do it too openly, especially if the woman objects, but not much worse than that.

This will not be enough, I know, to convince some women that for a husband or lover to watch porn is not a matter for shock-horror. But look at it like this. A newborn baby comes into the world with two urgent appetites: one is to feed, the other is to suck. Because the nipple is there to satisfy both appetites, the feeding/sucking distinction gets blurred for both mother and baby. If you are lucky, the baby's time at the breast or bottle is time enough to satisfy the sucking instinct. If you're not lucky, the baby, though fed to completion, cries, chafes and vomits yet goes on sucking desperately, as if it were monstrously hungry. At which point the wise mother goes to fetch a dummy, so everyone can get some peace. Then baby can suck, digest and sleep, all at the same time, blissfully. (Most babies simply toss the dummy out of the cot as soon as they're on solids and the sucking reflex fades, thus sparing the mother social disgrace.)

In the same way, in males, the instinct for love and the need for sexual gratification overlap but do not necessarily coincide. The capacity for love seems inborn; lust weighs in powerfully at puberty. The penis is there to satisfy both appetites. If you are lucky, the needs coincide in acts of domestic love; if you are not, your man's head turns automatically when a pretty girl passes in the street, or he goes to the porn channels on the computer. He is not to be blamed. Nor does it affect his relationship with you. Love is satisfied, sex isn't quite. He clutches the dummy.

An Unreliable Narrator

Bear in mind, of course, that you must take your instruction from a very flawed person. She wouldn't want to make you anxious by being perfect. Your writer spent last night in the spare room following a domestic row. Voices were raised, someone broke a glass, she broke the washing machine by trying to wrench open the door while it was in the middle of its spin cycle.

Domestic rows do not denote domestic unhappiness. They do suggest a certain volatility in a relationship. Sense might suggest that if the morning wakes to the lonely heaviness that denotes a row the night before, you have no business describing your marriage as 'happy'. But sense and experience also suggest that you have made your own contribution to the way you now feel. And the early sun beats in the windows and it seems an insult to your maker to maintain a grudge when the morning is so glorious.

You hear the sound of the vacuum cleaner downstairs. Soon it will be safe to go down and have a companionable breakfast without even putting on your shoes for fear of slivers of broken glass. Storms pass, the sun shines again. Yes, you are happy.

What the quarrel was about I cannot for the life of me remember.

Except of course now the washing machine doesn't work. When it comes to domestic machinery, retribution comes fast. In other areas of life it may come slowly. But it always does come, in terms of lost happiness, in distance from heaven, in the non-appearance of angels.

And since this book comes to your writer through the luminiferous aether, that notoriously flimsy and deceptive substance,

Victorian equivalent of the dark matter of which scientists now claim the universe is composed, what is said is open to interpretation. It is not the Law.

Why, Why?

Like it or not, we are an animal species. Darwinian principles apply. We have evolved into what we are today. We did not spring ready-made into the twenty-first century. The human female is born and bred to select a mate, have babies, nurture them and, having completed this task, die. That is why we adorn ourselves, sweep the cave, attract the best man we can, spite unsuccessful lovers, fall in love and keep a man at our side as long as we can. We are hardwired to do it, for the sake of our children.

Whether a woman wants babies or not, whether she has them or not, is irrelevant. Her physiology and her emotions behave as if she does. Her hormones are all set up to make her behave like a female member of the tribe. The female brain differs from the male even in appearance. Pathologists can tell which is which just by looking,

(Of course if a woman doesn't want to put up with her female destiny she can take testosterone in adult life and feel and be more like a man. Though it is better, I feel, to work with what you have. And that early foetal drenching in oestrogen, when the female foetus decides at around eight weeks that female is the way it's going to stay, is pretty final.)

11

In her young and fecund years a woman must call upon science and technology, or great self-control, in order not to get pregnant. As we grow older, as nurture gains more power over nature, it becomes easier to avoid it. A: We are less fertile. B: We use our common sense. The marvel is that there are so few teenage pregnancies, not so many.

To fall in love is to succumb to instinct. Common sense may tell us it's a daft thing to do. Still we do it. We can't help it, most of us, once or twice in a lifetime. Oestrogen levels soar, serotonin plummets. Nature means us to procreate.

(Odd, the fall in serotonin symptomatic of falling in love. Serotonin, found in chocolate, makes us placid and receptive. A serotonin drop make us anxious, eager, sexy and on our toes. Without serotonin, perhaps, we are more effective in courtship.)

Following the instructions of the blueprint for courtship, the male of the human species open doors for us, bring us gifts and forages for us. If he fails to provide, we get furious, even when we ourselves are the bigger money earners. We batter on the doors of the CSA. It's beyond all reason. It is also, alas, part of the male impulse to leave the family as soon as the unit can survive without him and go off and create another. (Now that so many women can get by perfectly well without men, the surprise is that men stay around at all.)

The tribe exercises restraint upon the excesses of the individual, however, and so we end up with marriage, divorce laws, sexual-harassment suits and child support. The object of our erotic attention also has to conform to current practices, no matter what instinct says. *'Under 16? Too bad!'* *'Your pupil? Bad luck!'* Nature says, *'Kill the robber, the interloper.'* Nurture says, *'No, call the police.'* The sanction, the disapproval of the tribe, is very powerful. Exile is the worst fate of all. Without the protection of the tribe, you die.

Creatures of the Tribe

We do not define ourselves by our animal nature. We are more than creatures of a certain species. We are moral beings. We are ingenious and inquisitive, have intelligence, self-control and spirituality. We understand health and hormones. We develop technology to make our lives easier. We live far longer, thanks to medical science, than nature, left to its own devices, would have us do. We build complicated societies. Many of us choose not have babies, despite our bodies' instinctive craving for them. We socialize men not to desert us; we also, these days, socialize ourselves not to need them.

'I don't dress to attract men,' women will say. *'I dress to please myself.'* But the pleasure women have in the candlelit bath before the party, the arranging and rearranging of the hair, the elbowing of other women at the half-price sale, is instinctive. It's an overflow from courting behaviour. It's also competitive, whether we admit it or not. *'I am going to get the best man. Watch out, keep off!'*

To make friends is instinctive. We stick to our age groups. We cluster with the like-minded. That way lies the survival of the tribe. A woman needs friends to help her deliver the baby, to stand watch when the man's away. But she must also be careful: other women can steal your alpha male and leave you with a beta.

See in shopping, source of such pleasure, also the intimidation of rivals. *'My Prada handbag so outdoes yours – crawl away!'* And she will, snarling.

And if her man's genes seem a better bet than your man's, nab him. Nature has no morality.

Any good feminist would dismiss all this as 'biologism' – the suggestion that women are helpless in the face of their physiology. Of course we are not, but there's no use denying it's at the root of a great deal of our behaviour, and indeed of our miseries. When instincts conflict with each other, when instinct conflicts with socialization, when nature and nurture pull us different ways, that's when the trouble starts.

'I want another éclair.'

Agony.

Well, take the easy way out. Say to yourself, *'One's fine, two's not.'* No one's asking for perfection. And anxiety is inevitable.

A parable.

Once Bitten, Twice Shy

Picture the scene. It's Friday night. David and Letty are round at Henry and Mara's place, as is often the case, sharing a meal. They're all young professionals in their late twenties, good-looking and lively as such people are. They've unfrozen the fish cakes, thawed the block of spinach and cream, and Henry has actually cleaned and boiled organic potatoes. After that it's cheese, biscuits and grapes. Nothing nicer. And Mara has recently bought a proper dinner set so the plates all match.

They all met at college. Now they live near each other. They're not married, they're partnered. But they expect and have so far received fidelity. They have all even made quasi-nuptial contracts with their partner, so should there be a split the property can be justly and fairly assigned. All agree the secret of successful relationships is total honesty.

After graduation Henry and Mara took jobs with the same city firm so as to be together. Mara is turning out to be quite a high-flyer. She earns more than Henry does. That's okay. She's bought herself a little Porsche, buzzes around. That's fine.

'Now I can junk up the Fiesta with auto mags, gum wrappers and Coke tins without Mara interfering,' says Henry.

Letty and David work for the same NHS hospital. She's a radiographer; he is a medical statistician. Letty is likely to stay in her job, or one like it, until retirement, gradually working her way up the promotional ladder, such is her temperament. David is more flamboyant. He's been offered a job at *New Scientist*. He'll probably take it.

Letty would like to get pregnant, but they're having difficulty and Letty thinks perhaps David doesn't really want a baby, which is why it isn't happening.

Letty does have a small secret from David. She consults a psychic, Leah, on Friday afternoons when she leaves work an hour earlier than on other days. She doesn't tell David because she thinks he'd laugh.

'I see you surrounded by babies,' says Leah one day, after a leisurely gaze into her crystal ball.

'Fat chance,' says Letty.

'Is your husband a tall fair man?' asks Leah.

'He isn't my husband, he's my partner,' says Letty crossly, 'and actually he's rather short and dark.'

Leah looks puzzled and changes the subject.

But that was a couple of weeks back. This is now. Two bottles of Chilean wine with the dinner, a twist of weed which someone gave Mara for a birthday present . . . and which they're not sure they'll use. They're happy enough as they are. Medical statisticians, in any case, do not favour the use of marijuana.

16

Sources of Happiness

Henry owns a single e, which someone for reasons unknown gave him when Mara bought the Porsche, saying happiness is e-shaped. He keeps it in his wallet as a kind of curiosity, a challenge to fate.

'You're crazy,' says Letty, when he brings it out to show them. 'Suppose the police stopped you? You could go to prison.'

'I don't think it's illegal to possess a single tablet,' says David. 'Only to sell them.'

He is probably right. Nobody knows for sure. Henry puts it away. It's gone kind of greyish and dusty from too much handling, anyway, and so much observation. Ecstasy is what other people do.

Mara's mobile sings 'Il Toreador'. Mara's mother has been taken ill at home in Cheshire. It sounds as if she might have had a stroke. She's only 58. The ambulance is on its way. Mara, who loves her mother dearly, decides she must drive north to be there for her. No, Mara insists, Henry isn't to come with her. He must stay behind to hold the fort, clear the dinner, make apologies at work on Monday if it's bad and Mara can't get in. 'You'd only be in the way,' she adds. 'You know what men are like in hospitals.' That's how Mara is: decisive. And now she's on her way, thrum, thrum, out of their lives, in the Porsche.

Now there are only Henry, David and Letty to finish the second bottle. David's phone sings 'Ode to Beauty' as the last drop is drained. To open another bottle or not to open another bottle — that's the discussion. Henry opens it, thus solving the problem.

It's David's father. There's been a break-in at the family home in Cardiff, the robbers were disturbed and now the police are there. The digital camera has gone and 180 photos of sentimental value and some jewellery and a handbag. David's mother is traumatized and can David make it to Cardiff for the weekend?

'Of course,' says David.

'Can I come?' asks Letty, a little wistfully. She doesn't want to be left alone.

But David says no, it's a long drive, and his parents and the Down's sister will be upset and he'll need to concentrate on them. Better for Letty to stay and finish the wine and Henry will walk her home.

Letty feels more than a little insulted. Doesn't it even occur to David to feel jealous? Is it that he trusts Letty or that he just doesn't care what happens to her? And is he really going to Cardiff or is he just trying to get away from her? Perhaps he has a mistress and that's why he doesn't want to have a baby by her.

David goes and Letty and Henry are left together, both feeling abandoned, both feeling resentful.

Henry and Letty are the ones who love too much. Mara and David love too little. It gives them great power. Those who love least win.

Henry and Letty move out onto the balcony because the evening is so warm and the moon so bright they hardly need a candle to roll the joint. On warm days Mara likes to sit on this balcony to dry her hair. She's lucky. All Mara has to do is dunk her hair in the basin and let it dry naturally and if falls heavy and silky and smooth. Mara is so lucky in so many respects.

And now Henry walks over to where Letty sits in the moon-light, all white silky skin and bare shoulders and pale-green linen shift which flatters her slightly dull complexion, and slides his hands over her shoulders and down almost to where her breasts start and then takes them away.

'Sorry,' he says. 'I shouldn't have done that.'

'No, you shouldn't,' she says.

'I wanted to,' he said.

'I wanted you to do it too. I think it's the moon. Such a bright night. And see, there's Venus beside her, shining bright.'

'Good Lord!' he says. 'Think of the trouble!'

'But life can get kind of boring,' Letty says. She, the little radio-grapher, wants her excitements too. Thrum, thrum, thrum goes Mara, off in the Porsche! Why shouldn't it be like that for Letty too? She deserves Henry. Mara doesn't. She'd be nice to him. Letty's skin is still alive to his touch and wanting more.

19

'But we're not going to, are we?' he says.

'No,' says Letty. 'Mara's my friend.'

'More to the point,' he says, 'David's your partner.'

They think about this for a little while.

'Cardiff and Cheshire,' says Letty. 'Too good to be true. That gives us all night.'

'Where?' asks Henry.

'Here,' says Letty.

All four have in the past had passing fantasies about what it would be like to share a bed and a life with the other – have wondered if, at the student party where they all met, Henry had paired off with Letty, David with Mara, what their lives would have been like. The fantasies have been quickly subdued in the interests of friendship and expediency. But Mara's sheets are more expensive than Letty's, her bed is broader. The City pays more than the NHS. Letty would love to sleep in Mara's bed.

'We could go to your place,' says Henry. To elbow David out of his own bed would be very satisfactory. Henry is stronger and taller than David; Henry takes what he wants when he wants it. Henry has wit and cunning, the kind which enables you to steal another man's woman from under his nose.

But Letty's envy is stronger than Henry's urge to crush his rivals. They agree to stay where they are. They agree this is greater than either of them. They share the e, looking into each other's eyes as if they were toasting one another in some foreign land. It is in fact an aspirin, but since they both believe it's ecstasy, it has the effect of relieving themselves of responsibility for their own actions. Who, drug-crazed, can help what they do?

They tear off each other's clothes. Mara's best and most seductive apricot chiffon nightie is under the pillow. Letty puts it on. Henry makes no objection. It is the one Mara wears, he has come to believe, when she means to refuse him. Too tired, too cross, just not interested. He pushes the delicate fabric up over Letty's thighs with even more satisfaction. He doesn't care if he tears it.

'Shouldn't you be wearing a condom?' she asks.

'I don't like them,' he says.

'Neither do I,' she says.

For ten minutes Letty is supremely happy. The dark, rich places of the flesh unfold and surround her with forgetfulness. She is queen of all places and people. She can have as many men as she wants, just snap her fingers and there they are. She has infinite power. She feels wholly beautiful, consummately desired, part of the breathing, fecund universe, at one with the Masai girl, the Manhattan bride, every flower that ever stooped to mix its pollen, every bird that sings its joy to heaven. And every one of Henry's

21

plunges is a delightful dagger in Mara's heart, his every powerful thrust a reproach to pallid, cautious David.

Then Letty finds herself shifting out of a blissful present into a perplexing future. She's worrying about the sheets. This is condom-less sex. What about stains? Will Mara notice? She could launder them – there's a splendid washer-dryer in the utility room, but supposing it broke down mid-wash? Henry could possibly argue that he spilt wine on the sheets – as indeed he has, and honey too, now she comes to think of it. She is very sticky. Can Mara's chiffon nightie be put in the machine or must it be hand washed?

'Is something the matter?' he asks.

'No,' she says.

But she no longer feels safe. Supposing Mara gets a call from her family on the way to Cheshire and turns back? Supposing she and Henry are discovered? Why is she doing this? Is she mad?

Her body shudders in spite of herself. She rather resents it. An orgasm crept up on her when she was trying to concentrate on important things. She decides sex is just mechanical. She'd rather have David, anyway. His penis is less effective and smaller than Henry's, but it's familiar and feels right. David must never find out about this. Perhaps she doesn't want a baby as much as she thought she did. In any case she can't have a baby that isn't David's. What if she got pregnant now? She'd have to have an abortion, and it's against her principles, and it would have to be secret because fathers can now claim rights to unborn embryos.

Henry rolls off her. Letty makes languid disappointment noises but she's rather relieved. He is heavier than David.

Henry's phone goes. He answers it. Mara is stuck behind an accident on the M6 north of Manchester,

'Yes,' says Henry, 'I walked Letty home.'

Now Letty's cross because Henry has denied her. Secrecy seems sordid. And she hates liars. And Mara? What about Mara? Mara is her friend. They've studied together, wept together, bought clothes together and supported each other through bad times, good times. Mara and her Porsche and her new wardrobe have all seemed a bit much, true, but she sees why Mara puts Henry down from time to time. He's not only irritating but untrustworthy. How could you trust your life to such a man? She ought to warn Mara about that, but how can she? Poor Mara, stuck behind an ambulance in the early hours in the far north while her partner betrays her with her best friend . . .

Henry is licking honey off his fingertips suggestively. 'Shall we do that again?' he asks. 'Light of my life.'

'No,' says Letty and rolls out of bed. Her bare sticky feet touch the carpet and she is saved.

Moral

Few of us can resist temptation the first
time round, and we should not blame
ourselves too much if we fail. It's the
second time that counts. Let sin pass
lightly on and over. Persist in it and it
wears your soul away.

Letty's sense of guilt evaporates, washed away in the knowledge
of her own virtue and fondness for her friend. Guilt is to the
soul as pain is to the body. It is there to keep us away from
danger, from extinction.

And good Lord, think what might have happened had Letty stayed
for a second round! As it was she got into her own bed just
minutes before David came through the door. His father had rung
from Cardiff and the jewellery had been found and the burglary
hadn't happened after all. Letty hadn't had a bath, thinking she'd
leave that until the morning, but David didn't seem to notice.
Indeed, he fell on her with unusual ardour and the condom broke
and he didn't even seem to mind.

If she'd stayed in Mara's bed David would have come round to
find Letty and at worst killed Henry — fat chance! — and at best
told Mara, or if not that then he'd have been able to blackmail
Letty for the rest of her life. *'Do this or I'll tell Mara'* — and she'd
have had to do it, whatever it was: go whoring, get a further
degree (not that there wasn't some attraction in surrendering
autonomy . . .)

But as it was it all worked out okay. Letty had her 10 minutes of sublime pleasure, felt anxious, felt guilty, and was rewarded by having her cake and eating it too. I don't know what happened to the sheets. I daresay Henry calmed down enough to put them through the washer-dryer and get them on the bed again before Mara got back. I hope he had the sense to rinse out her nightie in the basin at hand temperature, not hot.

I do know that in the following week Henry sold the Fiesta and got a Jaguar which could outrun the Porsche any day, and he used the joint account to do it. He felt better about himself.

I allow Letty, having observed the moon, to sleep illicitly with Henry once, but not twice. It is a balancing act and she got it right.

It is doing what you should, if only in the end, and not what you want which makes others respect and like you, and to be respected and liked by others is a very good way to be happy.

Save your moral strength for what is important.

The Inevitability of Anxiety

What makes women happy? Nothing, not for more than ten minutes at a time. Anxiety, doubt and guilt break through.

'Supposing my boyfriend comes back?' 'Have I left the fish out for the cat?' 'Should I be doing this?'

Blame nature.

It's the hormones doing it, interfering with our happiness, not the mysterious thing called *me*.

Instinct rewards us by gratifying our sensual appetites. It also punishes us if we go too far.

It is when we are following the promptings of instinct, doing what nature suggests, going through the motions of procreation – however unlikely they are to succeed – even in the midst of our triumph and greatest pleasure that other warring instincts set in. *'Clean the cave, keep the baby safe, are the food stores okay? What's that rustling at the back of the cave? Can it be the sabre-tooth tiger? We can't just lie here enjoying ourselves! Hasn't he finished yet? Is the fire going out? Might a vulture swoop down to get the baby? What's the woman in the next cave up to? Has he noticed my spare tyre? Is she a better bet than me? Will he go to her?'*

While he, the man, is thinking solely about pleasure and completion, concentrating on the task in hand, our female minds are already wandering.

He: *'Is something the matter, darling? You seem to have lost interest.'*

She: *'I just remembered I left the butter out of the fridge. Sorry. Now where were we?'*

Our instincts overlap and contradict each other: the one to make babies struggles with the need to look after the ones already there; the one to compete with our friends with our need to have them at our side. It leaves us confused.

Sex with the new true love brings bliss, optimism, unguarded delight – and then: *'Am I too fat, will he notice my varicose vein, will the baby wake, will his wife come back, should I have told him I loved him?'*

With the wedding, it's all *'Will the flowers arrive, should I have worn this tatty veil, should I really be doing this?'*

With the promotion, *'Will my friends hate me, will my new office be okay, will my partner leave me if I earn more than him?'*

The pleasure in the new baby is balanced out by the anxiety that goes with bonding. Bonding is one of the worst tricks instinct plays on us. The baby cries; the mother leaps to attention. It is a lifetime's sentence to anxiety. It doesn't get better with time. And it is not open to reason. Experience may tell us that the teenager late home is usually late home. But mother love is panicking: *'He's come off his bike. There'll be a call from the hospital.'*

The baby's quiet – and it makes you happy and proud to have got him through to the end of the day. *'But perhaps he's stopped breathing?'* Wake him and see!

There are so many things to be anxious about. The baby's not breathing. You only mascaraed one eye this morning. Sheer pleasure can trigger anxiety. When you're nibbling caviare, or taking a taxi home loaded, or feeling spaced out at a concert, what do you think? *'I shouldn't be here. I am going to be punished. I shouldn't be doing this. Something terrible is about to happen. I do not deserve to be happy.'*

Well, maybe you don't. That may be the trouble.

We are more than creatures of the cave, ruled by instinct. We are moral beings as well.

Guilt, Offshoot of Anxiety

Guilt also stands between you and enjoyment. It's an offshoot of anxiety.

'Shouldn't have done this, shouldn't have done that. Shouldn't have had a one-night stand. Shouldn't have eaten a bar of chocolate . . .'

It too is instinctive, hardwired in. It applies itself to any number of situations. When we succumb to 'inappropriate' sexual desire, eat the forbidden chocolate – anything that makes us feel bad – that's when the instinctive self, determined to satisfy its appetites, is in conflict with the socialized self.

'Ought not to endanger my relationship. Ought to lose weight.'

Feel it in its purest form when you neglect your children: *'Three in the morning, the baby's crying, but I'm too tired to bother.'* Baby wins: eventually you stir yourself, get out of bed and see to it. Thus Mother Nature, that unseeing, unthinking, callous creature, ensures the continuation of the race.

Whether or not you have children, the capacity to feel guilt is there. Stronger in some than in others. Certainly stronger in women than in men.

She: 'We need to get back, darling. The babysitter's waiting up.'

He: 'Oh, for heaven's sake. What do we pay her for?'

Guilt is society's safeguard. If you don't feel guilt at all they declare you're a psychopath and lock you up, and quite right too.

Let me add to that – just to counter the effect of so much Darwinian reductionism, which is true enough but there are other truths as well, namely that we have a spiritual life – that guilt is the soul's safeguard. And if the soul is safeguarded, we start from a higher level of life content than we would otherwise do. If you are good – abstain from bitchiness, doing others down, malice and complaint – people like you. If you are liked, you tend to have a good life.

Be good and you'll be happy. Be happy and you'll be good and go to heaven.

As a corollary, if you don't respond to the promptings of guilt, you might very well go to hell – in other words, fall into a depression, get ill and end up with no friends.

The Value of Guilt

You could see the 'oughts' and 'shoulds' which litter our lives as a nuisance, as contrary to our own self-interest. So our partner suffers because we were unfaithful, so our mother is lonely and upset because we didn't visit, so our children weep uncomforted. So who cares? *'I really deserve a holiday. I deserve it because I'm* me.' Stuff and nonsense.

'*Now at last,*' says the new-style granny, abstaining from babysitting, spending the children's inheritance, '*I'm going to do something for* myself.'

You won't enjoy it, you know. You will feel guilty and selfish every minute of your sun-soaked, pampered holiday, and so you should.

Therapists may well try and iron the emotion of guilt out of us, and some do, seeing it as 'negative'. By which they mean it's uncomfortable, painful and inconvenient, and aren't we trying to achieve happiness here? '*Look to your own skin,*' they advise. '*Do what you want.*'

Alexander Crowley, black magician, rapist and philosopher of Edwardian times, self-styled Beast no. 666, had this as his philosophy: *Do what thou wilt shall be the whole of the Law.* It was an attitude seen as very shocking at the time, even satanic. If it doesn't sound all that unreasonable now it may be our loss as, seeking validation for our bad actions, we virtuously pursue the 'authenticity of our feelings' ('*I have to leave you and the kids because I'm in love*') and decide we deserve every good thing, in the words of the shampoo ad, *because we're worth it.*

Self-esteem can go too far – a little low self-esteem might not come amiss as we consider our faults and failures. On our deathbeds the memory of the authenticity of our feelings might not seem as important as the love and company of our friends and relatives.

There is a truly simple answer to the pains of guilt: *If you feel bad about it, don't do it.*

Now there's an old-fashioned doctrine. Step by step, little by little, do what you *should*, not what you *want*.

Conscience is to the soul as pain is to the body. It keeps you out of harm's way.

Doing Bad and Feeling Worse

There are little everyday acts of meanness, little evils which are under our control, little tactlessnesses meant to hurt, which contribute to our own unhappiness. For hidden somewhere within us is the fear of retaliation. *'If I do this, you might do that.'* You get wary and untrusting. Meanness shows – it's bad for the complexion, gives you a dull skin, wrinkles and squinty eyes. You end up, in fact, with the face you deserve.

And then there are the great big destructive acts, like bringing your family toppling down like a house of cards. It's quite easy to do and you will always find allies.

> *Daughter: 'You were a terrible mother. That's why I'm such a mess. My therapist says so. I hate you. I'm not letting you see your grandchildren any more – you're such a monster you might do the same to them as you did to me.'*

Mother: 'But I did the best I could. You are the meaning of my life. I love you the way you love your own children.'

Daughter: 'Daddy, you must have abused me when I was a little girl. My therapist says there's no other explanation for my feelings of hostility and depression.'

Father: 'Perhaps you were just born that way. Perhaps you should go to church and not a therapist. Meanwhile, thanks a million for breaking up the family. I'm off.'

One day you come to your senses and wonder what it was all about, and you can remember everything, but there's no one to tell, no family shoulders left to cry on, and your own children don't seem to seek your company.

Conclusion

There are some truly bad therapists out there as well as some very good ones.

Proud, Defiant and Unhappy

You can take the proud and defiant path through life, of course. Some do and get away with it. You can decide you have problems because you let yourself be trampled on and go to assertiveness classes.

It has never seemed to me, however, that assertiveness classes have done anyone any good. My friend Valerie went to one, complaining that other people walked all over her. My own feeling was that she was the one who normally did the trampling, while worrying about her self-esteem and tendency to self-effacement. When she returned after her two-week course she bullied more, smiled less and her self-esteem was sky-high. It's true she got a rise, but she lost her boyfriend. Justice was on her side, but life wasn't.

The fewer the mini-nastinesses we do – and we all do them – the better able we will be to deal with the real, great, imponderable areas of unhappiness when they come along. Which they do, unasked, in everyone's life.

Moral

If you haven't anything nice to say, don't
say anything at all. Smile though you want
to spit. When in doubt, do nothing.

This flies in the face of contemporary wisdom, I know. Valerie was told to give voice to her anger (*or she'd get cancer*), speak emotional truths (*it was only fair to herself*), claim the authenticity of her feelings ('*I feel, therefore I'm right*') never fake orgasm (*it's a lie, an indignity*) and in general claim her rights and seek justice in the home and at work. Above all she must never be persuaded into making the office coffee, because she was worth more than that.

Valerie sounded off at her boss when he said it would be nice to have a cup of coffee, and he said that was the last straw, he was tired of being bullied, and he fired her. She told her mother she'd rather she didn't phone the office because of her Birmingham accent and her mother spent her savings – those that hadn't gone on Valerie's expensive education – on a little cottage in France and wouldn't be there to babysit when she was needed – not that there was much question of babies any more, since Valerie was 41 and her boyfriend got so nervous in the end about not 'giving' her an orgasm (which didn't seem in his power to give anyway) that the sex dried up altogether and he left. And she had to make her own coffee in her lonely home, while trying to find a lawyer willing to accept her unfair dismissal case, and these days caffeine gave her palpitations, and her mother was out of even mobile range.

An Alternative Therapy: Prayer

Suffer a pang of remorse when in bed with your best friend's boyfriend and act upon it by getting out of the bed, and you will have less sensual pleasure in the short term, but it is amazing how gratifying doing the right thing is. Your best friend may not see it quite like that, of course, concentrating only on the fact that you were in the bed in the first place.

But pray God she will never find out.

I mean that. Actually pray. Gather a few forces around you. The way to be happy, to forestall anxiety and guilt, is to be good.

The world being what it is, you may not know what praying is. (Look it up on the Internet and you can't find a definition.) But this is how it goes. You sit down. You create a mental space around you. Shutting your eyes helps. Hands steepled together helps: you're enclosing yourself within yourself, making a separation between yourself and what's outside you. Which, you will find, if you develop the antennae, is a kind of breathing presence, the majesty of existence itself. You are part of it.

Pray for others, not yourself. (Praying for yourself is vulgar.) Hold your friends in your mind, household by household. Direct your thoughts towards them, wish them well, enfold them and surround them with goodwill. Family too, of course, but anxieties and practicalities are more likely to break through here. Attention wanders.

You can link what you're doing with a known religion, the Father (*'Dear Holy Father'*), the Son (*'Dear Lord Jesus'*) or Holy Ghost (though very few pray to him because he is so hard to envisage), or any of the saints (*'Dear St Anthony, help me find my lost sentence'*), or Pan, I suppose, if you're a pantheist (*'Dear Lord Pan, help me find my lost virility'*), or Mother Mary (*'Help me get pregnant'*), but with all these what you are doing is using an intermediary to connect you.

Prayer is easier than meditation, which encourages self-centredness and too great a sense of *'Look at me, meditating!'* You seldom fall asleep when praying for others, as you do when meditating. You just stop when concentration fails.

Perfection is impossible to achieve, of course. But we can try, and angels will attend us, and we can take pleasure from the gentle air of their beating wings.

A Joke: Man Prays to God

'Dear God, let me win the lottery!' The voice is piercing, shrill and desperate, amongst all the others pleading to God for help. It goes on for week after week, Wednesday after Saturday after Wednesday: *'Let me win the lottery!'*

The Almighty does his best to ignore the voice, but finally he can't stand it any more. He speaks like thunder from the clouds. *'Okay,'* says God, *'tell you what, I'll meet you halfway. Buy a ticket.'*

The Major Enemies of Happiness

Forget guilt, forget anxiety. There are real enemies of happiness out there, real tribulations, which are powerful and not self-inflicted. Things that just happen.

Difficulties Along the Way

Old age

Illness

Bereavement

Isolation

Debt

Bitterness

Old Age

Make no mistake about it, money helps. It makes most troubles easier, while not necessarily solving problems.

Failing money, friends help – as does a long record of good behaviour and kindness to others. The comfort of strangers, if sought, is often there. What you put into life at the beginning you can take out with dividends at the end.

Old age seen from the outside can look horrific. But if you're in there in that derelict body it's still you; there are still pleasures and ambitions left to you. You are Ivan in the Russian story by Solzhenitsyn, the man in the prison camp who guarded his piece of dry bread successfully all day, and when he finally ate it, enjoyed incomparable pleasure. Seen from the outside, it was dreadful; from the inside, triumphant. May it be like that for you.

Illness

Illness is bad. But it can be very interesting, especially if it's your own. Symptoms are fascinating. It's another world, a bubble one, perhaps, and precarious, but those in it have already found a way to live with it. The skill of physicians and surgeons is inspiring. As is other people's selflessness. The walls of your experience may narrow to the width of a hospital bed, but it is still a stage, this is your drama and you are the centre of it. A good performance will get good reviews. Understand and please your audience: the visitors who may or may not cluster round your bed; at the very least the volunteer who brings round the library books or the man who wheels the trolley of newspapers and junk food.

'*How are you today?*' they ask. Well, tell them. That's pleasure in itself. If ill enough, you are excused selflessness and martyrdom.

And if you are temporarily in a hospital ward, try not to hate it. Go with the flow. The social life of the ward is rich and strange, never mind the routine. People elaborate their symptoms and treatments with a relish others share. They support and understand each other. They joke about death. The ward is a mini-tribe, sharing experiences.

In the private ward you have your comfort but you can be lonely, and another patient is more likely to come to your aid than a nurse. Sometimes money is not the universal solution.

When Children Are Ill

There is nothing good to be said about the serious illness of a child and not much comfort to be offered to the parents involved, other than to try to shift the perspective, see the small body as too frail and weak to support the intense existence of the mind and soul of this particular child. See how the latter exists, how clearly and powerfully it becomes apparent even as the body fails. The inner being makes itself clear – let the parents try to gain strength from it. Difficult, because parental distress is based in one of the most powerful instincts we have: to protect and save the children. The mind has little defence in these circumstances. The soul has. It is strong in the child. Those who suffer with children will understand the concept.

You can pray, though your sense of a benign universe will be somewhat blunted. That in itself is unsettling. The prayers would have to overcome your sense that you are picked out by fate for cruel and unjust punishment.

And it might help you, selflessly, to let the child go, to not struggle pointlessly for the continuation of its existence.

You could try Lourdes. I haven't been there, but they do say that a community of the like-minded, on the edges of despair, within which you don't have to explain yourself, with standards you can adapt to, however idiosyncratic and peculiar they may seem to the healthy and flourishing rationalist you once were lucky enough to be, can be a great comfort. You're with the tribe you have inherited. It might seem grotty compared to the one you were born into, but it is a tribe.

Bereavement and Isolation

We'll get on to these universal enemies later, and in more detail, when we are feeling stronger. I can be quite cheerful about bereavement, there are cures for isolation, and as for debt, well . . .

Debt

It's probably your own fault. You had a vision of yourself which did not accord with reality. You upgraded yourself to a wealthier sort of person than you actually were. It happens. You should have listened to the Voice of Guilt. You have my every sympathy. Earn your way out of it.

Bitterness

Very little in life is fair. Some of us are born with longer legs than others. Some of us are born into poverty in the Sahara desert, others into prosperity in leafy suburbs.

It's unfair that some are born thin, active, nervy ectomorphs and others are born rounded, easy-going endomorphs. Society these days smiles on the former rather than the latter, who have to spend their lives on diets, never eating what they want, except in those few places left in the world where obesity is valued.

Seeking natural justice is absurd: justice does not exist in nature. Seeking justice in the home is okay, but tends to end in exhaustion: it can be easier to wash his socks than argue that he should do it.

Resenting men, an emotion familiar to most women, is understandable but pointless. Don't let it make you bitter. Some things are just not fair. It is not fair that for men the culmination of sex is always an orgasm – or at least for 98 per cent of them – and for women it is not.

Sex

Sources of Envy

10 per cent of women never experience orgasm.

20 per cent occasionally do.

50 per cent sometimes do.

20 per cent usually do.

10 per cent always do.

Or so the current figures say. But figures change. Someone in the 10 per cent 'always' category suddenly goes down to the next division: *'My partner came back from his trip and he'd grown a beard.'* Someone in the 'never' group claims now to be in the 'sometimes' category: *'I met another man.'* But the broad pattern is clear. The pleasure so liberally bestowed upon men by nature is only grudgingly given to women.

Of course women resent it. Listen to any conversation between women when men aren't there: at the hen night, on the factory floor, over the garden fence, at the English Lit. tutorial. Women may laugh and joke, but actually they're furious. *'They can, we can't, unfair, unfair.'* They may not know what's biting them, but that's it.

But facts are facts and there we are. Deal with it. Life is not fair. Resenting the fact is no recipe for happiness.

Indeed, the less you think about orgasms the better, since the greatest bar to having one, if we're to believe the research, is wanting one. Best if they creep up on you unawares. Women are at their most orgasmic when they are least anxious, but wondering why you're not having one can make you very anxious indeed. Which is ironic, since what you want most you're going to get least.

But a lot of life is like that. Want too much and it's snatched away. An attitude of careless insouciance is more likely to pay dividends.

Because really, having an orgasm or not doesn't matter in the great scheme of things, just as having an éclair or not doesn't matter. Life goes on pretty much the same with or without. There are other pleasures. There's true love, trust and sensual pleasure. Or, if you're that kind of person, and I hope you are not, the victory of disdain. *'See, knew you were no good in bed.'*

44

But actually, it's as likely, if not more likely, to be your doing, not his.

Unfair – but what you are after is happiness. Sexual repletion is not a necessary ingredient. Sexual satisfaction can happen anyway, and is not dependent on orgasm. If women were not so often described as 'achieving orgasm' then there would be no sense of failure when they didn't. The word is wrong, not the thing itself.

'*I don't* do *orgasm*' might be a more useful way of describing yourself, initially, to a partner, and it's a bonus to both if it turns out not to be true. But having an orgasm is not a sign of true love any more than the lack of it is the opposite. I have read letters from girls who think they must end a relationship because sex between them and their true love does not conclude with an orgasm for her. Imagining sex has failed, they feel the relationship has failed. It hasn't – all that has happened has been that she *didn't have an orgasm*. So what? Better, more conducive to happiness, just to see orgasm as an additional extra, something special that happens, a bonus, a surprising gift from heaven which descends like manna from time to time, not your natural-born right – and then a whole raft of unhappiness will be wiped from your life.

In Any Case

Female orgasm has no apparent usefulness to the human race. This puzzles those who think that everything in nature has to have a purpose, those who personalize evolution as if it knew what it was doing and had some end of perfection in sight. Some say muscular spasms help the sperm on its way to the egg; others doubt it. It is not the longing for orgasm which makes the virgin girl fall in love – though it may be the boy's. Another inequality, another injustice!

The peacock's tail demonstrates sexual attraction in overdose as he struts before the female; his voice would be enough to put anyone off. I don't suppose nature was after fairness, trying to balance things in the scales of justice, when she gave with one hand and took away with the other.

Why different birds have different voices no one knows – and no one's worked out what they're *for* – but those with (to our ears) the sweetest voices are the ones who sing the loudest and seem to relish their singing most. I like to think that the thrushes in my garden sing because it occurs to them that it's a beautiful morning and they feel like acknowledging it. It's an irrational thought, but it makes me happy for at least ten minutes, wandering in the garden and listening, but then the sun gets too hot and I worry because I haven't got a hat.

Some say that, like male nipples and the appendix, female orgasm is a mistake which nature has failed to recognize as a non-necessity. Better to see it as a celebration and a reward just for being alive. But there are others – the exhilaration of ideas, conversations, the company of good friends and so on – which probably add up to more.

46

The Joy of the Fake Orgasm

Just fake. Happy, generous-minded women, not too hung up about emotional honesty, fake. Research tells us that when you do there is *'activity in the part of the motor cortex that relates to the genitals, the amygdala, but not the deactivation of the cerebral cortex that occurs prior and after a genuine orgasm'*. In other words you have to be happy to have an orgasm, but if you have an orgasm you will be happy.

Activate the positive. Deactivate the negative. That's what it's all about.

The more highly educated you are, the more likely you are to fake orgasm. I am not sure what we deduce from that. Is too much intellectual stimulation bad for the love life? Or does it just occur to clever women pretty soon that it's only sensible to fake it?

Genuine orgasm experienced, acknowledged and stored away as one of the uncompromisingly good things in life, you will then no doubt leap out of bed and make breakfast, or squeeze orange juice or pour champagne or whatever your lifestyle, with the words *'You are so clever'*, or however you express enthusiasm, ringing in his – or her, of course, should you be a lesbian – ears.

If you are sensible you will do exactly the same if you've faked it, because half the pleasure of sex is being nice to the other person, and half is better than none, on the half-full, half-empty cup principle. Clever, judgemental, honourable people who feel deception is unworthy of them, who say, *'But relationships must be based upon truth,'* are likely to be of the half-empty sort.

Remember you are not in pursuit of justice, you are seeking what makes women happy. You must catch it as it flies, and if it flies just out of reach, well, it was a nice sight while it lasted, wasn't it?

Faking is kind to male partners of the new man kind, who like to think they have done their duty by you. Otherwise they too may become anxious and so less able to perform. The more the woman rates 'performance', the more likely the man is to wilt and fail. Do yourself and him a favour, sister: fake it. Then, who knows, as a reward for your kindness, sublime pleasure may creep up on you unawares.

There is a great confusion here between the pleasures of love and the pleasures of sex. Both can carry on along parallel tracks, never touching, to the end of time. Or one day, who's to say, they may meet.

My friend Olivia, now 69, had an orgasm for the first time when she was 54 and nine years into her second marriage. It took her by surprise. But she said it was like learning to ride a bicycle: once you knew how to do it, you could do it all the time. She's been clocking them up ever since. Life does not begin at 20. She was doing well enough without them, was earning a salary at that time as CEO of a media communications firm and had seemed to me to be living a full, even over-full, love life since I first met her when she was 18.

Her first marriage ended in scandal and divorce – her husband, a writer, naming seven co-respondents. (In those days of guilty and innocent, sexual infidelity had to be proved. Illicit couples had to be discovered *in flagrante*, stained sheets produced and so on, before the judge would grant a divorce.) The press went to town. Oddly enough, the naming and shaming did Olivia no harm in the business world. Even then, everyone liked anyone who had their name in the papers. And then the sixties were upon us and a great deal of random sexual activity went on as a matter of course, and after that divorce was not a matter of right or wrong but about the division of property. Meanwhile Olivia rose rocket-like through the corporate world and who is to say, if she had had more orgasms, she would have bothered to reach such heights? A touch of discontent in the night may be good for all of us. Sexual satisfaction, sensual repletion and the irrational sense of gratitude which tends to go with them, may be the last thing a career woman needs.

Most women, I suspect, are after true love, rather than orgasm, though they will put up with many stages on the way, from pure lust to pride assuaged to boredom endured. And even if true love is not on your agenda, it is always gratifying to stir it in others. If faking it helps, do it.

The Naturalness of the Hen Night

Girls together is good, girls together is fun and usually noisy. But notice how bitterness against men seems to be hardwired, as if nature had bred us to be suspicious of the male, on the lookout for bad behaviour. There's something in us of the female cat, not letting the tom near the kittens in case he eats them. Put us together and there's no stopping us. Listen in to the talk and laughter at a girls' night out: anecdotes about the follies of men, jokes about the minimal size of their parts, tales of male vanity and self-delusion – their stumbling mumbleness, their crazy driving.

We egg each other on to disloyalty. We are the women; we close ranks in opposition to men. The food gets cold on the plate in our excitement. The wine is quickly drunk, and more wine, and vodka shorts. We are the Maenads just before Orpheus comes on the scene to get torn to bits.

And then the mirth gets bitter. It isn't really funny, it's real. Someone begins to cry.

Men who leave, men who won't leave, men who fail to provide, men who don't love you after all, men who are a sexual disappointment. Past husbands, vanished partners, the ones who never washed, the ones who had the *au-pair* girl. Men: ridiculous, pathetic, sad.

Sex

The noise diminishes and fades away. Silence falls. Time to count heads and divide the bill. Those who have partners slip away, feeling guilty and grateful. Those who haven't go home on their own, or walk each other to the bus, and tell themselves all they need is their friends.

I have in my time enjoyed such gatherings immensely. They are a great pleasure. Life is good. The trick is to pay and leave just before the silence falls. And try not to be the one collecting the money and tipping the waiter.

Go to Norway and Sweden and notice how the restaurants are full of men. Few women eat out. Yet in theory these are super-equal societies. The women, one supposes, can only prefer to stay at home. These all-male meals – tables for four, six, eight, ten, more – tend to be silent, grim affairs. Men like to sit side by side, silently, metaphorically locking horns, and don't seem to have nearly such a good time as women do. But they do seem to get happier as the evening progresses, not the other way round. Life gets better, not worse. It isn't fair.

Nothing's fair.

It's unfair that some people like sex a lot, some very little, some not at all. The capacity for pleasure is not doled out equally or fairly.

(It is probably a good idea that people with equivalent levels of sexual energy partner one another, if they want the union

51

to last. People need to wear each other out in bed. Three times a day, three times a week (the norm) or once a year – so long as both are suited, what's the worry?)

Mind you, the easy-orgasmers, the lucky 20 per cent, are not always popular with others. The papers this morning were in a state of outrage about Sandy, a feckless girl of 19 who went on holiday to Spain leaving her three children in the care of a 15-year-old. When summonsed home by the police and the media, she refused to go. She was having too good a time, she said. She had her photo taken burying her head into the bare chest of a semi-naked waiter. I bet she had orgasms at the drop of a hat. She knew how to enjoy herself. She was not anxious. She did not feel guilt. She well and truly broke the ten-minute rule. She stretched it to a whole week of drink, drugs, sex and ecstasy before guilt set in and she flew home. That's one way of doing it.

It Isn't Fair But It's a Fact

The fight for gender equality is bad for the looks. It makes no one happy, unless you find some reward in struggling for a justice that evolution failed to deliver. It will just develop your jaw, wrinkle your brow beyond the capacity of Botox to unravel, muddy your complexion so much that no amount of Beauty Flash will clear it, and in general do you no good.

Fight for political justice by all means – join the party, reform and re-educate. Fight for domestic justice – '*Your turn to clean the loo*' – if you must, though personally I don't recommend too much of it, it's too exhausting. But do not fight for physiological equality because it does not exist.

If you have a period pain, you have one. Accept it. Don't fight it. Sit down. Take a pill. A male voice raised is impressive; a female voice raised creates antipathy. Accept it. You are not trying to be a man. You are proud to be a woman. Do not shout your enemies down at the client meeting – leave that to the men. Get your way by smiling sweetly. The end is more important than the means.

Accept that for women happiness comes in short bursts and the ten-minute rule applies. For men it can last as long as a football match before they realize they're late picking up the child from school.

So is the sum of human happiness greater for a man than for a woman? I suspect so. Lucky old them.

Be generous. You can afford to be. At least you occupy the moral high ground, and they know it.

Occupying the Moral High Ground

It's quite nice up here these days. Women can look out over the urban landscape and know they are nicer than men, more co-operative, more empathic, better at communication, better at getting to university and better at getting jobs. Women multi-task – everyone knows. They can do many things at once. Men tend to do one thing at a time. If a woman loses a sock she finds another which will do just as well; a man continues the search until he has found it (albeit in the bin where he threw it), by which time the train has gone and the meeting has begun.

Women abjure the idle languorousness of sexual contentment and get on with things. Women leap out of bed after sex to feed the cat and wash out their smalls so that they'll be dry by morning. Men just go to sleep gratified and satisfied, happy that all is well. (Though if it's not his own bed he may well want to regain it before falling asleep. *'I'll call you in the morning,'* he says. Oh yes!)

Women worry in advance. They search through their bags for the dry-cleaning ticket before they even get into the shop. Men wait until they're in there and then hold everyone up.

Just Accept It
Accept gender differences, don't deny them. That way you make the most of what happiness nature did allow you as a woman.

Evolution has allowed you an intellect that's pretty much the same as the male's.

(Though the male bell curve when it comes to IQ is a little more flattened than for the female. That is to say there are more males at the extreme ends of the spectrum – extreme intelligence, extreme lack of it – which is why you get more male double-firsts at Oxford than female and more males held in police cells overnight than females.)

Evolution has also allowed you an aesthetic appreciation equal to that of the male. There are as many men as women listening to flute concertos at the Wigmore Hall, as many men as women wandering round art galleries.

(Nature might slightly favour the male when it comes to creative activity – men's books may be 'better', if less read-able, than women's, their paintings fetch more in the art market, and so on – but that claim would take a whole book on its own to discuss.)

The traditionally female qualities of caring and nurturing, sharing and co-operating were not always seen as admirable. Inside the home a woman did them for free; outside the home they commanded low wages. Society favoured to male virtues: dismissing and disposing, self-control and a stiff upper lip. But then women, released by technological advance from the domestic drudgery required just to keep the children alive, have used their new power brilliantly. Theirs are the qualities now most valued in Western society. Forget the old male values of never apologizing, never explaining – they're out-moded. Presidents weep, prime ministers apologize, monarchs explain.

To have to accept your genetic make-up, the femaleness of your body, its irritating habit of keeping menstrual time with the moon, is not so bad a fate. These cosmic forces are too great for you to take on single-handed anyway.

It isn't fair, but it's a fact.

If It Takes a Man to Make You Happy . . .

It's a dreadful assumption to make that just because a woman is a woman she must need a man. I know many a female who's lived happily ever after without one. They may well have a blip in their mid-forties when it occurs to them that being single looks like being a permanent state. That pang of doubt is nature's last-ditch stand against the nurture that persuades a woman that a man is an optional extra. But the automatic, instinctive pairings-off of the under-thirties are a long way behind her now. Crowded rooms are not for looking across in case she sees the man of her dreams, but for meeting friends, elegant conversation and making useful business contacts. She is the contented singleton. She tried sex and found it wanting. She never met a man she liked or respected enough to join forces with on a permanent basis. She has money enough to enjoy her life.

My mother, coming from a generation in which any man was better than none, would have described her as 'too picky'. And today's educated young woman is certainly in something of a pickle, what with both nature (her traditional selectivity when it comes to choosing a mate) and nurture (our current understanding that compared to women men are crude, loud-voiced, doltish creatures; look at any TV ad to see it) persuading her that nothing but a truly alpha male will do for her. That knight in shining armour crashing through the undergrowth to find her has to be better born than she is, better educated and richer – women have such a passion for marrying their superiors – and it gets harder and harder to find such a man.

And the girls of the tribe, the ones in her age group, will be watching and vetting to make sure she gets it right.

'*You can do better than that,*' they'll say. (That's tribe-talk too. Friends as arbiters of sexual choice is a timeless scenario.) Their judgement these days isn't so good, that's the trouble. It's self-conscious, and probably self-interested too. They need someone to sit next to in the cinema, to laugh and giggle with. The pleasures of a night out with friends outweigh the pleasures of a date. Men just look at films and grunt; girls *talk*.

But anyway, here she is, and life is good, and what should she want with a man? If she needs to change a tyre she can use her mobile and call a garage. Once she had to stand by the side of the road showing a leg. (She could do it herself, but whoever wanted to do that? My dear, the oil, the spanners, the weakness of the unaccustomed wrist!) The pang soon fades. She is happy again, and good for her.

But if you still believe that only with a man can you be truly happy, then you had better find one.

Finding a Man
There are two ways of doing it:

1. *He chases and you run.* This requires nerve, and you to be higher on the scale of partner-desirability than he. If you are convinced that you are – your beauty outweighing his wealth, for example – then give it a go. Female disdain is attractive, but you have to have looks to get away with it. Your handbook will be *The Rules.*

2. *You sit quiet and smile.* Never when in the company of the man you're after do you give him a hard time. You never argue, quarrel, demand your rights, reproach him, give him one iota of emotional, intellectual or physical discomfort. This is the best ploy for the 80 per cent of women who were not born with symmetrical features and a sexy body, who have wiry hair and a muddy complexion and cannot be bothered to have cosmetic surgery. Your handbook will be *The Surrendered Wife.*

A man, research tells us, plays the sexual field until he decides he's ready to settle down. Then he looks round the field of his female acquaintance and picks the one he likes the most. Let it be you. If that's what you want.

A woman, research tells us, goes searching for the perfect mate within her field of expectation (the rich marry the rich, remember, the beautiful the beautiful) and may go on searching too long. Her vision of herself can be inflated (*'Because I'm worth it!'*), her standards higher than is practical. That is why we have so many talented, beautiful, high-earning, intelligent, single young women about, while their male compatriots are safely tucked away in the suburbs, shacked up with some dim and dozy wife. Too picky!

Category 2 women fail when they behave as if they were in category 1. Only in romantic novels does Mr Darcy marry Elizabeth Bennett. He ran, she ran faster, he turned round and caught her. In real life he might have set her up as his mistress in Maida Vale, but marriage? No. On the scale of partner-desirability they did not match.

Let me tell you the parable of a woman who feared that she lived a dim and dozy life but found great happiness because she was good.

Happy Yuletide, Schiphol

And we'd been so clever. We would catch the 15.40 from Schiphol Airport on the 24th and be back in Bristol by 17.55 to pick up the hire car and be in Okehampton in good time for Christmas Eve dinner with goose, mashed potatoes, red cabbage and a fine Rhone wine. Christmas dinner the next day would be turkey, roast potatoes, sprouts, cranberry sauce and a good claret. My daughter and her husband, who live in Okehampton, are traditionalists. Chris and I tend to be salad and a slice of quiche people, but that's the way it goes these days. You go forward into a quicker, lighter future and the children hop off backwards into the past, staring at you and muttering 'Weird.' But we love to see our daughter, and we have a new grandchild, and our son and his new fiancée would be joining us.

We'd finished work in Amsterdam and had a host of presents already wrapped, which we'd packed into the suitcase, so we could just trolley them out at the Bristol end and then head straight down the M5. Yes, very clever. Well organized. My husband does all that. It's his thing, dates and timetables and being at the right place at the right time, and I trot along behind. He does consultancy work for a Dutch property company. I'm a writer; I fit in.

Too clever by half, of course. We'd reckoned without Christmas, or at any rate Yuletide. We'd reckoned without the waywardness of humanity. We'd not taken into account the seasonal urgency which sometimes catches us up like a tide, so we move as others do, in a group, and do what we must, not what reason says. Princess Diana's funeral, trolley rage at the supermarket just before the bank holiday . . . It was just the same when Thor cracked his thunder over northern skies and everyone jumped the same way at his command. Rituals must be observed. They have their own imperative.

Amsterdam is far enough north to still be partly the land of the Nordic gods, and Christmas is still Yuletide, their midwinter festival.

Sex

I have always suspected Schiphol Airport to be Thor's own place, all that cracking of the skies, the low thunder of aircraft breaking through the clouds, the tremble of the ground as the big jets land. Thor likes it; he hangs around. This year Christmas Day falls on a Thursday (*donderag* in Dutch), his day – all the more likely for him to put in an appearance. When the god roars out over the flat damp land, saying that it's time to shut the doors and bring out the drink, people do as he says, and who cares what the timetables say?

We got early to the airport and checked in the luggage. We'd allowed ourselves twenty minutes to look round the Rijksmuseum annexe before going to the gate. We like to do that. There is something refreshing, like cool clear water on a hot day, about looking at paintings in an airport. It restores you to sanity. There's currently an exhibition of Rembrandt prints which Chris particularly wanted to catch. But my attention was caught by a farmyard painting by Melchior d'Hondecoeter, 1636–1695. Two vain and disdainful peacocks look down their nose at a little, pretty, silly hen with four fluffy chicks, while a great gobbling turkey, stupid and amazed, looks on. I wondered which of them was most like me. I asked Chris, hoping, I suppose, for some kind of compliment or reassurance, but instead of answering he said, 'We can't be too long here. We don't want to miss our flight. Shall we go?'

Now I can't bear to be hurried. Chris can't bear to be late. And I was feeling tetchy – Christmas brings out the worst in me, not the best. I was tired. The trouble with family is you have to work so very hard at not saying the wrong thing. 'Don't panic,' I said, meanly. 'You are so neurotic about time. They have our luggage, they can't go without us.' And for once I didn't relieve him of his anxiety by consenting to leave at once, but lingered and let him fret. It is the kind of cruelty that even the fondest couples some-times practise – putting the other person in the wrong, pressing their buttons. It may fall short of an outright row, but it verges on one.

The elegant girl from the Rijksmuseum shop, the only member of staff left on the premises, was beginning to hover and look at her watch. That irritated me too. I am a customer; I have my rights. It was only ten past three; there were five full minutes before the place was due to close for the six days of the Christmas holiday. I was looking at Art. I shouldn't be hurried.

It was almost twenty past three by the time we left and the poor thing could hiss the doors shut behind us. She stalked past us as we left, long legged. She carried crimson and gold parcels, pret-tily tied with Rijksmuseum ribbon. She was one of the peacocks, disdainful.

In the space of fifteen minutes Schiphol had stopped being a busy, noisy, excited place and become a lonely expanse of empty walk-ways. Shops had closed, passengers gone their ways. Lights were muted. Even the all-pervasive smell of coffee was fading. 'Yuletide!' said the notices, 'Happy Christmas! Bon Noël!' But here and there 'New Year Sale' signs had gone up.

The passport booth was closed and empty. Barriers were up. We had to find another one, and the Information desk was closed. The moving walkway slowed and stopped while we were on it.

Sex

The languid warning voice dropped a tone and droned and was silent. We ran. Even I ran. We ran down a flight of steps – the escalator had stopped – to gate C4, where our flight was closing. Even as we ran we heard a gate change. Now it was gate C6. We ran some more.

And then we sat, because when we got there, there was no urgency, the flight was delayed. One minute we were racing, the next we were staring into space. Airports are like that. And we sat, and sat and sat.

'We could have taken our time,' said Chris. He is very good. He could have said earlier, as we ran, 'Told you so.' But he didn't.

There were six of us: one little old lady who had been drinking, one shabby businessman who looked as if he had been up all night and a young engaged couple. She was plump and blonde and fidgety and reminded me of the busy little hen in the painting. He was the turkey, cross and awkward, with a nose too big and a chin too small. But he loved her. He kept trying to hold her hand, but she pushed him away. She was upset. There were tears in her eyes. I don't know what they had quarrelled about but it seemed quite bad. Two hours passed.

Pretty soon I had tears in my eyes too. The flight had been cancelled. There had been a technical fault. Thor was punishing me. I had been mean to Chris; I had been mean to the girl in the shop. I had not heeded the clarion call to the midwinter ritual. The last flights to Heathrow had gone. There was no way we could leave Schiphol that night. It was Christmas Eve. They were running a skeleton service. They would put us up in the airport hotel. They apologized for the inconvenience caused. We would be compensated. No, luggage could not be returned. It was already on the aircraft. There had been an industrial dispute and the baggage handlers had gone home.

There was a strange underwater feeling to everything. I could hear Schiphol breathing – or was it the air conditioning in the great echoey empty halls? In and out, very slowly. Thor's breath. The airline staff were very polite, very thoughtful, but they too were looking at their watches. Everyone wanted to be off. It was Christmas.

We were all silent. 'A Fokker F150,' said the businessman, looking out of the window as our plane taxied away, cute and antsy. As if the make made a difference. There was a crack of thunder from outside and lightning – only two seconds between the two – but no rain. 'Two propellers,' he observed. I think he was stunned. So was I. 'Nice little aircraft. Cityhopper. Doesn't usually go wrong.' But it was no use to us.

The blonde girl, whose name was Penny, threw her engagement ring across the floor. It skittered and bounced. The boy, whose name was Darrell, set his jaw and didn't go after it.

'That's it,' said Penny. 'That's it.'

'Yes, it is,' said Darrell. 'Goodbye you and goodbye Christmas.'

It seemed a great pity to me, the way the whole world had to suffer from the weight of my sin. The ring glittered under a plastic chair. I thought it was a diamond. The old lady said it was all right by her, she didn't like Christmas anyway. I longed to be at home in bed.

They bussed us to the airport hotel. The rain broke as we stood outside waiting for it to arrive. We were soaked. Thor was letting me know who ran things round here. I had no face cream; Chris had no sleeping pills. The young couple still weren't talking. I was distressed for them. It seemed such a waste of life. I was sure neither of them would find anyone better. I told Chris so. He said it was projection; personally, he was distressed for *us*.

The hotel was crowded. Industrial dispute, fog and storm had wreaked havoc with flights. They gave us tickets so we could be called in order to the reception desk. Someone from the airline came over and said they would try to get us out first thing the next morning. Christmas Day. She was the other peacock, the disdainful type.

'Now I must be off,' she said. 'In Holland we take Christmas Eve seriously. It is our most important festival.'

We made phone calls. We said, 'Don't expect us tonight, we've been delayed, we'll be in touch when we know more.' We were past caring about having no night things. There were plates of free food in the bar, but I wasn't hungry. Chris gnawed on a chicken leg. Our numbers came up. There was one room left, a double. They gave it to Chris and me. Everyone else would have to sleep in armchairs and on sofas in the lobby. I said to Chris, 'Please can we give the room to them,' meaning the young couple, and he looked at them and looked at me and said, 'Okay.' He is not a man of many words. We slept and partly slept, and outside the storm died down.

In the morning everyone said 'Happy Christmas' to each other, and there was big notice up with an arrow saying 'Yuletide breakfast this way', and there was, too, fresh bread and good coffee and fine eggs. The young couple came down from the bedroom. They had made it up. They smiled soppily at everyone. Chris looked in his pocket and handed them the ring. He had actually stopped to pick it up.

The young couple leant into each other in the Cityhopper, the Fokker F150, all the way home. An oil seal had been mended. We had missed Christmas Eve goose and our hire car, but my son-in-law would pick us up and we'd be in time for Christmas lunch. We even had the presents with us.

'Look at you!' said Chris, as we disembarked into brilliant morning sun, 'you're smarter than a peacock, nicer than a mother hen, and not one bit like the turkey,' and I glowed, and marvelled at the rich splendour of the world.

Moral

Nothing is as good as you hope or as bad
as you fear.

Food

The Fleeting Happiness Food Brings

Next to sex, food, being such a basic source of the most wonderful pleasure, is also the most basic source of exquisite anxiety and all-pervasive guilt.

Wanting to eat is instinctive. It's like sex – you find yourself wanting to do it. If you didn't want to, you wouldn't do it, and you'd starve to death, as anorexics do.

Anorexics lack the urge to eat and eat some more, before the winter comes and there's only the fat you stored in the summer to get you through the hungry days. Anorexics are out of touch with their species selves. They are all mind and soul, spiritual, brides of Christ, rejecting the flesh.

Bulimics are all instinct: eat and eat and eat, and only when the craving's stopped do mind and soul cut in, and by vomiting demonstrate repentance.

The person with the food disorder cannot get the balance right. Bulimic and anorexic swap and interchange. Nature says, '*Eat.*' Nurture says, '*Don't. Thin is best.*'

Eat for ten minutes and then feel the anxiety begin. '*How many calories was that?*' Now the guilt. '*Was I mad? Did I just eat strawberry jam?*'

Bananas

I looked in the fruit bowl just now and found a bunch of bananas, rapidly going brown from lack of anyone's interest. (I try to eat one a day, to keep my potassium levels up, but keep forgetting.) It seemed a pity to waste them. So I took the over-ripe bananas, peeled them, sliced them in two down the middle, criss-crossed the halves in an oven dish, added butter and sugar, and slid them into a very hot oven. Thirty minutes later I removed the dish and squeezed lemon juice over the now caramelized, buttery, amazingly interesting bananas.

I put them to one side. The struggle with the self began. '*Should I eat them? Shouldn't I eat them?*' Food makes you fat. It also keeps you alive.

I thought about adding ice-cream: cold and hot together add to the taste buds' delight. But I had run out. The double cream in the fridge was well beyond its sell-by date and smelled bitter.

There is no diet in the world which will allow you to eat banana, sugar, butter and lemon juice, forget cream, at the same time, and at will. And in quantity, because one spoonful of the disallowed will always lead to another.

Three Types

We fall broadly into three different physical types:

Endomorphs: rounded and happy

Ectomorphs: skinny and anxious

Mesomorphs: athletic, muscly and busy

No one's going to be wholly one thing or another, but the predominant traits are going to be visible to everyone. You can have the sharp elbows of the ectomorph, the muscular calves of the mesomorph and the double chin of the endomorph all on one body – and God help you. But one type will be favoured.

You will mostly find endomorphs (I'm one) on the Atkins diet, on which you're allowed to drink alcohol and eat everything that in your previous dietary life has been forbidden. It is also probably going to ruin your health and make you ill (what do you care) and you will put it all back on (fine) and more (not so fine). Atkins dieters are self-indulgent and always hopeful. Their self-discipline is not good. They run to fat around the middle. They should certainly not be eating caramelized bananas cooked to stop good fruit going to waste.

Mesomorphs, in my experience, go on GI diets. They're the healthy-looking, broad-shouldered, narrow-waisted energetic girls you see in the gym, especially on the weights. Everything they eat will be healthy, reasonable and balanced. They would look first at the caramelized bananas and then at you as if you were insane. They're the ones who lose weight successfully. They're the broad-shouldered healthy-looking celebrities, the film stars who have their babies and six weeks later you'd never have known it.

Ectomorphs would smell the aroma of the caramelized bananas, run it to its source and simply reach out and eat every scrap, having restocked on ice-cream and charmed a (male) neighbour into lending them some cream first. They're skinny and they have long legs and they eat everything and never get fat. See them putting aside their hamburgers before shimmying down the catwalk. See them sitting in reception while the mesomorphs haul the post and the endomorphs hide behind the filing cabinets. (Mind you, it can be quite exciting back there – think President Clinton and Monica Lewinsky, an endomorph if ever there was one.)

Now that a girl can have a boob job to order and small breasts need no longer bother her, contentment should be complete.

But it isn't. Species inheritance affects all physical types. Anxiety and guilt strike all of us, though ectomorphs least of all when it comes to food.

Personally, I capitulate to the bananas. Of course I do. I eat. I leave a bit on the plate and then think, '*What the hell*,' and go on and finish the lot. I am an endomorph. I prefer present pleasure to future benefit. (I may also be a bit more inclined to depression than my mesomorph and ectomorph sisters, so have less sense of future than they do. Sure, if I don't eat this I will be thinner *then*, but this is *now, now, now*.)

Nothing, I know from experience, is more delicious than caramelized bananas eaten in the privacy of one's own home. It's like forbidden sex – all the more delicious for the prohibition.

I eat. I am happy for three minutes. Yummy!

Then, oh, guilt and anxiety dawning! I have enjoyed myself. I don't deserve to be happy. I will be punished. I shouldn't have bought the bananas in the first place if I didn't mean to eat them properly.

And what was that I heard myself saying? *Yummy?* Revolting. I remember the girl who used to come in to help with my children, years back, and how she'd rub my three-year-old's tummy after he'd eaten and say, '*Yummy*.' I never liked it. There was something somehow wrong with it. She might give him a weight problem for life – too much emphasis on the '*Yummy*' content of food and not enough on the '*Swallow it down and get on with it.*'

I was right. It transpired that she was having an affair with my then husband.

And now I feel sick, and serve me right.

Eat, Eat

It is no use beating yourself up, reproaching yourself about being greedy. That is what you are. That is what you are born to be. '*Eat!*' says nature. '*Eat!*' You do.

The eye sees the food!

The hand takes the food!

The mouth eats the food!

The teeth chew it!

That's what they have all evolved to do!

At the same time it is not good to be fat. Bad news in the mating game – nurture in the form of our socialization has seen to that. Slim wins the alpha male, fat gets the leftovers. But you have to eat to be fit enough to bear a baby, even though you want to be thin to get the best mate. Two instincts clash. You suffer.

There's no fairness here, either. Some women can be as greedy as they like and stay thin:

Ectomorphs, who are lucky. Born thin and nervy, they stay thin and nervy. They can live off fish and chips and Mars bars if they want.

Mesomorphs, the born exercisers. They put on weight and take it off again, down the gym. It works for them.

Endomorphs are unlucky all round. Born plump and placid and prone to depression, they are also the least likely to diet successfully.

But they're the ones people like to have around. When nature and nurture clash in them, nature plainly wins. And those in whom instinct triumphs tend to be nicer people than those in whom it is subdued. They're spontaneous and loveable.

But I would say that, wouldn't I? I'm an endomorph.

Still, fat people are the nicest people, and increasingly in the West the *most* people. Perhaps, just as Mother Nature puts berries on the yew trees to warn of a cold winter ahead, she makes us fat to warn us of hard times to come?

That's the kind of myth the tribe likes. It doesn't really bear investigation. It's what is called the pathetic fallacy, attributing emotions, intent and the power of prophecy to a force incapable of it, namely 'nature'. But it's nice to speculate.

It's also nice to be nice. And to be thin. The tribe unites in making fat people unwelcome, uncomfortable. So nice people are not necessarily the happiest people.

Moral

Be good about the diet and you'll be happy
to be thin.

At the Mercy of our Greed

The eating of food being such a pleasure, so hardwired and yet so in conflict with society's current loathing of fat, it is not surprising the conflict tears us to pieces. Body mass index not within normal limits? *'Hang your head in shame, you fat person.'* Guilt and anxiety race in almost after the first mouthful of delight. As if life wasn't hard enough without this.

Did evolution stop just before the first good harvest? Is that it? Before the age of plenty? To all intents and purposes, yes. Evolution bred greed into us – *'Take while you can, as much as you can, who knows when it will come again?'* – and the pleasure of satisfying appetite – *'Oh yummy, yummy'* – and the yawning repletion of appetite satisfied – *'My, that was good!'* It has not yet had time to evolve us into persons fit for the age of McDonald's. That may take another millennium or two, left to nature, but no doubt the genetic scientists will get there first and turn us into a race of skinnies who can eat what they like and still stay acceptable in polite society. (When no doubt the plankton will dry up, there'll be a universal food shortage, women will long for curves and the scientists will have to return us to what we once were.)

As it is, lumbered with *now*, as we are, nature says, *'Forage, cook, feed the man who keeps the children fed. Keep strong, keep fat.'* Nurture says, *'Push away the plate half-eaten. You keep the children fed yourself, you don't need him. Keep thin, welcome hunger – the skinnier you are, the more you'll get paid at the office.'*

(*Fact:* Obesity lowers perceived status. The higher your status, the longer you live and the healthier you are. A vicious circle. Being fat is associated with poverty, depression, ignorance and being on benefit. Being slim is associated with the Duchess of Windsor: *'You can't be too rich or too thin.'* The phrase has stuck, 70 years or so after it was uttered by the runaway would-be queen Wallis Simpson, because everyone believes it to be true – other than the families of anorexics, who are in great distress.)

Nurture and nature, which should in a perfect world go hand in hand, when it comes to food simply do not. It's not surprising that the country is in the grip of one big eating problem. The more we feel distaste for being fat, the more cookery books we read. The more we long to be thin, the more obese we get, as we try to comfort ourselves, deny cause and effect.

Fashion also dictates that thin is best. Being slim is associated with wealth, choice and purchasing power. Designers challenge us, '*Fit into our clothes. Don't expect us to make clothes to fit you.*'

Way Out

If you feel guilty and anxious about eating, stop eating. Who are you trying to destroy there? Yourself?

Easily said – and people say it – but the trouble is that food breeds anxiety, and anxiety requires food to quell it. It is a vicious circle. But people do break it.

Remember what research tells us: that skinny women earn more than fat women, marry richer husbands, have more lovers, go to smarter restaurants and die with more jewellery. They wear more designer clothes than fat women and look far, far better in them.

(Tallness is to men as skinniness is to women. Tall men earn more, live longer, marry prettier and nicer wives, have more lovers and go to smarter restaurants than short men. They tend not to accumulate so much jewellery, though.)

Food

So be thin.

Convince yourself it's winter and there's simply no food to be had. That it's an eternal winter. That you can take it.

Remember, oh unfortunate endomorphs, with your legs shorter than your torsos and your tendency to run to fat around the middle, how great is your achievement if you manage to get thin and stay thin. Mesomorphs, luckier in that they can exercise and lose weight with comparative ease (though their ribcages will stay wide), deserve some credit. Ectomorphs, you fragile, lightly muscled things, elegantly and effortlessly slim, realize that though for you summer is always here, the rest of us can't afford to think like that. You see us as greedy, without self-control. You don't *understand*.

The way through again, if I could venture so outrageous an idea, lies not in this diet or that, but in seeking virtue. Not, *'Oh, I've eaten no carbohydrates today, aren't I good?'* or *'Oh, I've eaten lots of carbohydrates today, aren't I good?'*, but to go back to the old idea of our great-grandparents, that the body is the temple of the soul, and the preoccupation should be looking after the soul rather than the body. Not *'What will this food do to me?'* but *'How will this food benefit the temple?'*

It is your duty to look after the temple. Keep it not too fat, not too thin, not inviting ill-health, well exercised, allowed its proper pleasures, indulged a little but not too much – in

77

as perfect and cheerful a state as age will permit it to be. Pursue a fit shelter for the soul and the body will look after itself.

Friends

It's natural to have friends. You feel unhappy and lonely if you don't. The tribe troops together to keep danger at bay. It exchanges information, ideas, experience. That way survival lies.

In particular women need other women. If only to act as midwives.

We may live in cities, but we are still people of the tribe. We tend to cluster in our own age group:

Little girls congregate to discuss their frilly socks.

Teenagers get together to work out their seduction techniques.

Singletons go to the cinema in giggling groups.

Young mothers meet up in the park.

Older women meet for lunch.

Yet older women talk on the landline.

And the fun to be had is immeasurable, and the level of anxiety and guilt low.

Of course little girls squabble and brood, teenagers plot, singletons get competitive, younger mothers can be bitchy. Older women can decide never to speak to you again for reasons only known to them. Yet older women can forget all about you, through no fault of their own. But by and large having friends seems to be an activity encouraged and unconflicted by instinct. Nature encourages it as part of the cohesion of the tribe.

When a man turns up, as everyone knows, everything changes. Women complain the spark goes out of the party. It's not the spark, it's that something judgemental enters in – nature reminding us of our destiny, our obligation to the future. It isn't worse. It's just different.

Sure, the mating game takes precedence. Any sensible girl stands up her friends when a hot date comes galloping over the hill.

I know it is irritating to speak as if women were people who had babies, and that was their only definition, but Mother Nature is hopelessly old-fashioned. That's how she sees them, doling out the oestrogen like nobody's business. She does it in dollops. If she makes a mistake, and it's not rare, she'll dollop out testosterone to a girl in the womb, and she'll grow up to be an astronaut or an engineer. Good for her. She won't be unhappy. She'll just earn more.

The girl who at 13 is a clumsy stolid loaf of lard can turn suddenly into a bright-eyed, attractive, shapely lass. That's oestrogen. Now she's ready for the mating game. Nature says now, and makes her silly, vulnerable and sexy.

Our genes dictate when enough is enough and we're to stop producing oestrogen. Our skin dries out, our waists thicken, we are post-menopausal. We get depressed, overlooked and disregarded by the still fertile. We are fit for nature's scrap heap.

Fortunately, not for society's.

Nature also gave us brains surplus to our survival requirements and the ability to get round her strictures. We add the stuff artificially. We're back in business.

Nature doesn't care. Nature doesn't know. Nature is blind, deaf and dumb. Following her strictures in the modern world is pretty pointless. All she knows about is Darwinian evolution. She knows nothing about the soul.

The Pleasure of Friends

You can do without partners, husbands, lovers, children, jobs and money, so long as you have good friends. It is advisable to try to accumulate the others as you go through life, because then happiness is maximized, but you can do without if you have to.

In the good times friends are fun. They're to laugh with, drink with, eat with and refine ideas with. They're the mini-tribe you set up around you.

In the bad times friends are essential. They take you to hospital, give you a bed for the night, take in your children and lend you money. They listen to you for hours on the phone when you're in distress.

You do the same for them, or should. Be good to your friends and they'll be good to you.

No one's life is so in control that they know what's going to happen next. Aircraft fall out of the sky, tsunamis hit, husbands have heart attacks, children get meningitis. Friends turn up trumps.

For the most part friends make you happy. They can also betray you, give you bad advice, lie to you and tell tales about you out of school. They can spread malice and dissent. They can turn out to be still 13 at heart and decide to perse-cute you.

I had one good friend who I think somehow got me mixed up with her string of husbands. Left without one temporarily, she decided to divorce me. Losing friends is very painful.

Friends

Friends are powerful people. They can influence you too much, especially if you're at the courting stage in life. The gaggle of teenage girls, noisy and defiant, crude and lewd, is nothing alarming, not the end of civilization as we know it, it's just more tribal behaviour, only nowadays with the help of sex, drink and drugs. The process was the same in Victorian days. Young girls gather together in groups, working out their relationships with each other, trying out their own gender for size, as it were, before starting on men. One by one they peel away to create families of their own. Or should. The group can get over-possessive and destructive.

Intent is all. Motive matters.

Tell your best friend her new boyfriend is crap, she can do better than that, and next time he calls she'll put down the phone. Or might, at least. So only say it if it's true, not because she's the one who helps fill your own lonely evenings, because you shop together, go clubbing together, because her mother gives you tea and sympathy and you don't want to lose her.

It's not what you say, but the reason you say it that counts. And people sense it, and like you or leave you accordingly.

I have a rich and fashionable acquaintance who sees friends as social accessories. Once a year she gives herself a birthday party. She flies the 'friends' in from all over the world. It costs her a bomb. This is the only time she ever sees them. She makes an emotional speech after dinner and talks about how many friends she has and how they have supported her and how important they are in her life. Everyone feels warm and friendly. Then they all go away and she is left with the cook, the butler and the personal trainer, who are her real friends, but do not, of course, get asked to dinner.

Well, why not? If this is how she wants to spend her money, good for her. 'Friends' are whatever you define them as. I tend to define mine as the people who wander into the house and collapse exhausted and distraught at the kitchen table, but each to their own.

I read in the paper that anyone who has six friends can call themselves 'happy'. I can do that easily, if I include the guy who sells the *Big Issue* outside the supermarket. We always smile and say good day. And e-mail makes good colleagues of us all.

But already I'm worrying. Why haven't I heard from Wendy? Have I said something to upset her? And I should have called Stacey for the latest on her heart procedure, but it went out of my head. Anxious, guilty? But usually with friendships these are quickly allayed:

If the anxiety is of the free-floating variety and can be applied to this circumstance or that, breathe deeply and dismiss it. *'No, you have not upset Wendy. Stacey doesn't expect a phone call.'*

If the Wendy guilt is reasonable – you told her to stop moaning, it was getting on your nerves – *call and apologize.* Don't text – in these circumstances it's an evasion.

If the Stacey guilt is well founded, *call her and find out what's happening.* The longer you leave it, the worse it will get.

Let me tell you a parable about a girl who knew she was better than others, knew she was right, and made sure others knew it too. She kept to the rules and made sure everyone else did too, and it did her no good.

It's another Christmas story because it's at Christmas, or whatever mid-winter festival we keep, that we tend to meet ourselves as we really are.

Sometimes I Feel Like Crying

I like Christmas Eve. The office closes at midday. I reckon to get all my Christmas shopping done in the few hours available before the big stores shut. That's usually around 4.00 or 4.30. Colleagues marvel at my efficiency, but I explain it's just a question of being organized.

'It's not that I'm so great,' I say, 'it's just that you lot are so inefficient: you worry and fret and get neurotic. All you have to do is forward plan, know exactly what you mean to buy and go to any big department store of which you have previously obtained a floor map. By leaving it to the last moment too, you can save money. By 24 December the stores are setting up for the post-

Christmas sales, a lot of stuff is already marked as reduced and sales staff are too exhausted by the seasonal long hours to keep up any argument that everything is meant to be full price until Boxing Day. "Marked down is marked down," say I, and they capitulate.'

It's not that I'm mean, you understand. I just don't like spending money unnecessarily. I see so much of it. I work for a large insurance company, monitoring claims. This year I was promoted to head of department. I take the responsibility seriously. People waste so much money just because they can't be bothered to read the small print. It appals me. I'm sorry for them sometimes, but what can I do? So an owl flies in an open window and leaves a nasty trail across the wedding feast, including the cake, and you put in a claim. 'But bird damage is specifically excluded in your agreement,' I say. 'You get nothing.'

There it is, bold as brass, in the small print. Well, 'bold' might not be quite the word – I reckon the font's about eight – but there it is all the same.

'But I've spent £900 a year for the last 15 years on insurance and never claimed a thing,' comes the response. 'Now my daughter's wedding is ruined. Is this all you can do for me?'

And all I can say is 'Sorry, you should have read the agreement before you signed it.' I think before my promotion I might have stretched a point – we do have some discretion – but not now. I see my duty as being to my employers.

Mind you, the toy department can be a bit tricky by Christmas Eve. Things do sell out, and one may have to revise one's list pretty quickly, but there's always the educational toys to fall back upon. If staff act reluctant and say, 'But it's so late, Parcel Collection in the basement must just about be closing,' I remind them of their Christmas ads and put it to them that they don't want to be in contravention of the Trades Descriptions Act. The whole store is advertised as open, not just bits of it. They soon enough find a messenger to take whatever it is first to gift-wrapping then down to the basement to await collection.

A ceiling of £10 a present and ten presents to buy and that's exactly £100 for Christmas, plus train fares home to my parents for the family get-together. Not bad. I book the train well in advance to make sure I get a good reduction. If there's any nonsense I demand that they call head office and get the management to read them the small print on discounted fares. It's best to book such tickets in person, in the rush hour. A long queue behind you, pressing for attention, usually brings results.

Anyway, at 4.26, gift-shopping complete and only £89 spent, it was time to turn my attention to me. I went on up to the Bargain Bin on the third floor – that's Fashion – to look for a glitzy top to wear with my jeans for the New Year's party. I have just about a perfect figure – 34, 26, 34 – which I've dieted and exercised and liposuctioned to achieve, so most things look okay on me, they don't have to be expensive.

I found a piece of really agreeable glitter, low cut to make the most of the 34. It was reduced from £90 to £8 – not bad at all.

I do rather rely on the New Year's party to find my escort for the year. Around September I tend to get fed up with them and say goodbye, then I give myself three months solo in which to firm up my friendships. That done, my bed begins to feel a little empty and by Christmas I'm quite looking forward to filling it with someone new. I'm only 28, too young to settle down.

As it happens, last year's escort actually dumped me before I could dump him, and that's made me nervous. His name was Corin.

'I don't know what's the matter with you, Jacqui,' he said as he walked out. 'Every day you seem to get meaner and tougher. Perhaps it's your job.'

I am not tough, I am not mean, I am just practical and hate waste. If anything, I'm too soft. I even trained as a nurse. My heart bled for humanity – so much so I had to give up because of the stress. Now at least suffering humanity only comes to me through the post, or at the end of a phone if reception slips up and lets the calls through.

I should be feeling happy and relaxed, here in the bosom of my loving family, at the time of year I most love, in that blissful torpor that descends on the land between Christmas and the New Year, when the office is closed and the streets are empty and you have time to have baths and read books and think about yourself. I don't often do that. There isn't time, is there? I often work a twelve-hour day.

Friends

Yet for some reason I feel like crying. I've turned soft and gentle. See what just five days away from the office can do for a girl? I sit in my childhood bedroom looking out over the bare garden and think of Corin. I miss him.

I can hear my mother pottering about in the living room below, doing her annual lament at the too-early falling of the Christmas tree needles, and my father tangling with the streamers as ever, and my twin nieces and one nephew arguing over their toys.

I don't know how my sister Effie had the courage to have children; I don't know how any woman has. You have no control whatsoever over what comes out, and no insurance. If ever I have children I'll have them by cloning, thank you very much. Fortunately Effie's kids seem just about okay and I love them and they love me.

But anyway, my gold top. I had quite a tussle with this particular sales girl. She had greasy blonde hair with black roots. She said the top had got into the Bargain Bin by mistake and was a designer piece and the asking price was £900 and I had to pay the shelf price. That was absurd. Black-roots was temporary Christmas staff; they can be greater sticklers than the regular girls. I noticed her hand was trembling. I knew then I would win.

I demanded to see the manager, and when Black-roots claimed she'd already have gone home, inasmuch as the store was now closed, I said oh no the store wasn't, not while my stuff was down in the basement waiting for me to turn up. First I made her call down to Parcel Collection to confirm that they understood this.

Then I made her come with me to the managerial level on the sixth floor and we banged on doors until we found some woman still packing up, who, after I had explained the situation in detail, said, 'Oh give it to her for £8, for God's sake just give it to her,' and we went downstairs. When I said I wanted the top gift-wrapped Black-roots began to cry and I relented and said, 'Okay, just shove it in any old bag,' and she did. I do have a kind heart. I even said, 'I do hope you get to the hairdresser before tomorrow, so you can get your roots done.'

It was 5.10 by the time the janitor had unlocked Parcel Collection – can you imagine, they'd just shut up shop and gone home, their business unfinished? I would never have done a thing like that. As a result I actually missed my train and had to get the next one, and you can imagine what happened next. The conductor said my ticket wasn't valid on the train, I argued that it was the crowds on the platform as result of a couple of their cancelled trains that had held me up, so it was the railway company's fault, not mine. I got my way, but only after a short unscheduled stop while the transport police were called, and somehow I didn't feel the normal stab of triumph. In fact I felt rather depressed. Why is everything always so uphill?

If I go on getting value for money like this, I will have the deposit of a house saved within a year. But who will there be to help me with the mortgage? No lovers in sight and friends pretty thin on the ground. My bright idea for giving up smoking was never to buy cigarettes but always to ask others for them and let social embarrassment stand between me and the wasteful, unhealthy habit. But I think my s.e. threshold is rather high. It must be. I smoked just as many cigarettes and ended up with fewer friends.

Downstairs someone opens a window.

'Now all the robots are broken,' one of the twins is saying, 'we've only got what Auntie Bug Meanie gave us.' Me, Auntie Bug Meanie?

'Hush. She'll hear,' says my sister. 'We don't want to upset her.'

'Why not?' asks the niece, in the manner of small children.

'She's upset enough as it is,' says my sister, and I suppose that's true. Since Corin walked out I've been unhappy. I haven't seen why other people should be having a good time when I'm not.

My father says I've grown obsessive about money, but he's a fine one to talk. He's a gambler, he spends money obsessively, the way I save it. And they even make him pay an entrance fee to get into their bloody casino. I'd never stand for that. He's too soft.

I begin to cry. Time stretches forward and back in an odd way. Forward to the New Year's Eve party where I just might meet Mr Right, with the aid of a gold top which I should have paid £900 for and paid £8. Back to Christmas Eve when I bought it, and that poor girl with the black roots crying. I hope she got to the hairdresser. Bet she didn't. And then Christmas Day, and my mother opening her diary and my father his wallet – you can get both in leather goods – and my sister her gardening gloves and my brother in law his secateurs – both from gardening, the next section along – and the children their educational gifts, just down the escalator, and all their faces as they opened them, and how the adults seemed both polite and somehow concerned, and the children just plain unbelieving.

It's true that once I was famous for the originality and extravagance of my presents and would never, never have had a store gift-wrap anything. It would be all wicked paper wrap and coloured string and tags and bows and glitter and so forth, done by me. And I wondered what was happening to me.

I call Corin on his mobile. I know the number by heart, though it's been six months since we split.

'I think you're right,' I said. 'I blame my job. If they pay you to be mean and tough, that's what you become. If you get paid for reading the small print, you get into the habit.'

There was silence at the other end of the phone. Then Corin said, 'You could try blaming yourself.'

So I put the phone down. He was a pompous prat. I'd quite got over him. But I thought I might call by the store and leave a box of chocolates for Black-roots. She might even become my friend. I might even, who knows, chuck in my job and go back to nursing. Try living by the small print and everyone hates you. I give up.

Moral

If you let life and times work upon you, if
you can listen to what is being said to you,
and reform – and indeed repent – you will
have your reward.

I can tell you that Black-roots, whose real name was Rachel,
did indeed become Jacqui's friend. They went out for a coffee
and Rachel told Jacqui that to have black roots was
purposeful, trendy and a gesture of defiance to her employers.
'They don't like it,' she said, 'but no way can they fire you.'

Jacqui had her own hair done the same. It was easy. You
get your hair bleached all over and then just wait for nature
to run its course. By the time the roots were an inch deep
Corin was back, and liked Jacqui's new style. He could see
that she was loosening up.

Jacqui is not the warmest of people, though she shows
promise. She felt remorse and acted upon it. All the same
she needs her soul strengthening to make her truly likeable.
There are exercises which can be done. Treat the soul, like
the brain, in the same way as you would a muscle. To make
it stronger, use it.

Rachel could join Jacqui in a quest for culture, and general
elevation of the spirit. The more you perceive the difference
between the mundane and the divine, the more responsive
you become to the latter.

Exercises to Strengthen the Soul

Seek exposure to the arts, since they are God given.

(The Darwinians deny it, I have to admit. No God, they claim. No intelligent design, no supreme Maker, not even one who set the clock of the universe ticking. Music and dance are survival friendly, that's all. Art is sympathetic magic, cave painting just part of the religious ritual of fools. Literature likewise – random variations on the holy books of the primitives. These claims may be true, but other things are true as well.)

Exposure to the arts refines the spirit. Exposure to what is best in the arts increases our resistance to the shoddy, the brash, the ugly. If you listen to music long enough and hard enough, you can just about hear the music of the spheres. If you look at enough paintings, you will automatically choose the least offensive sofa in the shop.

All those parents trailing their unwilling children around art galleries do them a great service. Those who see only what is ugly – concrete and graffiti – grow up to be ugly of spirit and negligible of soul.

Certain shopping malls clear their centres of hoods by playing Bach over the sound system: vampires scatter when presented with a cross. Think about it.

Exercise 1: Go to a Concert

Jacqui and Rachel need to go to a concert. They've mostly only ever heard muzak, or sound delivered directly into their brains via iPod, which drives out any possibility of reflection. Like a hot, hot wind the iPod dries out and shrivels the tender green shoot of a growing soul. Silence now makes them nervous.

A Beethoven string quartet at the Wigmore Hall would be a good shock introduction, but perhaps too much of one. Jacqui and Rachel could only marvel at how it was that so many delicate and refined-looking people – women with long earrings, men with ridiculous large glasses – could sit for so long, listening to the screeching of strings? Tell them that the audience strains to hear the music of paradise and all they'll say is 'weird'.

A night out at the Proms would be less rarefied, and perhaps more advisable; the 169 golden angels on the Albert Memorial could waft them through the great doors of the hall, and the rolls of drums and the suggestion of a tune, though only now and then, might pacify them enough to make them stay. And perhaps if they listened hard enough they might just hear the music of the spheres and exult. It is not beyond the bounds of possibility. Exultation is to the soul as Baby Bio is to the Busy Lizzie.

Failing that, let them go to any concert – rock, pop or hip hop. At least live music disturbs the air and is a real and not a virtual thing, and sharing tunes with the like-minded can do your soul no actual harm. Jacqui needs to feel herself at one with others, not just a reader of the small print but part of a whole which might start in Hyde Park but stretches and stretches to include Great Britain, the world, the universe and all creation. Awe is what the soul feeds upon.

Exercise 2: Go to a Gallery

Jacqui and Rachel can cross London and go to the National Gallery. Their eyes will no doubt glaze over at first. They will want to go to the café and to the shop, but won't find much they want to take home, let alone wear. It's all so middle-aged and middle class.

But a poster of a Van Gogh chair quite takes their eye. It is the one used to advertise the gallery. It is the same chair which hangs in one of the galleries upstairs, essence of chair – woven rush seat, yellow painted wood, tiled floor, blue curtain – but put through a clever technological process for the benefit of the gallery promotion, distorted until it seems to be somehow liquidizing. Demons might laugh with joy to see it.

Jacqui and Rachel stare at the poster a little bit. 'That's wicked,' says Rachel, accurately enough. But Jacqui has a vague memory from school that it's not really like that and they trip all the way up the stairs and through the tourist throng to see the original. Jacqui's right. The chair is not liquidizing. It's still there, as ever, solid, imposing its vision on posterity. 'I prefer this one,' Jacqui says, and angels dance, and pin a gold star on her soul, or whatever they do, just to encourage it.

On the way down the steps Jacqui has a strange pain in her heart and tears come into her eyes and she can't think why. It's the sudden sharpness of the pin, no doubt.

Exercise 3: Go to Church

Not some dreary place of worship, the pews gone and chairs put in their place, fixed together for easy handling so they creak when you move, with bongo drums, jingle music, social worker vicar and counselling after the service, but a proper old-fashioned church. They could try Westminster Abbey.

They might be impressed by its ancient magnificence, the idea that their forebears felt at home in such places, went to extraordinary efforts to afford and build them, to the greater glory of God. They might be moved by sheer marvel to take their iPods out. They might even stay to a service, with any luck in the old-fashioned language, which you can only half-understand, but in the half-understanding catch a glimpse of something mysterious and infinitely desirable and definitely *there*.

They might sing a hymn of the old-fashioned kind, in which you have to struggle with the syntax but the rhymes are so satisfactory, the puzzlement adds to the sum of the parts. All glory, laud and honour, and so forth.

They could pray for the sick – and as the list of names is read out, wonder about the lives they lived, and how no man is an island. Some phrase they've heard from somewhere. Rachel could think how really she ought to go and visit her grandfather in an old persons' home, properly run and inspected, but lonely. They could repent of their sins, and giggle because obviously it was absurd to think of the elderly congregation, kneeling at the communion rail with ankle-less legs and wrinkled stockings, committing sins of fornication, let alone getting down to sweep up the crumbs under anyone's table. No-one today has sins. They have issues which need to be resolved. Same thing.

But for a fraction of a second Jacqui could remember how her nephews call her Auntie Bug Meanie, and resolve to do better.

They could listen to the choir for five minutes – a spot of polyphony in the sepulchral gloom. They could long to leave but not quite like to push their way through the lines of old folk. Already they're more moral creatures.

When they leave, Rachel and Jacqui will shiver a little and say, 'I don't want to die' and wonder briefly what happens after death. They are right to waste no time on it – nobody can possibly know. That in itself intrigues them. They're doing really well.

Exercise 4: Go See a Landscape

Jacqui and Rachel can take a coach from Victoria to a beauty spot within easy reach of London – hills and valleys, ripe for exultation, patchworked by the green fields of man's endeavour. There's nothing to *do*, though at least there's a stall where they can get a Diet Coke, and a fellow tourist says, 'Listen, is that a lark?' and they take out the plugs in their ears and forget to put them back. The wind in their ears is strange and interesting.

Or instead they could just go up to Hampstead Heath on the bus, after half an hour in Covent Garden, where you can buy lucky rose crystal rings at £15, and get off at the Kenwood entrance. Walk along past Kenwood House, and catch a glimpse of a Fragonard through the windows, and a note or two of Handel's 'Water Music' from the outdoor concert hall drifting through the air, and climb a hill or two amongst summer grasses and see the misty view over London, way over to the Surrey hills and the streaks of sunset red in the western sky.

Red sky at night, shepherd's delight.

'Does the sun always sink in the west?' asks Rachel.

'Duh!' says Jacqui. 'Everyone knows that.'

'Well, I don't,' says Rachel.

'I think it does move a few inches or something,' says Jacqui kindly, 'either way.'

Which shows you how she is improving. A month back she'd have hugged the idea of Rachel's ignorance to herself and rejoiced.

A last gleam of sunlight strikes her black-rooted blonde head and looks for a moment almost like a halo.

I hope they did go up to Hampstead because on the way back in the bus they would then sit behind two students, one called Jude, doing design at Camberwell, and Ralph, studying marine biology at the Imperial Institute. Jacqui and Rachel fell into conversation about the Proms, Van Gogh's chair, the many-skirted girls of Fragonard, and Jacqui said, 'What was that thing about no man is an island?'

At which Jude turned round and quoted a John Donne poem he once learned by heart for an oral English exam. He stumbled a little but remembered most of it:

> No man is an island, entire of itself,
> Every man is a piece of the continent, a part of the
> main.
> If a clod be washed away by the sea
> Europe is the less, as well as if a promontory were,
> As well as if a manor of thy friends or of thine own
> were.
> Any man's death diminishes me, because I am involved
> in mankind,
> And therefore never send to know for whom the bell
> tolls.
> It tolls for thee.

After that, with their strengthened and well-exercised souls, they all got on like a house on fire, and though Jacqui felt enough loyalty to Corin to stay with him, Rachel eventually moved in with Jude.

I am not suggesting that a good man is necessarily the reward for virtue. On the other hand, there is nothing like an enthusiasm for the arts to help you leap class and educational boundaries.

The elevated soul calls to the elevated soul.

Family

Families make you happy.

Your sister turning up at the door unexpectedly, bearing gifts.

Your mother saying she's proud of you.

Your father saying the same.

Your brother lending you his car.

Your grandmother – the happily married one – leaving you her wedding ring.

Your children asleep, safe, sound and smiling.

Your husband bringing you flowers.

Your stepchild giving you a kiss.

That is, if you're a happy family to begin with.

If not, we can see quite another scenario:

> Your sister turns up. You pretend to be out.
>
> Your mother and father say they're not going to pay back your student loan.
>
> Your brother's car's a death trap. Is he doing it on purpose?
>
> Your grandmother's putting a guilt trip on you: she wants you to get married.
>
> You couldn't get a babysitter and you could be at a party. Why did you ever have children?
>
> What's he trying to hide?
>
> Little toad.

How did you get into this state? By spite, meanness, malice, carelessness, a general '*Why should I?*' and '*Who do you think you are?*' That's how.

You got into this state by flirting with your sister's partner, spending your student loan on drink and drugs, driving your brother's car for a week with the oil light on, telling your grandmother you've got chlamydia, habitually keeping the babysitter until dawn, being unfaithful yourself and pointing out to your stepchild that you're not her mother and never will be, when the child's real mother is an alcoholic.

You're not likely to do *all* these things, I agree, but just one or two is more than enough to make for very unsatisfactory family Christmases. I should make do with friends, if I were you. The family might be happier without you. Your 'making do' might be more like them 'putting up with'. You might even have to treat all your friends to Christmas lunch at some fancy hotel to make sure they turn up.

But you too can be loveable, if you would only change your ways. Remember that if you can't say anything nice, it's better to say nothing at all.

Remember that if you want to be happy you'd better be good.

The Instinctive Approach to Family Life

The Darwinians and neo-Darwinians take a stern, harsh, horrid view of family life. They see the child as using up the parents' resources of food, care and attention and when it's sucked them dry spitting them out and discarding them, leaving their poor depleted husks behind. As a sideline the child does its best to elbow its siblings right out of the nest – the more parental nourishment and attention that goes to them, the less left for it.

If the father has any sense, he's off too, before the growing son takes over as head bull and gores him to death. He may well have gone already, of course, to build another family, spread the selfish gene.

See instinct in unhappy action in the child who grows up and leaves home and never gets in touch again. It happens. Just a card at Christmas if you're lucky.

See innate sibling rivalry in the way the older child beats up the younger and the younger uses cunning to get the older into trouble.

It's there in all of us. In the least socialized of us, in whom the soul is least elevated, it's there the most.

If the culture tells you the life of the instinct is okay, it's easy to believe it. It suits us. *Do what thou wilt shall be the whole of the Law.* If the culture says it's every man, or woman, for themselves, that's the way it will very quickly be. So hell might quickly come to Earth.

Yet other forces are at work, too. Natural affection, given a chance, and when mixed with oughts and shoulds, is remarkably resilient.

See it on the train as Jacqui did, going home for Christmas – so many returning family members, so many gifts and ribbons and a kind of thrill in the air. Even those who most hate Christmas feel they ought to go home and do.

See how siblings love to reminisce, old feuds forgotten. Except at funerals, when they flare again. Who gets the oak table, who gets the silver cutlery, who got the most love and attention? Then the self-serving instinct subsides again, family affection reasserts itself, sibling speaks to sibling again and former wrongs are forgotten. This one stores the furniture, that one guarantees the rent – a mini-tribe within the tribe, that's the family.

So value it: subdue self-seeking instinct; bury the spitting, fighting, snarling aspect of family life. Don't remind your mother of the time she got drunk. Don't say to your child, *'If you can't remember what it was you said, it can't have been very important.'* It's mean and rejecting. Try blaming yourself, not them. Then the family will make you happy, not unhappy, because virtue is on your side. They will look to you and love you: you occupy the moral high ground. The bitchery and resentments will stop, the eating up of the soul in gripings, and brooding about wrongs done to you and vengeance planned by you.

And keep your motives clear. Think not, *'One day I might need them.'* Rather think, *'Today they need me.'*

Did you, reading that, think, *'Oh yuck!'* Did the gorge rise in your throat at such sentimentality? The *'yuck'* moment is when sentimentality (nature) and rationality (nurture) collide. The more educated you are, the more able nurture is to win over nature and the sooner you'll say *'Yuck.'*

For sentimentality is instinctive: the surge of emotion, the lump in the throat, is to do with the protection of the young and helpless. Any mammal with eyes which are large in proportion to the head causes the '*Aaah!*' reaction in any adult. Wolves will suckle human babies. Farmer's wives will spoonfeed lambs. Think kittens, think Audrey Hepburn, think Goldie Hawn. Starving children in Africa speak to us more than their starving mothers. We can't rest until they are fed.

If the sentimentality leads us to moral action, that's fine. Doing good, as we know, makes us happy. But for how long?

Let me tell you a parable about Jason, William and Zoë, three young people who thought they could save the world, their parents Doug and Gail, and Janet, who came along for the ride. You might think the world is in such a state that it is beyond saving, but that is the voice of an older generation speaking. Take no notice.

The Joyous Multitude

Gail looked at her children across the breakfast table on Sunday morning and wondered how she and Douglas had done it. She had always considered herself rather dull, plain and dumpy, and Doug was frankly rather short, thin and gangly, with eyes too close together. She had married him in a fit of generosity to make up for his mother being so nasty to him and because her mother said looks in a man didn't matter. Yet between them they had produced three singularly attractive young people, Jason, William and Zoë, with cheerful dispositions, kindly natures, broad brows and wide-apart eyes, all granted by the grace of God the ability and desire to pass exams and at the moment all back from college, recovered from Glastonbury, recovering from Live 8 in London on the Saturday and intending to be at the G8 demo on the Monday. If the Toyota held out. Douglas would not let them take the Mercedes. Yet some of Gail and Doug's contemporaries, better looking and posher, had managed only dull, inward-looking and neurotic children, dropouts and drug addicts who were a perpetual shame and worry to their parents. Luck of the draw, Gail supposed, and they'd been lucky.

At the moment, in between eating scrambled eggs and bacon, the young people were singing Sting's 'We'll Be Watching You' in chorus, and, what was more, in perfect harmony.

Douglas was opening the post. Whatever it was didn't please him.

'Hang on a bit,' said Gail. 'I thought it was "I'll Be Watching You", the stalker's anthem.'

'It's "we" now,' said Jason. 'Everything's changed since you were a girl. The people of the world have got their eye on the leaders of the world, that's what last night in Hyde Park was all about.'

'Sting was fabulous,' said William. 'Bush, Blair, Chirac — all the villains, named and shamed. The West can't get away with it any more.'

'I want to get to the shops to buy white clothes for Edinburgh tomorrow,' said Zoë. 'White bands aren't enough. It's Janet's fault. All my white T-shirts are grey. She put them in the wash with Jason's black Armani underpants. That girl is really and truly thick.'

Janet was 22, dyslexic, and helped Gail out sometimes in the house and garden.

'There were eight loads of washing after Glastonbury,' said Gail. 'Perhaps Janet just got fed up with sorting. You three couldn't be woken.'

'That's Glastonbury for you,' said Douglas. 'Mud and exhaustion. Thank God our water isn't metered. Yet.'

He put down the letter. It was from his accountant. It was not cheerful. His business was failing. Another twenty skilled staff would have to be laid off. The demand for British-made high-quality reusable medical instruments was falling. Since AIDS, mad cow disease and the prion scares – prions can survive even steam sterilization – more and more hospital equipment was required to be throwaway. And now China was entering the market in a big way. Meanwhile Zoë and the boys needed to be kitted out in white to save the whale or whatever it was this time. Their bracelets ran up their wrists like rainbows to their forearms. They were good children and he was proud of them. He had saved them from the harsh lessons of life and with any luck they need never learn them.

The doorbell rang. It was Janet. Her mother was an alcoholic and her father a chronic depressive, but together they had produced a sweet, pretty, blonde girl who worked full time in a baker's shop, part time as a hairdresser and in her spare time for Gail. She was saving up for the deposit on a house and had been since she left school at 16. She spent nothing on herself if she could help it and had £23,000 in the post office.

Family

Seeing the family was still having breakfast, Janet went straight out into the garden and started dead-heading roses and stripping the unsightly yellow rose leaves which had appeared overnight. The garden was to be opened to the public for the first time on Monday morning as part of the National Gardens Scheme. The gate takings were to go to the charity of Gail's choice. It was a great honour to be accepted onto the scheme. Gail had worked for fifteen years with this in mind, breaking stones and sifting earth, laying down lawns, planting trees and shrubs, and now her roses were the best in the neighbourhood. Never let it be said that just because she was a stay-at-home mother she didn't work hard. Janet had been helping Gail in the garden and house since she was 10.

'Janet is so embarrassing, Mum,' said Zoë. 'It isn't right to employ domestic staff. It's okay when she does the garden, but it feels unethical when she cleans up after us.'

Zoë liked Janet less than the boys did. Janet looked fragile, but wasn't. Zoë looked zippy and confident, but wasn't.

Janet came in for coffee. She told Gail she was having trouble with the sprinkler. The water pressure from the mains was so weak it was hardly enough to make it rotate. There was talk of a hosepipe ban in the area.

'That's nuts,' said William. 'It was raining most of last week. And you should have been at Glastonbury! The mud!'

'Yeah, I noticed,' said Janet. 'But here the ground's so hard the rain just runs off. And the water table's falling. It's the new estate up on the hill. Eight hundred new houses.'

'A hosepipe ban!' shuddered Gail. 'I might as well just give up on the garden. Those dreadful little houses!'

'Don't be such a snob, Mum,' said Jason.

'You're such Nimbys, you two,' said Zoë.

'Nimbys?' asked Douglas,

'Not in my back yard,' explained William.

Doug refrained from saying it was all very well for them, they were away at college a lot of the time, or in bed, or at festivals, or concerts, or parties. They didn't notice how busy the roads had become, or how crowded the trains, and how with the coming of the supermarket all the small shops had closed.

William was now explaining to Janet about the Make Poverty History concert and why it was important. How noble Bob Geldof was going to Make Poverty History, and how all the good people were going along to the G8 summit in Edinburgh to make sure world leaders noticed.

'I've never been to a concert,' said Janet. 'Why, when you can download the stuff for free? I've never been to a demo either.'

Family

'A protest virgin,' said William appreciatively.

'But I'd quite like to go one day,' said Janet. 'Just to see what it's like. It might be exciting.'

'Why don't you come to Edinburgh with us this evening?' asked William. 'There's a spare seat in the car.'

Zoë gestured *no, no*. She hated travelling in crowded cars and Janet would be a drag. But William and Jason didn't seem to notice.

Douglas opened the letter he had left until last. It was from the Inland Revenue. It said his appeal had been turned down; the disputed £37,000 was indeed owed. He had hoped to get the children through college without student loans, so they didn't have to start their lives loaded with debt. He could forget that.

'We'll be dangerously squashed,' said Zoë. 'Unless of course Dad lets us take the Mercedes. Did you know that for every extra student in a car the accident rate rises exponentially?'

'Perhaps you'd better,' said Douglas. The clapped-out Toyota was a safety risk; the M1 horrendous. The word 'squashed' brought horrific headlines to mind: 'Protesters in motorway mayhem horror.' He'd had too much bad news lately. You got to expect more.

'But they're depending on me at the baker's,' said Janet. 'We're short-staffed.'

'Saving the world is more important,' said Jason, 'than serving the already overfed with cakes and buns. You know how many children die every in Africa from starvation? One a second!'

Click, click, click, they went with their fingers.

'One click, one death,' said Zoë.

'That's awful,' said Janet. 'I'll come.'

The M1 was busy. Old bangers, coaches, all converging on Edinburgh. Everyone dressed in white. Jason driving, Zoë in the passenger seat, William and Janet in the back. Make Poverty History. So much goodwill! Of course it would happen.

'Isn't it exciting?' said William. His hand was on Janet's slender knee. Any minute he'd put her arm round her. It wasn't going far, because she worked in the local baker's and aspired to nothing and he was taking a philosophy degree, but you never knew.

Janet thought William was a bit of a twat, like the rest of his family, but she liked his fingers. They felt quite electric.

'I don't know anything about politics,' she said. 'I've never taken an interest. You'll have to tell me.'

They told her.

'Those G8 leaders must be real scumbags,' said Janet, horrified. 'Starving all those poor little African children!'

Family

'They don't want to share,' said Jason. 'They want all the wealth for themselves.'

'But if we give more to Africa, does it mean we'll have to pay more tax?' asked Janet.

'The West can afford it,' said Zoë.

'I can't,' said Janet. 'You should see my pay slips as it is! And I don't know how long my job is going to last. Krispy Crème Donuts are opening down the road.'

There was slightly awkward silence. Then they tried to explain about debt relief and free trade, but it wasn't much use.

'I'd be ashamed to have debts,' said Janet. 'I was brought up to pay my own way.'

She was very difficult. Jason and Zoë wished they hadn't brought her along, but William was holding her hand.

They talked about Bush's satanic empire, about the illegitimacy of the Iraq War and the problem of obesity, which was not theirs.

An old banger passed them at dangerous speed, its many occupants making slitty throat gestures.

'Just being in a Mercedes,' said Zoë crossly, 'doesn't mean we're rich.'

A coach passed. The passengers were draped in white, with white face masks and black holes for eyes.

'Like the Ku Klux Klan,' said Janet. 'Spooky.'

'I'll look after you,' said William.

'I still don't understand why it's our fault the Iraqis are blowing themselves up,' Janet complained.

'Bush started it off,' explained Jason patiently. 'He destabilized the region. He should have left well alone. It wasn't democracy he was after, it was oil.'

Douglas had filled the tank for them before they left, which was just as well, there were such queues at the petrol stations.

'You mean Saddam Hussein was a good thing?' Janet sounded surprised. 'My dad said he cut out people's tongues if he didn't like what they said. And that's what he'd do to me if I didn't shut up.'

William gently disengaged his hand from Janet's. What was he getting into? Her home life sounded a bit strong for him. Sorry for her and all that, and it must be hell to be dyslexic, but even so.

'My mum likes Tony Blair,' Janet continued. 'She says the government's doing all right. She gets free detox sessions.'

'Tony Blair!' the others shrieked. 'Bush's poodle! All those refugees sent back to Zimbabwe, back to torture and death!'

'But we can't keep everyone,' said Janet. 'The whole of Zimbabwe would be over here if they could. Who'd want to live there when they could live here?'

They were in a traffic jam now, cars from all over the country converging on Edinburgh. Flags, banners, laughing, singing, everyone of one mind – fabulous. In the free car park the sounds of Pink Floyd, Sting and Madonna came floating through the crisp early morning air, warring for precedence.

'I bet that concert was just a money-making scam, nothing to do with Make Poverty History at all,' said Janet.

They were sorry they'd brought her.

'And I expect that's what all this Geldof stuff is really about too,' she went on. 'If we make Africa a better place to live in they won't want to come over here. It's just all one big conspiracy, isn't it, the way you say.'

Too horrified for words, they managed to lose her when the march was forming. They didn't feel good about it, but how could you communicate with someone so stupid?

They marched in the slowly winding procession up towards the castle. Make Poverty History! It was hard to see how the world would not be saved with so much hard work, organization and goodwill all focused here.

Round about teatime William worried a little about losing Janet. Would she be okay?

'The Janets of the world will always survive,' said Zoë. But even as she spoke her mobile buzzed and fluttered in her pocket.

It was Janet. She was in the infirmary. She'd got caught up in a riot of some kind. The doctors were keeping her in overnight and possibly longer. She had concussion and they didn't want her brain to swell.

'But she hasn't got a brain *to* swell,' said Zoë, and the others giggled before they shushed her for her wickedness. She didn't think Janet had heard.

It was a great nuisance. They couldn't just leave her. They'd have to go and check her injuries out.

A&E was crowded with casualties from the march. There had been some trouble – not much, they were told, but of course Janet had managed to get caught up with the anarchists and on the wrong side of the riot police. She was a bit battered around the head and had a nasty black eye. They were keeping her in for observation, but there was no need to worry.

Jason, William and Zoë agreed they couldn't wait for her, they had a party tomorrow. Janet said it was okay, she'd just take the train back once she was discharged. But then she complained about having to spend money on the fare home, which was a bit much – everyone knew she had £23,000 in the bank.

When Jason, William and Zoë got back home on the Tuesday night their mother was in tears on the lawn. The water pressure had finally fallen so low the sprinklers had stopped rotating and there'd been no one to put up the *'Open to the Public'* signs. She'd only had thirteen visitors, after all of those years making the desert bloom.

'But what's the matter?' they asked her.

'Nothing, darlings,' she said, as was her wont. 'Nothing important.'

On the Thursday the bombs went off in London and all Gail thought mattered was that her children were safely home.

Moral

We could try charity begins at home. Never were there three more self-centred, self-righteous and bigoted young persons than Jason, William and Zoë. Selfish too. Mud at Glastonbury is a joyous thing so long as there is someone else to clear it up. They never lift a finger to help their mother in the garden. It never crosses their mind that their father has business worries. They spend all their energy being good.

But they are happy. And by many people's standards they are really quite good. They are at least trying. When it comes to charity, though they may see 'home' as starting far away, in distant places, they shake boxes, go on marches and do their best, so long as it does not inconvenience them too much. None of them will stay with Janet; she does not agree with them and it is easy to dismiss her as stupid. And no one they know takes any notice of concussion.

You could also quarrel with Jason, William and Zoë because they look past the beggar outside their new supermarket, not meeting his eye, though noticing that his dog looked well fed enough, and reproach their father when he gave voice to his marvel that Social Services gave extra money to claimants with pets, out of his taxes.

'You are such a right-wing fascist, Daddy,' Zoë often complains, while he signs the cheque, and when her mother murmured once, of the beggar, 'I hope he spends all that money on bones, not drugs,' she pouted about the house for hours, saying her mother was drug phobic, and it was dangerous to give dogs bones, anyway, they could splinter.

But she loves her mother and her mother loves her. They are a happy family. It is too easy to be irritated when it comes to other people's happiness, and we should not succumb to the feeling. We must give them credit where credit is due, and remember that young people do learn.

This lot will have to. Douglas is to go bankrupt, and the house to be sold by Inland Revenue at a knock-down price.

120

Family

Fortunately Gail has a little money of her own and they end up living in a pretty cottage in Ireland, in a lush spot with a high rainfall. Her garden wins prizes locally. The children visit frequently. Jason becomes an estate agent, selling rural plots for business development, William has given up philosophy and is a banker, and Zoë, who always did have too much of a liking for drugs, took up with a Rastafarian and has two children and no money.

Janet did not have concussion but lost her job. The baker's did close. But she married the manager of Krispy Creme and sits on the Town Council where her contribution is most valued. She has a keen eye for waste, and expenditure has been cut to the bone. She taks about her visit to Edinburgh when she was a girl as a real eye-opener.

And really, actually, all of them except Janet could be described as happy. That's what comes of having a loving family.

Shopping

We gather in stores, in the good times, to keep ourselves going through the hard times. (That's a pun. Gather in stores of grain in the cave. Gather in stores to shop together, in the new world. See?)

We do it with food. Our bodies lay down fat in order for us to feed from it in times of scarcity. Think of the brown bear, plump as can be after a good autumn, but skinny as a rake when the thaw comes and she emerges, skin hanging in folds, from hibernation.

The Atkins diet works by tricking the body into believing it's starving, that it's got to break down fat if it's going to survive.

It's just a pity the times of scarcity never come. Strawberries were a once-a-year treat. Now they're always growing somewhere in the world – just snap your fingers and they're there. *'How about some caster sugar? And lashings of cream?'*

We like to have the cave nicely filled with *things*. In case we run out. A hefty pile of moss to put the baby on. An extra bearskin. Wood for the fire. *Gather in, preserve, save, collect.*

Of course we shop. Always have. Or bartered. Your nose bone for my beads.

It's instinct, at it again. The urge to ornament the self. To get yourself a super man. He brings the meat back, though you gather the berries. *'That's a pretty red! Let's have it!'* Excavations of prehistoric peoples always turn up some female ornament or other.

Socialization brings us the credit card, the bank account, the bargain offer. How can we resist? Some men like us to spend. *'My wife, she shops till she drops!'* Proud.

The alpha male deserves the alpha female. The brave deserve the fair. So don't beat yourself up about this either. The urge to acquire is in your genes. Acquisition. It's Mother Nature at her fiendish work again.

Just remember, twelve pairs of shoes are fine, but twenty-four are pushing it. Twelve are forgivable, twenty-four or more are bad, an offence against the sumptuary laws. Sell surplus shoes on eBay and give to charity. You're never going to wear them and only a few of them will fit.

Shopping? Just Do It!

I have a bright-blue and yellow mug which carries the slogan *'Shopping? Just do it!'* It is my favourite mug. On it is a giddy-looking and totally happy girl, of the garage pin-up kind.

Happy, yes, but for how long? What happens next? *Bills.* Shopping is a source of great pleasure and also, naturally, a source of female guilt and anxiety.

If a woman has children there's no end to it. *'Now how am I going to buy their clothes? I've signed up for this new car and what about their maths tutoring? They will never pass their exams and it will all be my fault!'*

If she hasn't got children it's not much better. *'Why on earth did I buy that? It's the wrong colour/too large/too small/too cheap/too dear for what I wanted. There's no space left in the wardrobe as it is. If I saved instead of spent I could buy a house or get a pension.'*

And on the way home on the bus, the seat next to you piled with bags in shiny white and pink, bursting out with folds of white tissue, or the soft cloth of a shoebag, your breath starts coming in short gasps. A fully fledged anxiety attack: sweats, trembles and all. And no amount of breathing into a brown paper bag as recommended (first find one!) will stop it. Anxiety has struck and it's not even free-floating –

it is specific to shopping. (More about free-floating anxiety later.)

You could step off the bus and leave the bags behind, and with it the evidence of your guilt – it's not as if you actually needed anything you bought – but it would be an even worse waste of money. You could sell the stuff on eBay. Yes, that makes you feel better.

The normal advice – *'If it makes you feel guilty, don't do it'* – doesn't seem quite to apply. Stopping it would make you extremely unhappy. And who wants to drink from a mug that says, *'Shopping? Don't do it!'* Not me.

Your writer was brought up in a poverty-stricken household. She's never quite got over it. Schoolfriends would look in shop windows, say, *'I rather like that,'* and just go in and buy whatever it was. It seemed an infinitely desirable kind of life and she assumed it would never be hers. She was accustomed to averting her eyes when passing a shop window in case she was overwhelmed with longing for something she couldn't have.

Yet in the end she too could say, *'I like that, I'll take it'* or *'Let's go by taxi, it's quicker'* or even *'Let's hire a car with a driver, it's so much less effort.'* Now she is simply not good any more at frugality, and not inclined to wish it on others.

All I'm going to say for once is if you want to shop, shop. Shop some more. Put up with the boring details of what comes later. Debt, ruin, misery. Shopping? Just do it!

(I all but bought a pair of Roman earrings once, a bunch of purple grapes in a gold setting. I didn't buy them. I had a feeling they might be 'funerary objects' and had been found in some tomb. Then I changed my mind. I just wanted them. When I went back to the shop they had gone. I have lamented them ever since, and that was eight years ago. You know how it is? When it comes to shopping those who hesitate are lost.)

Driven to Ruin

Emma, in Flaubert's novel *Madame Bovary*, was driven to suicide by her passion for shopping. It wasn't disclosure to her husband of her many affairs which did it, it wasn't the sheer boredom of his presence, it was because, my feeling always was, she brought ruination on him by buying pretty things. She offered to sell her pretty proud self to the shop-keeper to whom she owed all the money – M. Hereux, but he pushed her aside. He didn't want her, he wanted his money. He'd encouraged her to run up debts. He despised her.

And when the crunch came, her lovers declined to help her. They were married now, they had other commitments, it was inconvenient. Love's love and then it's over! And she had so believed and trusted it was for ever, that it was a sacred thing. In love! And things, the pretty things, the silly things that you find in shop windows, were her ruination. Money is real, love is not.

She bought silk embroidered slippers for one lover, a silver case for another and little gifts for her husband. She bought pretty clothes for her daughter and lit the candles every day, not just on formal occasions. Her mother-in-law knew it would all end it tears, but her husband adored her and couldn't bear to stop her. She bought a new cloak lined with silk to run away in and a new studded trunk to take with her. But the lover she was absconding with didn't turn up. Perhaps because she'd warned him in passing that the daughter was coming too. And Emma went on spending, and the interest kept rising. She forged her husband's signature and in the end there was no way the family could be saved. She took her life, but her husband was ruined anyway.

Mind you, the story was written by a man. I think if it had been written by a woman Emma would have got away with it. One of the lovers would have turned up trumps. An admirer would have left her a fortune. Something. She would have lived happily ever after, lover after lover, and her husband would never have found out. That's much more like real life. And who is to say, as she grew older, being happy, she might have been good, and being good, she might have been happy – if only for lack of opportunity.

Shopping with the Hungry

Let me tell you my experience of going shopping with four Hollywood wives. They were all as skinny as rakes and as glamorous as hell. (Your writer has other things to think about than her appearance, and it shows, but they were good enough to take me out window shopping and endure the embarrassment.)

'Not shopping?' I asked, disappointed.

'Just window shopping,' they said firmly.

We trooped along an avenue in Century City. It was lined with restaurants, confectioners, delicatessens, cheese and chocolate shops, interspersed with stores selling Bach remedies, crystals, healing essences and so forth, as if the latter somehow neutralized the former, absolved you of the sin of being fat.

The wives' limbs were thin and sun-bedded, their manicures bright, their clothes in many tones of beige. Their gold jewellery clanked. I stomped around in flat shoes for wide feet; they wore Manolos even to shop.

We looked in windows. We studied the cream cakes, the mammoth Easter eggs, the little tins of caviare, so exquisitely expensive. As we walked, and loitered, and loitered and walked, we discussed, in principle, without of course tasting, the difference between Belgian chocolates and Manhattan chocolates, the merits of Italian garlic salami as opposed to French and whether maraschino cherries should be described as bitter or sweet. We talked only about food.

The wives seemed to have total recall of every morsel they had ever tasted. They recalled but did not eat. They found their pleasure where they could, enjoying the view from the dietary moral high ground. Elbowing others off with their thin, sharp elbows.

They came to a café which seemed familiar to them. It was midday. Their jewels were glittering, their chins were stretched, their eyes were wide.

'Shall we go in for just a cup of coffee?' asked one nervously.

They seemed to ponder.

'Black coffee,' said another.

'Of course black,' they chorused. But it was obvious that the one who had first suggested coffee was the weakest and had lost status.

We all went in and had black coffee. Around us men were eating heartily. The aroma of roasting chicken assailed us.

'I think I'm just going to have a salad,' said the one who'd first suggested coffee. Well, what did she have to lose? She was bottom of the pile.

'Without dressing,' she added.

Shopping

The salad came. Everyone stared at it. She ate it, leaf by miserable leaf.

'Tell you what,' she said, 'I'm going to have a piece of chocolate cake.'

'Chocolate cake,' she said to the waiter, and he instantly brought out a great square of cream-filled chocolate cake which practically filled the table and four plates and spoons and handed them round.

The wives all ate voraciously until there wasn't a scrap left. I didn't need to. I'd had breakfast.

'Happens all the time,' said the waiter to me, as we left. 'I know that sort by heart. I save them the embarrassment of asking.'

It just goes to show, challenge instinct too much and instinct fights back and wins. Train youself to relish hunger, which dieters should do, but even so it's hard. The body fights back. The appetites of the flesh are huge and those of the spirit can get a little attenuated.

Use one instinct to control another. Play off the instinct to acquire against the instinct to eat. We should have stopped off at Tiffany's and bought some jewellery.

This is the parable of Emily and how she achieved happiness by falling in love and not going shopping.

Nothing to Wear

It was at half-past four on Tuesday, 6 June that Charles realized he had a problem. He and Emily had plans for the evening. They were to have tea at the Ritz – he'd booked it for five – and after that they were to go on to the summer exhibition at Burlington House. They have been invited to a private view.

Tea at the Ritz was mostly for Charles, for when he visited his old mother in her care home on Sunday afternoon and gave an account of his week. Tea at the Ritz was a useful talking-point, being a concept the old lady could still understand, and there were allied subjects to discuss, such as how no one knew how to make cucumber sandwiches any more, let alone how to blanch cucumber. And Emily quite liked the Ritz. She said she found it relaxing.

Then they'd go on to Burlington House across the road and if they got there early, Charles might well meet up with his friend Marlowe. Then he could casually mention the good studio property about to come on the market in South Ken., a snip at two and a half million. He knew Marlowe was looking. If it worked, there'd be a good commission in it for Charles.

But it was already half past four and here was Emily not even dressed and not quite sitting but somehow crouched, folded on the bedroom carpet, wailing, 'I've nothing to wear.'

She crouched in her silk slip, pretty as a picture by a slightly astigmatic painter, her legs so long and her hips so slim – backèd like a swan, as the folk song had it – that for the first time it struck Charles that there was something unreasonable about her looks. Other girls were pear-shaped, or had short necks, and complained of not being able to find clothes to fit. But Emily was the one designers liked to lend clothes to for grand occasions, because she showed them off so well. She catwalk modelled sometimes, when she could be bothered, which was not often. She gave the impression of having sprung to life not from between human thighs but from a sketch in some couturier's notebook. Yet her mother was dumpy enough.

I've nothing to wear,' she repeated, 'not a thing.'

They had been married for five months and Charles realized by now that Emily had dressing problems the way other girls had eating problems, but he loved her and he indulged her, or at any rate had until now, when he suddenly found himself irritated. She sat surrounded by Blahnik shoes, and Ferreti dresses, and Etro jackets, and leather skirts by Versace, and Westwood corsets, torn from their hangers and flung anywhere on the floor, and the price of them added up was beyond belief. His pocket was not bottom-less: he had to wheel and deal like anyone else, and it was not easy.

'I don't want us to be late,' he said rashly. 'Just put on any old thing. You always look fantastic.'

'Men always say that,' she said. 'It isn't true. I look absurd. For one thing my head is too small for my body. Haven't you even noticed?'

'I think it's about the same as anyone else's,' he said, but he could see what she meant. She went to the gym every morning: exercise developed her shoulders but not her head, so she did seem a little out of proportion.

'I'm a monster,' she said. 'A freak. My eyes look like that alien's in *ET.*'

'You could eat more,' he suggested and she threw a boot at him and laughed. He loved her laugh. 'Seriously, though,' she said, 'I haven't a thing to wear.'

He picked up a filmy silk thing without much top. 'How about this? It's a nice colour.'

'Don't be absurd,' she said. 'It might work for the summer exhibition, but then there's tea at the Ritz as well.'

He could see that it had become his fault that she had nothing to wear, because of his mother.

'People will be looking at their sandwiches and the paintings, not at you,' he said, though it wasn't true and he knew it. He didn't want to miss Marlowe. It would be difficult enough finding him in the crush.

'That thing you wore to Ascot,' he suggested.

'That's the whole *point*, I wore it to Ascot. And it's no good without a hat anyway. And nobody who isn't weird or my mother wears a hat to an art show.'

Shopping

'I just wear a suit,' he said, 'and it could be any old suit.'

'That's simply not true. I married an Armani man. Don't go and change on me!'

Her wardrobe took up the whole wall. Scarcely a day went by without her buying something new. Sometimes she just shoved the bags at the back of the cupboard to open later and forgot all about them.

'I've nothing to wear,' she said again.

'You're turning into a weirdo,' he said, losing patience. 'Just put something on and hurry up about it. I'll order a taxi now.'

Tears welled up in the enormous eyes and rolled down her thin cheeks. She was not accustomed to harsh words. He felt bad and after he'd ordered the taxi he sat on the floor with her to be companionable.

'But I'm not being unreasonable,' she said, snuggling into him. 'It's just the shoes are doing my head in. I'm going to have to walk from the Ritz to Burlington House and you can never sit down at private views, and supposing my feet begin to hurt? If the rest is right the shoes aren't and vice versa. And Genia Marlowe will be there and Marlowe's made her pregnant and she'll stand there with her six-month bump in stretch Versace being mobbed by the media. Babies are chic, but personally I think she looks totally yuck.'

'Look,' Charles said, 'if you want a baby I'm not all that set against it.' He had been married before and had two almost grown-up children and was well into his forties. Emily was not yet 30.

'Are you crazy? What makes you think I want to have a baby?'

'But you said you did,' he said, taken by surprise.

'Did I? That must have been a long time ago, before we were married. I've changed my mind. Genia Marlowe says she's going to breastfeed. I think that is so completely disgusting.'

'The taxi's here,' he said.

She uttered a shriek, stretched her long limbs out on the carpet and thrummed her pretty little fists into the white pile. She was a having a tantrum.

Charles hadn't seen this before. He was afraid she would damage her feet as they banged against the floor.

He called up her mother in the country to ask for help. He'd never done that before either.

'Oh dear,' said Mrs Julia Forrester. 'Not again! She used to do that all the time when she was little. The church bell would be ringing for morning service and there'd be our little Emily, throwing a tantrum because her ankle socks had frills, or didn't, I can't remember which.'

Shopping

Julia and her husband had recently downsized, perforce, and the big house was gone and now Julia grew roses in her cottage garden, and her husband read all the books he'd never had time to read when he was something in the City. They seemed happy enough. Emily's income fortunately came from a trust fund, but the expected inheritance would never come, which made it all the more important that Charles got to drop a word in Marlowe's ear.

'Perhaps it's because she's a younger sister,' Julia offered. 'She never quite thinks she has enough, and what she does have will never quite do. Or perhaps it's me. I've never wanted to wear anything other than a comfy jersey and an old skirt. I never liked being noticed and I never cared what others thought. I expect Emily likes to make up for what she sees as my shortcomings.' There was a tinge of acid in her voice.

'But what do I do with her?' asked Charles. 'I hate being late for things.'

'You're just like her father,' said Julia, 'a stickler for punctuality. I expect that's why she married you. Now Katherine takes after me. Very relaxed. Sit it out is my advice and she'll be good as gold for the rest of the day. That's what I used to do.'

Charles called Katherine. Emily was still in her slip and still thrumming and outside the front door of the pretty little Chelsea house the taxi meter was clicking up.

Katherine was older than Emily by two years. She favoured a neater and more expensive version of her mother's clothes and changed their style only as Marks and Spencer did. She was married to a barrister and had three children. She went to Ascot not to be seen but to look at the horses and meet up with her sister. They were quite affectionate with one another.

'Get her to talk to me,' she said.

Emily consented to take the phone. She'd calmed down, though still gulped air. Charles listened from the other side of the door.

'It's Charles's fault,' complained Emily. 'He's so weird. He only wants to go to the Ritz because of his dotty old mother, and I'm the living sacrifice, and he expects me to wear the same thing to both of them, and I've nothing to wear anyway.'

There was pause while Katherine spoke.

'That spotted la Croix thing? Are you joking? It's head to toe and last year's, and makes my bum look large, and nobody's wearing spots, and I have to show some flesh,' said Emily. 'Everyone will be showing flesh. Genia Marlowe will have a naked belly, I bet, with the navel pierced, if she can find it to pierce.'

Again Katherine spoke.

'Suede's cruel,' said Emily, 'you really are weird, Katherine. And it's far too solid, not in the least floaty, and floaty is in. I know you wear the same T-shirt three days running, but you live in the country where nobody sees you except kids and animals.'

Shopping

Charles gave up and was about to send the taxi away when Emily came dancing out of the house wearing a pair of jeans, a lilac beaded chiffon blouse with frills and pointy gold shoes cut so low they showed her toes and so insubstantial he didn't see how they could carry all six feet of her. The secret no doubt lay in their cost. Her eyes were a little pink and she sniffed, but she leant up against him trustingly in the taxi. At the Ritz she ate a whole plateful of tiny cucumber sandwiches and looked so lovely, fresh and happy that people stared and there was an incident when a Japanese guest tried to take a photograph of her and security appeared out of nowhere and confiscated the camera.

'I must tell Genia Marlowe about that,' said Emily. She had been to school with Genia.

They crossed the road to Burlington House. Emily stepped into the bus lane without looking and Charles had to pull her back or she would have been run down.

'It was coming from the wrong direction!' complained Emily.

'You should have read the signs,' said Charles. 'It wasn't the driver's fault, it was yours.'

'Why do you always take my enemy's side?' she cried. 'You're so like my father I can't bear it.' She looked at him for a moment almost as if she hated him, but quickly composed her face again and took his arm. She limped a little but denied that it was anything to do with the shoes.

They arrived at the private view half an hour later than Charles had hoped and the Marlowes had been and gone. There was a painting on the wall of a naked Genia, however, proudly pregnant. Journalists crowded round it and guests mobbed the painter, a burly, bearded young man in a tattered green jumper which looked as if he had slept in it. Certainly he had spilled soup down it.

Charles caught a glimpse of Tattery Abel the art dealer, a man reputed to be rich as Croesus, with four Edward Hoppers, three Jackson Pollocks and five Warhols to his name and who liked to dabble in painting himself. Failing Marlowe, he fell into conversation with Tattery and mentioned the fact that one of the best of the original studio houses in South Ken was coming onto the market soon, at about three mill. Tattery was undoubtedly interested and took Charles' e-mail address.

Charles looked for Emily and found her deep in conversation with the painter in the green jumper, while photographers from the gossip columns and the arts pages snapped away. She'd like that. No one seemed to take pictures of Charles any more, not since he'd taken a wife and stopped being the most eligible bachelor in town, even though it was Emily he had married. He wandered off to look at the paintings on the wall. He imagined Emily was persuading the artist to paint her portrait, and didn't doubt that she'd succeed.

Fifteen minutes later he came back to see how she was doing and found her sitting on a little gold chair while Green Jumper, on his knees, took off her shoes for her and put one in each pocket of his trousers, little heels sticking out. The artist helped her up, tucking her arm under his, and took off his sandals to keep her company, showing dirty toes, and the pair of them went round happily in bare feet, he deriding the paintings and Emily enthusing.

When next he went to look for Emily he couldn't find her. Fortunately, Marlowe turned up just then and said he'd seen her leaving with a weird-looking slob in a green jumper. They'd called a taxi. Charles mentioned the studio house in South Ken and was gratified by Marlowe's eager response. Now he could play Tattery off against Marlowe and the price would go up. He went home on his own.

The next time he saw Emily was when she opened the door to him a year later. She was living with Green Jumper in a dilapidated barn conversion in Essex. There had not been much to discuss in relation to the divorce; she'd left it all to his lawyers. Charles had claimed alimony and Emily hadn't argued, to the extent of leaving herself with barely enough to live on. She hadn't bothered to come back to collect her clothes.

Green Jumper hovered in the background while Charles got Emily to sign a few necessary documents. Charles stayed on the step and was not asked in. The house smelled of garlic, oil paint, dogs and turpentine. Emily was wearing a frumpy jumper like her mother's and a soiled suede skirt of an unflattering length, and she was pregnant.

If you had hardly anything at all to wear, he could see, having nothing to wear wouldn't matter too much, and the pain of it would be greatly eased. He was happy for her.

Parable ends.

And that is all I have to say on the subject of shopping.

Chocolate

'Time for myself, time for *me*,' is the desolate call of the new woman in a new age. Nurture overtakes nature. Her instincts have nowhere to go. Without the tribe she is desolate.

The birth rate falls, men become an optional extra, and love is neurotic dependency. Sex loses its savour. '*Because I deserve it, because I'm worth it!*' begins to sound hollow. Oh, hand me the chocolate bar, it's all I have left.

Six women out of ten, according to research, prefer chocolate to sex.

Can this be true?

An exhausted woman of 35 with three children and a career and a new baby in her arms might well prefer chocolate to what feels like male mauling – choose the soft melting of the sensuous stuff in the mouth to the demands of another's flesh.

A girl who is unhappy because her boyfriend has betrayed her and who never wants to have another man in her life might well claim to prefer chocolate to sex. Though experience suggests she will not feel like this for long.

A woman bored by the same sex with the same man in the same bed for too long a time might well prefer chocolate. But the situation is not likely to go on for long in modern society. One or the other will split. Probably him.

He: 'What's the matter? Do you have a headache?'

She: 'I'm just going down to the fridge to get some chocolate.'

And he thinks about the girl in the salsa class. He tried to give her a box of chocolates and she looked at him as if he were mad. But he likes a certain hauteur, a certain disdain, in a girl. And she's as slim as a whippet.

I am not saying that to frighten you. No woman should ever alter her actions because she is nervous that her husband fancies someone else. She should go to the fridge and come back to bed and eat the chocolate, under his nose, and offer him some, and then resume her love-making. She must appear indifferent to the interest he takes in other women. She must appear to take it as a compliment that though he says, 'Whoaar, look at that!' when a pretty woman passes by, he remains with her. It would be very odd if men did not fancy other women, since

144

they are creatures of nature as well as nurture. Nurture tells him it's bad manners, nature makes him spontaneous in his reactions. When he's not allowing himself to say '*Whoaar*' that's the time she should worry. He may be trying too hard.

Mind you, the craving for chocolate that affects so many women is hard to explain in Darwinian terms. It seems an entirely learned response. It is equally hard to explain in spiritual terms. Hard to imagine the Intelligent Designer perceiving his creation and saying, '*I know, the way to get this race to make moral choices is to create chocolate.*'

Mother love, male aggression, greed – all the kinds of things that play a part in the survival of the species and its better ability to glorify its creator, take part in the cosmic struggle between good and evil – all that, yes. But chocolate? Hardly.

Addictive, though. Chocolate, as most of us know by now, contains many of the substances which keep us happy and tranquil – the endorphins, serotonin, and so forth – though you'd have to take 240 lb of the stuff to get the effect of one marijuana reefer. That's why it's become traditional to give chocolate on Valentine's Day. (Though personally I think this is more to with the Chocolate Council and the card industry than tradition. My generation had never heard of it, any more than they had of Mother's Day.) So you eat it because you like it, because it's sold to you by skilful brainwashing and advertising, because you shouldn't, because you want to spoil your dinner, because life around you seems vaguely unsatisfactory, because *it's there*. And life has spited you in some way and so you deserve a little treat.

Well, perhaps you do.

Chocolate comes under the heading of little treats, of whatever gets you through the night, of feast days and holidays and on the seventh day thou shalt rest and do no labour, of trinkets and bangles and new lipsticks, new face cream, new nail polish – little exercises in hope and betterment, the very pleasure of frittering away what should be saved. The denial of prudence. Delinquency.

Delinquency may be what pushes the tribe forward to better things. A refusal to accept things as they are. Boredom with the status quo. *'Let's do it this way, not that.'* And so we end up with carts, trains, cars, aircraft, television, space travel, nuclear fission, modern warfare, wind farms and boxes of chocolate.

Eat, eat and be damned to them!

Whatever gets you through the night. And that's enough about chocolate.

To cheer us up, let's have the parable of Marigold, who, finding herself in an unfamiliar tribe, took delight in upsetting its rituals. The tribe, of course, exacted punishment. She was lucky to escape with her life. But she did learn.

A Solitary Person

I am by nature a solitary person. If I were to advertise in a newspaper for a partner – and who hasn't at one time or another been tempted? – the entry would go something like this: *'Reclusive blonde young woman (32), workaholic, sharp-tongued, hates company, children, loud music, country walks, wining and dining, likes crosswords, seeks similarly inclined male. No smokers, no Viagra users.'* Nevertheless, when Marigold asked me to Badger House for the Christmas weekend I was glad of the invitation. Around Christmas, aloneness, that normally enviable and superior state, can feel suspiciously like loneliness.

'You don't have to talk to anyone,' said Marigold. 'You can sit in a dark corner amongst the pine needles and wrapping paper and pretend to be the *au pair*. My family won't even notice you, I promise.'

'Well,' I thought, 'don't be too sure of that. I can make people notice me if I put myself out.'

I share an office with Marigold. Fortunately she, like me, is a silent person. We are both the offspring of noisy ducal families who, having taken to drugs in the sixties, dropped babies like flies and failed to make proper arrangements for their upbringing beyond sending them off to boarding schools. Now, for both of us, just to be in a quiet room alone is bliss. I, for one, seek it perpetually. In the same way, my mother says, those children who were kept short of butter in World War II grew up to slather it on their bread for ever. Thus she excuses her own obesity.

What Makes Women Happy

My mother decamped with a movie-maker to California some four years ago and one by one my younger siblings drifted after her – I was the oldest of five. I could have gone out to join this new ersatz family of mine for the festive season, but I declined. I mention this so you don't feel sorry for me or see me as the kind of person who is short of places to go to at Christmas. It's just that I sometimes fail to want to go wherever it is in time and then end up miserable. But I do like to feel I have removed myself from company, not that company has removed itself from me.

I also need, I think, to point out to you that the benefits of my temperament are such that my confinement in this prison cell is not in itself onerous. Don't feel pity for me on this account. I have faith in justice and assume that I will be found innocent of a murder I did not commit, and in the meantime I rejoice that I won't be expected to go to some party to see in the New Year. I understand that here in Holloway we just all sit silently and separately in our cells on the dreaded night and contemplate the past and the future. Suits me.

No, indeed, sir, I did not murder Lady Hester Walpole Delingro. Let me tell my story in my own way, as is normally done, from the beginning. Or are you in some great hurry? Perhaps you Legal Aid solicitors are on piece-work? No? When I hear from my mother she'll have the best lawyers in town take over my case; it's just that she's staying oddly silent, so you will have to put up with me for the time being.

Badger House! My heart sank on seeing the place, at the wrong end of a two-hour standing journey on a crowded train which smelled of alcohol and mince pies. Marigold had showed me photographs of her family home. It looked lovely enough in the summer, with rampant nature creeping up to its door, but in midwinter, standing isolated and denuded of foliage, you could see it all too clearly for what it was: one of those badly sited, dull, ostentatious houses built at the end of the eighteenth century by people with more money than sense. For one thing the house was situated too near the brow of the hill – the down draught would be bound to make the fires smoke – and faced north. Wall the sloping kitchen garden as you might to keep off the bitter wind, there would be endless troubles with drainage and slugs.

Badger House – badgers prefer valleys, actually, but I daresay occasionally wander – was the property of Marigold's grandmother, Lady Hester Walpole Delingro. (Delingro had the money, she had the title; the marriage, her third, lasted six weeks.) But she kept the name, if only because it stood out in the gossip columns, and she loved a smart party, as did all the family. It was here at Badger House, every Christmas, that the whole vast, noisy, extroverted, once-Catholic Walpole family assembled to celebrate if not exactly the birth of Jesus (except perhaps for Marigold's 93-year-old great-aunt Cecilia, who was a nun, but whose convent let her out for Christmas), then their survival as a unit for another year.

The taxi let me out by the great front door. It was half past five on Christmas Eve. Heavy crimson damask curtains had been pulled, but there was an urgent sense of movement and life behind them. I rang three times and no one answered. I pushed the door open and went inside.

What noise, what brightness, what Babel! I would have turned and left at once and taken my chances on a train back to the city, but the taxi had already left. In the great hall someone was playing a grand piano honky-tonk style and a group of adults had gathered round to sing Christmas carols out of tune, rivalled only by a cluster of teenage children singing the pop world's seasonal offering, *Have Yourself a Hip-hop Xmas and Other Tunes*, and jigging about in ecstasy frenzy. Decorations were plentiful, but without discrimination, organization or style. Dull paper streamers, of the kind made by earnest children, hung droopily over great distances from wall to wall. Vulgar tinsel draped old family portraits, and cheap Woolworths magic lanterns in gold, silver, scarlet and green hung from chandeliers and doorways wherever the eye fell, without order and without symmetry. Little children were running around to no apparent purpose, the girls dragging Barbie dolls around by their hair and the boys panicking and shrieking, pursued by clanking and fashionably cursing computer toys they seemed unable or unwilling to control. Fires had been lit in all the rooms and, as I had predicted, smoked. I was obliged to pull my scarf up to cover my nose and mouth and breathe through that to save myself from the worst of the fumes.

As I stood there dazed and horrified, I was approached by Lady Hester. I recognized her from the pages of *Tatler* and *Hello*. (Yes, she stooped to *Hello*. I assumed that there were financial problems.) Lady Hester was a woman well into her eighties, still tall and gaunt, bright-eyed and vigorous for her age. She wore black leggings and a waisted silver jacket which would have looked better on a cheer-leader. Old legs are old legs and look skinny, not slender, and that's that.

Chocolate

'You must be Marigold's friend Ishtar,' she said. (My parents had been deeply into Middle Eastern mysticism around the time of my birth.) 'Welcome! I'm sorry about so much smoke. Very cunning of you to think of the scarf. As soon as the fireplaces warm up, it gets better. It's a problem we have every year. Part of the ritual!'

And just as Marigold came running up, I was saying 'Personally, I'd abandon the ritual and put in central heating,' which Lady Hester obviously did not react well to, if only because it was sensible advice. But Marigold hugged me and said, 'Ishtar, please don't tell the truth, remember it's Christmas. Let us have our illusions, if only for the weekend!'

I had never seen Marigold like this, as if she were 6 again, tippy-toed. Her usually pale horse face was flushed and she looked almost pretty. With tinsel in her hair, wearing a low-cut black top which left a bra-strap showing, she was knocking back the punch as if it were Diet Coke, hotly pursued by the Seb she sometimes talked about, a young man with curling golden tendrils clinging to a finely sculpted head.

'This is Ishtar,' she was saying to Seb, 'I share an office with her. She had nowhere to go for Christmas, so we've all agreed she can be this year's Outsider.'

Well, thank you very much, Marigold. Who wants to be labelled an Outsider, an object of pity, the one invited to the Christmas festivities because otherwise they'd be on their own? It seemed to me a gross abuse of the laws of hospitality and if thereafter I did not behave like a perfect guest, who can be surprised? Nor had I liked the way Seb's eye had drifted over me and away even before he had heard me described as the Outsider. Prada, to the uninformed eye, can sometimes look too plain, too dowdy.

But what did I do, you ask me, to justify some twenty people and a host of sticky little children bearing false witness against me? First remember that the Walpoles as a family are notoriously mentally unstable. They have become so through generations of mismarriages, drug-taking, miscegenation and eccentric social mobility. Rest assured that a girl who goes to the best school in the country is as likely to end up with a Rastafarian or a truck driver, as a stock broker or a prince. And that what kept them united was the worship of Lady Hester and the Christmas rituals over which she, as deity, presided.

I didn't do much; I just made sure that what I did was noticeable. Shown to an attic room with three makeshift beds in it, with twigs and soot tumbling down into the empty fireplace every time the door slammed (the chimneys were not even netted against the rooks), I explained that I would have insomnia if I did not have a bedroom to myself and that I needed sheets and blankets, not a duvet, and after much apology and discussion ended up sleeping in Marigold's room and her on the sofa under the Christmas tree, so that Seb was unable to join her that night – I am sure that had been their plan – and the children did not get their normal sneak 2 a.m. preview of the presents.

People should not invite guests if they cannot house them adequately.

Chocolate

Earlier I'd found a gold dress in Marigold's wardrobe and put it on. Well, she offered.

'Isn't that one too tight? The navy would be more you.'

'Oh no,' I said. It was tight, of course, and incredibly vulgar too, but what does an Outsider know or care? I draped myself round Seb once or twice and pole-danced round a pillar for his entertainment. Then I let him kiss me long and hard under the mistletoe, while everyone watched. Marigold fled from the room weeping and flinging her engagement ring on the floor.

People who put up pagan mistletoe at a Christian ceremony must expect orgiastic behaviour.

Before going to bed I used the machines in the utility room to launder the damp towels I had found on the floor of Marigold's bathroom. I had searched the linen cupboard for fresh ones but found none – what else could I do? The washing machine was faulty – there was no warning note to say so; is one meant to read the mind of machines? – and overflowed and caused some kind of havoc with the kitchen electrics, so the deep-freeze and the fridges cut out. This was not discovered until well into the next day.

People who stuff turkeys with packets of frozen pork and herbs deserve what they get and must risk E.coli if the power goes off.

On Christmas morning, leaving Seb in the bed, I rose early when only small hysterical children were about and restrained the ones who assaulted me too violently, or made me sticky, and escorted them to where their parents were sleeping in their drunken stupors and asked them to take charge of their offspring.

People should not have children if they do not have the moral wherewithal to control them.

I spent the morning assuring enquirers that Seb was nothing worth Marigold having, and in all probability was not her cousin but her half-brother, and preserving the Christmas presents from the ravages of the children, standing up to their wails and howls.

Then came the adult giving-ceremony. The custom was for every adult Walpole to bring what they called a tree-present, a gift acceptable to all ages and genders, to the value of £15, to place under the Christmas tree and when the time came to take another out for themselves. Thus everyone came with a gift and left with a gift. It was a system fraught with danger. Simply by taking one out and not putting one in, I caused mayhem. The nun Cecilia, being slowest on her feet, was left without a gift and made a terrible fuss.

Lunch did not happen until three. Some thirty people sat in a triangle formed by three trestle tables. The table setting, I must admit, was pretty enough and decorated with Christmas crackers and the heavy family silver had been taken out of storage. But thirty? How this family bred and bred!

I had been seated at the jutting end of one of the tables, as befitted the Outsider. This did not improve my mood. I declared myself to be a vegetarian just as the three turkeys – one for each side of the triangle – were being carved.

Chocolate

People who have thirty to a meal must surely expect a certain proportion of them to be vegetarians. I mentioned the deep-freeze débâcle, a number of the guests converted to vegetarianism there and then – all those, I noticed, who had married into the Walpole Delingros, those born into it were hardier.

Next to me was Cecilia, rendered incontinent by the morning's upsets. When all were finally served, I enquired what the strange smell could be. A faulty drain, perhaps? One or two got to their feet, and the children, seeing the adults rise, found the excuse to leave their chairs and run hither and thither, sniffing around under the table overexciting the dogs and pulling crackers out of turn.

People should look after the elderly properly and make sure they do not drink too much or lose control of their bladders.

It was at this point that Lady Hester Walpole Delingro rose to her feet and, pointing across the festive triangle at me, arm fully extended, asked me to leave her table, since it was clearly so unsatisfactory to me. I too rose to my feet.

'Thank you for making me your Outsider,' I said, 'at the annual feast of the Walpole Delingros. I would hate to be an Insider.'

This was no more than the truth, but Lady Hester's noble horse face contorted, reddened and went into spasms. She grabbed her heart, her hand fell away, she fell dead into her plate. It was over in five seconds. She can hardly have suffered. Rage and pain get confused. Nevertheless, it was a shock. Silence fell. Even the little children returned to their seats and sat silently.

And then something even more shocking occurred. A group of male Walpole Delingros carried off the body to the next room and stretched it out on the sofa under the Christmas tree, shut the door, returned to the table and behaved as if the death had not occurred. Lady Hester's plate was removed; her daughter, Lady Rowan, Marigold's mother, moved to fill the now empty chair. Everyone moved up one, even Cecilia, leaving me isolated but with one damp, smelly chair next to me.

'Shouldn't someone call a doctor, an ambulance?' I asked. No one replied. 'You can't just eat Christmas pudding as if nothing had happened!'

But they could. Curtains were drawn, lights put out, heated brandy poured over hot Xmas puddings to be set ablaze and carried in with ceremony. I was offered none. It was as if I had ceased to exist. Only after coffee had been made and served and crackers pulled – those the children had left – and the dreadful jokes been read out and scorned were the doctor, the ambulance and the police called.

And that, I swear, is exactly what happened. Even if thirty, not twenty, Walpole Delingros swear that the death happened after dinner and that I took Lady Hester's head and deliberately banged it on the edge of the marble fireplace during the course of an argument about the cause of smoking fireplaces, so she fell dead, suffering a cardiac infarction on the way down, I cannot help it. This was not what happened. If there is a nasty dent on the side of Lady Hester's head, why then, one of the family did it while she lay on the sofa, with a blunt instrument, the better to incriminate me.

Chocolate

It won't work, of course — one of the children must surely blab, or perhaps Marigold will remember she is my friend. I believe she is back with Seb. In the meantime, while I wait for my mother's call, I am happy enough in this cell.

But perhaps you could arrange to have *The Times* sent in, so that I can do the crossword? And could you ask the governor to stop people playing their radios and TVs so loudly? Or at any rate to tune them to the same station? I am feeling a little insecure. I am accustomed to having enemies — the honest and righteous always are — but it was my bad judgement to make so many, in one place, and in that particular season. It is never safe to disturb the ritual, however much fun it may be.

Moral

The honest and the righteous are a real pain to be with. They are the scribes and Pharisees you read about in the Bible. They are often friendless, and if you are a nice person you will feel inclined to ask them to share your family and social rituals, but remember virtue is its own reward.

Though actually there is a brighter side to virtue:

> Be happy and you'll be good, be good and
> you'll be happy.

Things turned out well for Marigold and really rather badly for Ishtar.

TWO

Saints and Sinners

Death, bereavement, loneliness and shame: these are the four horses of the modern apocalypse. They circle our new reality, now we are people of the city not the cave. Their riders, the horsemen, are a fearful lot: they are called despair, depression, isolation and self-doubt. But being so fearful they are easily unhorsed and it's simple enough to get out of their way. It's just not nice to find them champing the grasses in your back garden. You need to *do* something.

Skip these next few chapters if you are young, believe that none of these things will happen to you or in general believe that ignorance is best. You may be right. *Why know now what you can put off until tomorrow?*

The news is not totally good, though there are a few things here for your comfort. Your writer believes quite strongly in the afterlife and does not believe that when we die the light is switched off. It glimmers on elsewhere.

Our perceptions are based in our senses; our brains give us a mere three-dimensional readout. Mathematicians, whose models of the universe seem on the whole sound, give proof that other dimensions exist. This being the case, anything can happen, *and may well do.*

Angels and ministers of grace attend us!

Death: The Gates of Paradise

I have had various experiences of the 'other side' – enough to make me think that when people fear death, they really have no need.

I saw my one-time (a long-time) husband in the mortuary after he had died. He was cold like marble and had 'gone away'.

I sat by my mother while she died. Her attention turned inward; she forgot the world. She had no pain. She seemed to be learning something she was reluctant to learn, coming to terms with the end of life. The struggle was inward, with something I didn't understand, but it was resolved. But it was in no sense 'the end' when her eyes closed. She too had 'gone away'.

I had an out-of-body experience when I was in my mid-twenties, under anaesthetic. Lots of people have these and psychologists take pleasure in telling us 'Oh that's nothing but *an excitation of the pleasure centres of the brain!*' Though to me it seemed far too active an experience to be issuing from the brain cells, self-induced out of nothing.

I travelled down a warm dark tunnel – the birth canal, the romantics will tell you. If so, it was an easy journey, not punctuated by the squeezing of muscle and the compression of the head that must accompany birth from the baby's point of view. No wonder babies cry – they must all suffer from post-traumatic stress disorder for a long, long time, unless they are lifted gracefully and carefully from the womb by the surgeon. Doors opened on both sides as I travelled, and people came out to me, some I knew well, others I scarcely remembered, all in perfect form, spirit rather than body, and at their best, not their worst, so I was truly pleased to see them. I knew we were all in this together. At the end of the tunnel was a bright light, which was my destination – and then it faded and I woke up in my hospital bed. But it was enough to make me sure that 'the other side' existed, and I haven't worried about death since. But now I am not so sure. It might be more worrying than I, in my young naïvety, assumed.

Just a year ago I all but died from an allergic reaction. The hospital rang my family to say they'd better come quick. My heart had stopped. Crash teams worked on me and brought me back to life. I had a vision then of the gates of paradise. They filled edges of my vision and indeed they were pearly white but tinged with pink, merging into a rather vulgar orange and red – the colours you see in Hindu temples.

The gates were double-glazed and they slid aside a foot or two to give me room to enter and the inner space was filled with a kind of fog.

I was passing through, but then hands and voices struggled to hold me back, while from the other side some gaunt and terrifying creature with long limbs tried to entangle me and pull me through. I saw a drawing in a gallery recently by the German expressionist painter Kathe Kollwitz, done in the early 1930s. It was called 'Death and Child'. Death, long-armed, gaunt and determined, snatches the child from its mother's arms. And that, I realized, was a vision of what I had encountered. It is not all sweetness and light over there, at least it won't be for me. But there is, I am convinced, an over there. Kathe Kollwitz saw it too. You may do better than me. Angels may attend your entry. I hope so.

I asked my vicar whether he thought I had encountered Cerberus at the gates of hell. He said he hoped not.

The gates of paradise, I warn you, can be rather a shock to the aesthetic soul, trained to appreciate shades of taupe and stone and dim sepulchral gloom. Colour, on the other side, is vigorous and startling.

Nature is not your Friend

Lay the blame for the four enemies of happiness, the four new horses of the apocalypse – death, bereavement, loneliness and shame – at nature's door. All are attendant upon ageing. We can ameliorate their effects, but it is as well to acknowledge that nature is not our friend. Blithely, she discards us. Better treat her as an enemy. She is concerned with our children, not with us, and though our interests may overlap, they do not coincide. Nature has no interest in us once we are past a certain age – and even for the young she can prove an uneasy ally. She certainly takes no steps to make our endings happier, brittling our bones, drying our skin and rheuming our eyes.

It is misleading to personify her in the way I do, shorthand for the sum of cause and effect through the ages in the organic world. '*Nature wants us to do this, nature means us to do that*' – it leads us to believe that she knows what she is doing, that she is driving us forward to a perfect world. She is not. She just *is*. If she intends anything, it is for a tree to fall on us when we're 30, which we couldn't dodge in time because of our advancing years, or a pregnancy to kill off anyone remotely unfit, or starvation to carry off those not lucky enough to lay down fat in the good times.

'She' makes mistakes. Every mutation is a mistake. Occasionally these mistakes benefit humanity: we are far, far cleverer than we need be to survive. Nature, in her incompetence, has succeeded in breeding a race who need medicines to keep them going as they grew older, and as the centuries pass, and the fat beget the fat, a breed given to obesity. The advantage of being fat in the cave far outweighs any disadvantage.

In our later years nurture is thoroughly out of kilter with nature. We must stop thinking '*I won't take those pills, it*

isn't natural.' 'Nature wants us take exercise, so on my bike!'
'Surely it's the healthy option to have my baby in a field, as
nature intended.' What nature intended was that the weakest
and oldest would die in childbirth. Not for nothing, in the
days before pre-natal care became so sophisticated, was any
woman over 30 called an 'elderly primigravida' and seen as
being at special risk.

Our orthopaedic hospitals are full of elderly sportspersons
who overtaxed their limbs in their youth and ageing ballet
dancers with crumbling ankles. They had glorious youths –
and good for them and it may well have been worth it. But
old age goes on an awfully long time – medicine, interfering
with nature's scheme for us, makes certain that it does.

(There is a theory that grandparents exist to help look after
babies, that nature designed them so to do, but that seems
to me to be pushing it. Nature is a blind, deaf, maddening,
senseless, wholly amoral creature. 'Grandparent' is a term
that applies to the world of nurture, not of nature, of central
heating, fridges, telephones and steady heartbeats on CDs to
soothe the baby. The heartbeats of the elderly aren't nearly
as steady and reassuring as those of the young.)

Nature wins in the end and carries us off – though scientists are working on that too. There is a gene which plots
the long-term destruction of all cells – 'the suicide gene' they
call it – and if they could only breed it out of humanity we
could all be born, grow to our optimum size and just stay
that way, never growing old. We could have our babies at

the age of 106, 206, there being no inevitable ageing in our cells.

Then let them worry about elderly mothers.

If, of course, accident, global warming, floods and hurricanes, not to mention biological warfare, have spared us. Personally, I'd rather take the cloning option: it puts a bit more – not much more, but some – variety into the mix.

I wouldn't really be afraid of dying, if I were you. If wavering, open up Hubble on the Internet and consider the beauty and scale of the cosmos. Yet we can hold all this within our comprehension, and the smallest component of the atom too.

Nature, that imperfect energy, keeps the race going. It seems our souls need housing. The body withers and perishes, but the soul goes marching on, though God alone knows where. Somewhere in the starry void no doubt there's room. If infinity exists – and mathematicians keep telling us it does – everything is always *somewhere*.

Bereavement:
Unseating the Second Horseman

Forget the five stages of bereavement – traditionally denial, anger, bargaining, depression and acceptance – before the 'moving on', when you're meant to forget, start again as if nothing had happened. I think that's terrible. It's brain-washing. The dead are there to be remembered and honoured, not moved away from. They are still part of your life and times, even though their bodies are no more.

But time passes, other events crowd in. Treat grief like flu, something physical. Recovery is quicker – if 'recover' is what you want to do – if you understand the physicality of your own reaction. Don't seek forgetfulness – your loss is none the less because time passes – but normal life does need to resume. We have a duty to enjoy life, since we put such a premium upon it. Pleasure is the best weapon we have against the four horses and their riders. It is our answer to death. Rejoice! Bring out the best bottle of wine.

Grief is not a rational response to death; it is born out of instinct. It is to do with nature, not nurture. It is similar to bonding. If the baby is to survive, the mother needs to love and protect it. If a healthy young member of the tribe dies then he or she is out of the mating game. It won't do. Grief is nature's way (again the personification; I'm sorry, see it as shorthand) of making us careful that the tribe survives and the individual, and that this kind of thing doesn't happen too often.

Trapped submariners, stuck potholers, pile-ups on the motorway – see how the tribe rushes to help. Go into the trauma room in a hospital, see the shelves piled with boxes of this, packets of that, labels scrawled *'in case of this'*, *'in case of that'*. *'Paediatric tracheotomy.'* *'Adult appendectomy.'* It is the equivalent of having everything you might possibly need in an emergency in your pockets. Reason says, *'Let them die.'* Instinct says, *'Save at any cost!'* Terrific cost.

With the old we say, *'Well, they had a good life.'* We miss them, sometimes very badly, but we come to terms with it. When the young die, it is an outrage. Every quiver of our instinctive being rises up in protest. How will we live now? The cave echoes to our wails. Time fades grief as the power of bonding lessens – to an extent, never totally; nature is not so merciful – as the child grows.

See grief as to do with the survival of the tribe. Mothers send sons off to war for the good of the tribe (well, they used to) more easily than they let them ride a motorbike. We grieve for our own, but rejoice at the death of the tribe over the hill. We even drop bombs on them. All the more for us! We can rush over the hill and steal the women, grab the genes and loot the caves.

To grieve for someone who dies isn't reasonable, it's just natural. Grief sweeps over us and absorbs us. It stops us functioning (unless other even more powerful instincts are at play, such as feeding the baby or killing the enemy). But those who have died have merely joined the ones who went before, as we all must do. They are beyond pain or grief of their own. We should be happy for them. It is reasonable for us to grieve for *ourselves*, because we've lost a parent, a lover, a child, a friend, and now have to do without them. But for them? Not really.

I once had a goose that died of grief for her gander. The fox got him. She wouldn't eat. She just walked about mournfully for a week and then sat down and breathed her last. Well, I understood that. I don't suppose she did. That's what I mean by instinct.

Depression: The Second Horseman

Death's rider is despair. Bereavement's is depression. What's worse, he has friends.

Free-floating Anxiety – Depression's Friend
Only to recognize this particular brand of anxiety for what it is can be helpful. It's not like ordinary anxiety, which is

rooted in a particular circumstance. It's called 'free-floating' because it floats free like a cobweb of a bright morning, alighting here, alighting there. Free-floating anxiety is attracted like a magnet to real fears – betrayal, infidelity, growing old, suspicious pains, how to pay the bills – but if none of those are around it lands anywhere and you start worrying about whether you've got split ends and they're getting worse or why the children aren't back from a party. You know there is something that ought to be done, but you don't know what it is, and you can't quite locate the source of the anxiety because it's already floating off, attaching itself to something else in your head.

If it has the habit of alighting on you, you must treat it like flu – something disagreeable that goes away. Cosset yourself until it does. Go to bed early, have hot milky drinks, that kind of thing. (Unless the 'milky' makes you worry you're going to get fat, in which case make it hot water.)

Free-floating anxiety comes in different degrees: it can consume you, make your breath come in short gasps, be bad enough to give you pains in your stomach or trifling enough to make you restless because you're convinced your skin is feeling tight and you haven't got any moisturizer with you. Explain to yourself that this is a physical state. It's a sickness of the imagination. It will pass. Easier said than done, I know. But once I had the phrase 'free-floating anxiety' in my head, it ceased to be the plague it once was for me. Simply as if naming it was a talisman against impending disaster. Once I'd noticed how it alighted here, alighted there, it lost power. I could sit it out and wait for it to pass, and soon it lost interest and went away.

Know your enemy!

Another Friend

This is another good friend of depression – you're used to sex and it stops. A sudden cessation of sexual activity can bother a woman a lot, until she gets used to it. Here she is, in a nice home, long-time married, good relationship, children grown, roses growing in the garden or geraniums in the window boxes, sex calmer than once it was but still very much ongoing. Then something *happens* – heart attack, stroke, prostate – and that's the dramatic end of that. Or else the sexual interest of the other just fades away.

And there you are, stranded. Life racing away at the speed of knots behind you.

The warmth and companionship of the double bed remains, and you don't want to disturb that, but unsatisfied longings swell in the loins, and you develop restlessness in the limbs, and it's amazing how much you can want something you can't have, at least within a normal domestic context.

When you had it you didn't take much notice of it. What can really bug you is what you haven't got.

So what do you do? Advice will vary on this point. Mine would be to put 'domestic' behind you. Develop a secret life while you still have the health and energy. Not too many questions will be asked if you go away for the odd weekend. Partners in these circumstances don't want to *know*, but they want you to be happy. Otherwise you might leave, and then what would they do?

Life is short; the grave is long. Just do it.

Use the Internet, use online dating agencies. Just do it.

If it all goes wrong, nothing is lost. You're old and experienced enough to tell a serial killer from a con man from a creep from a weirdo. And there are many, many people out there just like you, not wishing to disturb existing relationships, but longing to meet someone.

Loneliness:
Unseating the Third Horseman

Loneliness, the third horse of the apocalypse, is the one most of us fear the most, and rightly.

Loneliness can strike at any time. Even when you're in your prime. It's terrible. We are people of the tribe, happiest when clustering with others. Sometimes we can't. Sometimes we don't want to – we would rather be right than sociable, as was the girl who wrecked the Christmas party in the parable. Sometimes we have brought it on ourselves; sometimes we can't help it.

The Loneliness of Youth

It can happen when we are young. In our teenage years. You change schools, you know no one. The friends you have gang up on you. Boyfriends reject you, teachers hate you, your mother quarrels with you, your father's left home. There's nobody to talk to. Just when you need to talk about yourself the most, just when you're at your solipsistic zenith, there's no one to talk to. That's bad.

(I was bought up in a world where there were no teenagers. The word did not yet exist. We belonged to the coy and discreet world of the young unmarried girl, who the tribe dictated should be shy and self-effacing. Then nurture came along and moulded us into a market and gave us consumer power and self-determination. But nature still gets through to us, and when it does we suffer.)

But at least when you're young loneliness passes. There is time for things to change, for friends to court you, boyfriends to want you, teachers to admire you, your mother to forgive you, your father to return – and then all you'll want is a bit of peace and quiet. *'I want to be alone,'* you'll cry.

The Loneliness of Later On

You move house. Friends drift away. You work from home. (You never much enjoyed the company of other women and it seemed such an opportunity. Now you wonder.) Children leave home. Husbands go, or you throw them out, for good reasons or bad. Then you rather wish you hadn't. You quarrel with your mother and think she should be the one to apologize first.

You have everything you need. You have done very well in the world. You are warm, housed, clothed, fed and safe. How those in the cave would envy you if they could see you now. This is the world that the men of the tribe built, for good or bad, by their incessant tinkering, their curiosity and their craving for power, a world far above and beyond the needs of survival, just as the peacock's tail is double the size needed to attract a mate.

> (This is not to say that women freed from ill health and child bearing and rearing would not have invented television and the space shuttle. But I doubt it. Really, from a woman's point of view, these things are rather absurd and unnecessary. Television, mind you, is a good babysitter, as is a computer. It might have happened.)

Thanks to your own efforts, building upon those of others in ages past, your house is smart, your TV screen large, your iPod perfect. You wear Prada, there's a delicatessen next door, you have money in the bank, you have intimidated your suitors so they don't call and you have a pension. You have everything you want, but you don't want it any more. Because if you don't have friends it adds up to a string of beans.

Without people to talk to, without family, friends and colleagues, you can begin to believe you don't exist. We define ourselves as the sea defines the shore and the shore defines the sea: by the people around us. Speak to no one all day and then say hello to the girl in the supermarket, and your voice belongs to a stranger.

Solutions

Of course there are solutions to loneliness, namely (mostly) other people. You can go to a gym and while honing your perfect body to more perfection still you can pick up a friend or two there.

Or you can let yourself grow fat. People are nicer to you if they feel sorry for you and don't have to envy you. You could make a friend of the girl in the supermarket while discussing different brands of chocolate.

Try the Internet. In the chat rooms you can be who you like, change your gender, invent a history, be a fictional person, hook up with others as fictional as you are. As long as you don't assume anyone is speaking the truth about anything, there is no harm in it. A friend of mine, an actress, now aged 63, after a lifetime of emotional disasters met a museum curator on the Internet and developed a suitable interest in archaeology and now they live in married tranquillity at the foot of a Stone Age fort in the West Country. He really was a museum curator, GSOH, NS, just rather shy. She'd lied about her age, said she loved animals when she didn't, said she'd been married three times when it was five, and so on. When she met him she told the truth and he didn't seem to mind at all.

Inviting the Third Horseman In

Some people do it. It's madness. They quarrel with others. What's that but inviting loneliness in? They may not see it as quarrelling, just as a reasonable response to other people's bad behaviour, but they end up lonely just the same. The horse of loneliness champs and paws outside their front door. He's a grey and steely nag, rather thin and dour. Isolation, the third horseman, dismounts and knocks. And there's no one to answer. It's like the Walter de la Mare poem *The Listeners*, where the Traveller's horse champs the grasses of the forest's ferny floor, and he knocks upon the door a second time but still no one answers.

(My grandmother, who knew Walter de la Mare, said to me once, when I quoted the poem to her, 'Yes, *and if they knew it was Walter standing out there I'm not surprised they didn't answer.*' I don't know what she had against the poet. Perhaps he just wasn't very affable.)

What you don't want is the lonely horse and the lonely rider to come sniffing around your door. Both have gaunt, wild and terrible eyes and bony ribs. They don't like friends. They don't like family, particularly mothers. If they get a whiff of real maternal concern, they're off. Never, never quarrel with your mother. It is no use being censorious about them; mothers are the source of your life.

Being Lonely in Company

Being lonely in company is almost worse than being lonely on your own. You have done everything you can to keep the third horse away, but still he stays, champing the grass on the forest's ferny floor. And the chatter of small children and the booming of a male voice can add up to an oppressive stillness in the air.

It is possible to be lonely when there are quite a lot of people in the house – when no one understands anything you say, when the children are too small to conduct a conversation, though they chatter and fill your head with noise, when your husband doesn't seem to know you're there, and even seems to wish you weren't.

It happens.

And then I think it is understandable if you leave. The female heart can only stand so much unhappiness.

This is another true story of what once happened at Schiphol. I love Schiphol, Amsterdam's airport. It seems to be a place where the convergent dynamics of many lives meet and make sense. In the swirl of humanity you begin to see patterns. It is the nexus of the new world.

Why Did She Do That?

Sooner or later all roads lead to Schiphol Airport, if only for an hour or so, on the way from here to there, in transit.

We perched on high stools at the Oyster Bar where zones C and D meet. My husband had a new-season herring and a glass of beer and I had a brown shrimp sandwich and a modest glass of white wine. After that we planned to go to the art exhibition in the new extension of Rijksmuseum situated where Zone E meets Zone F. The exhibits change every month or so and there is always some new skating scene, some famous soldier on a horse, some soothing Dutch interior to be seen, some long-dead artist's glimpse of that love and trust that exists within families or between mankind and nature. Thus fortified, we would fly on to Oslo, or Copenhagen, or on occasion further afield along those curving, separating lines on the KLM map – Bombay, Los Angeles, Rio de Janeiro, Perth, wherever.

And if we were lucky, on the return journey the Rijksmuseum exhibits would have been changed and there would be yet more to see. That is, of course, if delays and security checks allowed us the time we expected to have to spare in that strange no-man's land called Transit.

Lucky, I say, but thinking about it I am not sure. The paintings in the Rijksmuseum pull you out of the trance that sensible people enter while travelling, checking out from real life the moment they step into the airport and coming back to full consciousness only when once more entering their front door. The technical name for the state is derealization, or dissociative disorder. Too much of it, they say, and you can actually shrink your hippocampus, that part of the brain from which the emotions fan like airline flight paths on the map, never to recover. It might be wiser just to stare at the departure board like anyone else.

But I am with my husband, a rare bird who has never in his life experienced a dissociative state, and is enjoying his herring, and I am emerging from mine in preparation for the Rijksmuseum and am even vaguely wondering whether I am drinking Chardonnay or Chablis when there is a sudden commotion amongst the throng of passengers.

The Oyster Bar is by a jeweller's booth, where today there are diamonds on special offer. 'The new multi-faceted computer cut' — whatever that might be. Presumably habitual buyers of diamonds know. But can there be so many of them as the existence of this shop suggests — so many enthusiastic or remorseful husbands or lovers who want to buy peace and stop off to purchase these tokens of respect and adoration? Though I daresay these days travelling women buy diamonds for themselves.

Next to the diamond boutique is a shop selling luggage and a booth offering amaryllis bulbs at ten euros for two. As a point-of-sale feature I see they're using a reproduction of that wonderful early Mondrian painting you can see in the Museum of Modern Art in New York, 'Red Amaryllis with blue background.' I bet that cost them a bit. It's midday by now and comparatively quiet in Schiphol, few customers and lots of staff, like a church when the congregation has left after a big service and the clerics are busy snuffing out candles and changing altar cloths. How do these places ever make a living? It defeats me.

A woman and her husband walk past us in the direction of departure gates C5–C57. They are in their forties, I suppose. I notice her because she walks just a little behind him and I tend to do the same whenever I am with a man. It is a habit which annoys husbands, suggesting as it does too much dependency, too little togetherness, but in a crowded place it seems to me practical. You don't have to cut a swathe through potentially hostile crowds, and passage can be effected in single file.

Couples who face the world side by side, I am prepared to argue, assert coupledom at the expense of efficiency. And it must be remembered that Jacob sent his womenfolk to walk before him when angry neighbours obliged him to return to Esau and the family farm, so that the wrath of Esau would fall first upon the wives and not upon him. As it happened Esau wasn't in the least angry about the business of the potage and was simply glad to see his long-lost brother again. But lagging behind is always safest in a world scattered with landmines both real and metaphorical. This woman seemed well aware of their existence.

I was hard put to decide their nationality. Probably British, certainly northern European. They had a troubled air, as if worried by too much debt and too little time ever to do quite what they wanted to do, always grasping for something out of reach, disappointed by the world, not as young as they'd like to be or as rich as they deserved to be. I blame the Calvinists and the work ethic: people from the warmer south have easier ways, less conscience and more generous hearts. Something at any rate was wrong. The flight had been delayed, or it was the wrong flight, or they didn't really want to go where they were going, or they didn't want to go together, or she was thinking of her lover or he of his mistress. But I didn't expect what was to happen next.

She was, I suppose, in her mid-forties: a respectable, rather pudding-faced, high-complexioned, slightly overweight stolid blonde with good legs and expensive hair piled up untidily in a bun. She was trying too hard. Her skirt was too tight and her heels too high and slim for comfortable travel. She wore a pastel pink suit with large gold buttons. The jacket stretched a little over a middle-aged bosom, that is, it was no longer perky but bulged rather at the edges. She carried a large shiny black plastic bag.

The husband who walked before her looked like a not-very-successful businessman: he wore jeans, a tie and a leather jacket, not high street but not Armani either, and you felt he would be happier in a suit. His face was set in an expression of dissatis-faction, his hair was thinning, he had the air of one beset by responsibilities and the follies of others. There was no doubt in my mind that they were married. How does one always know this? We will leave that as a rhetorical question, it being parried only with another: 'Why else would they be together?' – and the import of that exchange is too sad to contemplate.

But I thought of that tender 1641 Van Dyke painting of the newly married pair, William, Prince of Orange, aged 15, and Mary, Princess Royal of England, aged 10, and took comfort. The weight of the world is upon the young pair, and all the troubles of state and domesticity, and they are brave and beautiful in the face of it. And I sipped my Chardonnay, or Chablis, and watched the couple walk by, and wondered about their lives. They were on their way, perhaps, to visit a first grandchild and had never approved of the marriage in the first place, or to visit her parents, whom he had never liked. Something like that.

And then one moment she is walking beside him – well, a little behind him, as I say – and he says something and she suddenly falls on her knees before him. It is quite a movement: she seems to shoot out from behind him to arrive at floor level, twisting to face him. It is the same movement you see in the Pinter play, *Homecoming* I think it is, the one in which the man proposes to the woman, shooting right across the stage on his knees to entreat her to be his.

A few years back, when Harold Pinter was playing the part himself at the Almeida theatre, he remarked at one of those theatre evenings when the audience quizzes those on stage that his knees were no longer up to it. He was 60. The part really needed a younger man. I stood up in the audience and proposed a solution, namely that he altered the part to suit his knees. Let the actor propose from a sitting position and write a few lines to convey the power of the entreaty. It was, after all, his play. He could do what he liked with it. But the playwright was shocked and I sat down reproached. The lines were sacrosanct, they had entered into the canon, they were no longer Pinter's to change. They were derealized, they dwelt with other sacred texts in some dissociated state of their own, stage directions which had to be served and suffered for, by the writer too. I really admired that.

Picture the scene that day at Schiphol. Now the woman is wailing aloud like an animal, a human bereft, a cow that has lost its calf, hands clasped towards her husband in entreaty, her hair toppled around her face, her red-lipsticked mouth smeary and gaping wide, her back teeth dark with old-fashioned fillings. Her heels stick out oddly at the end of lean shins, as if someone had broken her bones, but people's legs do look like that sometimes when they kneel at the communion rail. Her skirt is rucked up, too tight and short for this sudden, passionate, noisy activity. She is not like a virgin, beautiful in prayer; she is a fat middle-aged woman with thin legs having a mad fit. She is praying to him, beseeching him, 'Have mercy. Lord, have mercy. Angels and ministers of grace attend me!'

At the Oyster Bar glasses pause mid-air. People all around pause in their transit and look to see what's going on. The husband takes a pace or two back, embarrassed and bewildered, and stares at the wife. He is trying to look as if she is nothing to do with him. At least he does not disappear into the crowd. Perhaps she has his passport.

Something stranger still happens. Women staff come out of the shops, first hesitantly, then with more deliberation, and move towards the source of the noise. There are two young girls with bare midriffs, but most are brisk and elegant older women in crisp white shirts and black skirts and sensible shoes. They cluster round the wife, they help her to her feet, they brush her down, soothing, clucking, sympathizing. She stops the wailing, looks round their kindly, consoling faces. She feels better. She manages a tremulous smile.

An armed policeman approaches. He is dismissed by this Greek chorus of female nurturers with a look, a dismissive flick of a hand, a derisive finger, and he melts away. It occurs to me that the Nurturers, even more difficult to sight than the Norns, who weave the entrails of Nordic heroes to decide their destiny, or those Mediterranean Furies, who drive us mad with guilt, have actually put in an appearance at Schiphol. Like the Lover at the Gate, unseen until the hour of need, who fills up the bed when the husband departs, these benign creatures turn up in an emergency, so long as it is dire enough. I have always suspected they existed, though unsung in fable, but I had never sighted them until now. And in an airport! I am privileged.

Then, as if this was her destined fate and this was their purpose, the Nurturers propel the woman towards her waiting husband. She does not resist. She is tentative and apologetic in demeanour. The expression on his face does not change: '*I am a man beset by troubles, bravely enduring.*'

The Nurturers turn back into shop assistants and disappear behind their counters. The couple walk on as if nothing had happened, towards Zone C, she is still just a little behind him. She pushes her hair back into its proper shape and wobbles on her heels. She may have hurt her knees.

Back at the Oyster Bar things return to normal. Eating and drinking continue. The crowds close behind the couple. Schiphol flows on. Lunchtime is approaching, noise levels are increasing.

'Why did she do that?' my husband asks, bewildered. 'Is she mad?'

'He may well have driven her mad,' I say. 'She will not have got there on her own.'

And as we make our way to the Rijksmuseum, I tell him how I imagine the day has gone for the blonde woman and how she has been driven to distraction, to the point of falling upon her knees in a public place and wailing, imploring her husband to stop, just stop, her state of desperation so extreme that she managed to summon the Nurturers. What I tell him is, of course, only one of a dozen possible scenarios.

'Marcelle,' he said to her this morning – I will call her Marcelle, she looked like a Marcelle, and we will call him Joseph, perhaps in the spirit of mild irony. Joseph, after all, stood steadily stood by Mary in the hour of her need: he did not take a step back and try to disown her when she embarrassed him so – 'Marcelle, did you remember to call Sylvia about Alec last night?'

Marcelle is busy packing a suitcase not quite big enough for all her needs. They are up early. They have a flight to catch.

Marcelle and Joseph will live in a detached house with thick carpets and good reproduction furniture and a designer kitchen. He will have one married daughter by an earlier marriage and they will have two teenage children between them and a neat garden in which anything unruly will have been cut down to size. She will use bark chippings, that ugly stuff, to keep the weeds down.

Loneliness: Unseating the Third Horseman

Joseph: 'Ugly, what do you mean, ugly? Well, you should know. But I am not made of money. We cannot afford a gardener more than once a week, for God's sake.'

Once, long ago, Marcelle dreamed of romance and roses round a cottage door, and once indeed Joseph picked a single cherry in an orchard and brought it to her. That was when she was first pregnant with Alec and Joseph was emotional about it. She kept the pip for ages and even tried to make it sprout by putting it in water. Then she would have a whole little tree covered with cherries, but nothing happened except that the pip just lay there and the water grew cloudy and sour and she had to throw it out. All that was left was a ring round the glass which no amount of scouring would remove. Still, even that was something. A memento of something good.

She would really like another suitcase just for her cosmetics, but Joseph doesn't like heaving cases about. Who does? Jars are heavy and bulky, and creams for the eyes and the neck and the lips and the bust are probably interchangeable, but she is nervous of being without a single one of them. She can't make up her mind. She packs and repacks. She slips jars into her shoes to save space, but the weight is un-avoidable.

Joseph: 'Couldn't you do without the gunk for just a couple of days and nights? It's not as if it seems to make any difference. You're over 40, nearly 50. Surely the days when face creams would help have passed? Take them to the charity shop and be rid of them.'

As if charity shops took half-empty jars of cream, however expensive. What do men know?

'I called but there was no answer,' lies Marcelle.

'Did you leave a message on Sylvia's answerphone?' asks Joseph. He has already packed. It takes him five minutes. He is decisive.

Joseph: 'One of us has to be.'

Now he is brushing his teeth. Marcelle cooked him breakfast but had none herself. He likes a good breakfast; she is never hungry first thing in the morning. Joseph has good teeth; Marcelle spends a lot of time at the dentist.

Joseph: 'My mother made sure I had milk every day. You really shouldn't let Alec and Carla drink those disgusting sweet drinks all the time. It's not as if they have particularly good dental genes – at least not from your side.'

But how do you stop teenagers from eating and drinking exactly what they want? It wasn't as if Joseph was around all that much at mealtimes to train them to do anything at all, let alone sit down when they ate and drank.

190

'I couldn't,' says Marcelle. 'It wasn't switched on.'

'That's strange,' says Joseph. 'Sylvia is usually so efficient.'

According to Joseph, Sylvia is elegant, Sylvia is intelligent, Sylvia has perfect teeth. What a good dress sense Sylvia has. So slim! Such a pretty figure. Sylvia is like a sister to Joseph, and tells everyone so, though of course they are no blood relation. Sylvia has twin girls of 15 who are very smart and well behaved and no trouble at all.

Joseph: 'Sylvia knows how to bring up children.'

The only thing wrong with Sylvia is her husband Earle. Joseph thinks Earle is something of a slob, not worthy of Sylvia. Earle and Sylvia are Joseph and Marcelle's best friends, and their children like to spend time together. But over the last five years Earle has crept up the promotion ladder and Joseph has stuck on a certain rung while others have clambered up over him.

The fact is, Marcelle did not want to call Sylvia. It was late, she was tired, and now, thank God, it is too early.

Seven years ago Joseph spent a night with Sylvia in a hotel at a sales conference. He had come home in the morning smelling of Sylvia's scent.

Joseph: 'Why do you never wear scent any more, Marcelle?'

191

Marcelle: 'Because I am too busy. Because I never remember to wear it. Because it made the babies sneeze and I got out of the habit.'

Then he had confessed and apologized and Marcelle and Sylvia had talked it out and had agreed to forget the incident, which had been, well, yes, both unfortunate and unexpected.

Joseph: 'I am so sorry, Marcelle. It should not have happened. But she is such a honey, such a sweet dear, you know how much you like her, and she is having such a hard time with Earle. I can only conclude somebody put something in the drink or it would never have happened. It meant nothing – it was just a silly physical thing. And she is your friend. I feel much better now I've told you.'

Yes, but in a hotel? A whole night? Full sex? Behind the filing cabinets would have been more understandable.

Sylvia: 'I am so, so sorry, Marcelle. I would never do anything to hurt you. I will always be open with you. It was a silly drunken thing – someone must have put something in the office drink. It was completely out of character and will never happen again. We both have our marriages and our children to think about, so shall we both just say "closure" and forgive and forget?'

So Marcelle had. Or had tried to.

Loneliness: Unseating the Third Horseman

Sylvia was a psychotherapist who worked in the human resources department of the haulage business where Joseph worked as an accountant. Earl was now director of acquisitions at the same firm, earned far more than Joseph and had an office to himself and a good carpet. He was away from home quite a lot visiting subsidiary companies abroad. Sylvia was brave about his absences but sometimes she would turn up at Marcelle's door at the weekend with red eyes and talk about nothing in particular and Marcelle felt for her. And Marcelle could see that bedding Sylvia had been a triumph for Joseph, a feather in his cap, so great an event it was now what sustained him in life.

Joseph: I was the one who bedded Sylvia, Earle's wife, at the office party seven years ago.

But Marcelle still did not want to call Sylvia about Alec. Alec had been found taking drugs at school and was in danger of expulsion. Joseph reckoned that Sylvia could help with advice and wisdom. She after all being so good with young people. Her twins would never take drugs, or be anorexic, like Carla. They were calm and orderly and dull.

'I'll call her when we get back from Copenhagen,' Marcelle says to Joseph, looking up from the parade of jars: different makes, different shapes, some gold-topped, some white, some silvery, all enticing. They are going to visit the new baby and will only be staying two days. She is glad it is not longer. Her step-daughter has always been a bundle of resentments at the best of times. Now she will be sleepless and ordering Marcelle about as if she were the maid.

What Makes Women Happy

Joseph: 'What can you expect? You stole me from her. Now you have to put up with it.'

It will not be an easy trip. Joseph does not like the new husband.

'That's all very well,' Joseph says to Marcelle, 'but you promised me you'd call her and now you haven't. I really don't understand you.'

'I expect it will have blown over by the time we get back,' says Marcelle with unusual firmness. 'Schools always over-react. And I really I don't see why Sylvia needs to know every detail of our business.'

'She's a good friend to you,' says Joseph. 'Better than you'll ever know.'

What does he mean by that? Has something else happened between Joseph and Sylvia? Has he tried to restart the flirtation and she refused, for Marcelle's sake? Or is that just what Joseph wants Marcelle to think, because he's annoyed?

She gives up on the throat cream and then thinks of Sylvia's smooth and perfect neck and repacks it. Perhaps she can do without the eye cream? Sylvia is seven years younger than Marcelle. Sylvia has beautiful clear bright eyes, widely spaced, and good cheekbones. Flesh seems somehow to have shrouded Marcelle's.

She feels suddenly hungry and goes to the kitchen to have a cup of coffee and a piece of toast. Joseph follows her into the kitchen.

'Sylvia says the way to keep slim is never to eat carbohydrates before breakfast,' he observes. 'And I don't think this matter of Alec is simply going to melt away, however much you hope it will. You have such a problem with reality! I don't like to say this of Alec, but there is a history of criminality in the family. Remember the time when he was eight and you found money missing from your purse? I don't think you dealt with that properly. Sylvia said the whole thing should have been talked through, not just swept under the carpet. Now this drugs business. Where has the boy been getting the money?'

Marcelle's father, a respectable builder, had served four months in prison for petty theft very shortly after Joseph and Marcelle were married. He had taken a lathe home, he said by accident, but the client had reported it to the police and the magistrate, no doubt in the middle of his own building work, had seen it as a gross breach of trust.

Marcelle had always had an uneasy suspicion that if her father had turned into a jailbird before the wedding, not after, it would never have taken place. Somehow the feeling was always there that she was lucky to have caught Joseph – a surgeon's son, well educated, good-looking, an accountant with a degree in mathematics. Joseph's family photographs were in real silver frames. Marcelle's were in plastic.

She saw herself with a terrible clarity: good legs and bosom, but with a tendency to put on weight, no conversation, no dress sense, no brains and no qualifications, a too-shrill speaking voice and a vulgar laugh. And both children took after her, not him.

195

They were a disappointment to Joseph. If he'd married someone like Sylvia, one of whose sisters was now the wife of a peer of the realm, albeit non-hereditary, he would have had children as perfect as the twins. Though Earle had once said something really nice when they were round to dinner.

> Earle: *'Say what you like about those children of yours, Marcelle, they're never dull. They're like you – a pleasure to be with.'*

Marcelle had been serving a chocolate mousse at the time. Sylvia never served sweets, only cheese. She didn't believe in sugar. Sylvia had made quite a face when Earle had said that to Marcelle and had looked disdainfully at the mousse and tried to smirk at Joseph, but Joseph for once had taken no notice. He had even seemed pleased at what Earle had said, as if he too were being complimented. Men were strange. They were pack animals, no doubt about it, and very aware of who was top dog. Sometimes Marcelle was surprised that Joseph had never actually offered her to Earle in recompense for the office party incident, just to even things out. She wouldn't have minded too much if he had; she liked Earle. But Sylvia would not have liked it one bit.

Marcelle knows Joseph loves her, and she certainly loves him. She feels for him acutely as the world looks by him and over him. She wants to protect him. She knows why he is trying to upset and disturb her: there was a letter in the post recently about his pension and the assumption was that he had reached the ceiling of his career and would never earn more than he did now.

They will never have a swimming pool like Earle and Sylvia. They will have each other, of course, but that in itself is a disappointment to Joseph. How can it not be? There are so many beautiful and brilliant women in the world that will never be his.

Marcelle also worries about Alec and Carla, because Joseph cuts them down to size all the time, as he does her, and she knows that children grow into their parents' plan for them. She wishes that he would just sometimes *pretend* to love and admire them more. It would help them.

'I hope you're going to change before we leave?' he asks. She is wearing black trousers and a dark-blue cashmere sweater, soft and comfortable but rather over-washed.

'I wasn't going to,' she says.

'Why don't you wear that nice pink thing? Sylvia always says how much it suits you.'

She changes into the pink suit, which is too tight for her and makes her look vast. She has not worn it for a few months. She can't admit it's unwearable, she will only get a lecture on Sylvia and carbohydrates. She will just have to hope Joseph doesn't notice.

She goes back into the kitchen. He looks her up and down and says nothing. He is not looking forward to the trip, either.

What Makes Women Happy

His son-in-law is a man he does not like or respect. He is a small-time Danish architect who came to Marcelle and Joseph's house to discuss plans for a conservatory in the days when they could have afforded one. The plans came to nothing, but he went away with the daughter.

> Joseph: 'Marcelle, I can't forgive you for this! When you knew they were seeing each other, why didn't you stop them? It's a disaster.'

Now he has to go and see the baby, fruit of this union, and try and look pleased. He never saw himself as a grandfather.

'Well, I don't want to be a grandmother either,' thinks Marcelle, with a sudden burst of inner petulance. 'Two can play at this game, and it's your fault, not mine, that I am, since I married a man with a child, more fool me.' She knows better than to say so. She takes a spoonful of conserve straight from the pot and puts it into her mouth without even bothering about the toast, and Joseph, with a sharp intake of breath, leaves the room.

Marcelle solves the beauty problem by slipping such small jars as she can into the case of Joseph's laptop. With any luck he won't notice the extra weight. She wears her highest heels. She knows they are impractical for travel, but her morale needs boosting. Since the only good thing about her that Joseph is prepared to admit to at the moment is her legs, she will make the most of them. Sylvia may have the eyes and the cheekbones and the salary, but Marcelle has the legs.

Loneliness: Unseating the Third Horseman

They get to the airport in good time. Joseph cannot abide being in a rush and Marcelle has learned not to hold him up. She has to pay extra because her bag is so heavy.

Joseph (the week after the wedding): 'Now, about our finances. We will each pay proportionate to our earnings and keep careful and accurate accounts. I will be paying the lion's share out of the joint account, but that is right and proper: I am your husband. I am not complaining. Personal extras must come out of our separate accounts – by "extras" I mean jaunts to the café, having your friends to lunch, parking fines, excess luggage, petrol for unnecessary outings, that sort of thing.'

And Marcelle had agreed, without asking for clarification as to who decided on the interpretation of 'unnecessary'. Her mother had told her at the time to get everything straight within the first week of marriage because if it wasn't done then it never would be. But that had been the week her father had gone to prison and her mother had been told she had cancer. She hadn't been concentrating.

On the Cityhopper flight to Schiphol Joseph said, 'I am disappointed you didn't get through to Sylvia. It's very unusual for her to leave the answerphone switched off. When we get to Amsterdam I'll call her on her mobile and you can talk to her then.'

What Makes Women Happy

'Did you bring the number with you?'

'It's on my mobile,' he pointed out.

'Well, it would be, wouldn't it?' Marcelle said. That was rash.

'I don't know what's the matter with you,' he said, looking at her with disdain. 'Next thing you'll be wanting to go through my numbers called to check up on me and Sylvia. It really is sick, Marcelle. So jealous of your best friend you'd risk the future of your own son! And your mascara has gone odd. There are little lumps of it under your left eye. Why do women want to plaster their faces with that stuff? It makes them look worse, not better.'

She could have pointed out that Alec was his son too, and if he were so sure Sylvia would know how to deal with the situation he could always have called her himself, or popped into her office for a consultation on how to conduct his family affairs. No doubt he did that all the time, anyway. But she said nothing. There was a strange kind of bubbling feeling inside her. Was this what blood boiling felt like? Her ears popped as the aircraft began to descend and she felt more normal again.

Joseph called Sylvia from Schiphol to check up on the status of her phone and Sylvia reported that it was fine, as far as she knew. Perhaps Marcelle had dialled a wrong number. It was easy to do, they made the keys so small these days. She'd be delighted to talk to Marcelle about Alec — when they got to Copenhagen, perhaps, and had a little more time. It might be that Marcelle was the troubled one, not Alec?

'Did you hear that, Marcelle?' asked Joseph. 'You might be the troubled one, not Alec. We'll have to think about that. Sylvia always has a fresh slant on things. I knew we ought to talk to her.'

Joseph and Marcelle made their way towards the gate for the Copenhagen flight. After the brief good cheer of his conversation with Sylvia, Joseph's mood was worsening.

'I wish you'd keep up, Marcelle. And why are you wearing those stupid shoes? And pastel pink? For travelling? The skirt's too short for someone your age and weight. You look absurd. The only gold buttons in this whole airport belong to you. Sometimes I think you do it on purpose.'

And that was the point at which she threw herself on the ground in front of him, on her knees, hands clasped like a supplicant, wailing, *'Stop it, stop it, stop it, come back to me, love of my life!'* so piercingly loud in her heart that the Nurturers heard and came to her rescue and returned her to him and him to her.

These things can happen beneath our very noses. I like to think that so shocked was he, so brought to his senses, that he didn't say a single mean thing to Marcelle, or even mention Sylvia, for the rest of the visit. That he even picked up the baby – it was a girl – and smiled at it and said, 'You're a pretty girl, just like your grandmother. And you have her lovely smile.'

'So that's why she did it,' I said to my husband. 'He drove her mad.'

'It's obvious you can't resist a happy ending,' he said. 'Personally, I felt very sorry for the poor man. I hope she's ashamed of herself.'

By that time we were at the Rijksmuseum, but found it was closed, because they were changing the paintings.

Shame:
Unseating the Fourth Horseman

The fourth horse of the new apocalypse is shame and his rider is self-doubt. A nasty, shabby pair.

These days the nag shame tends to get called 'low self-esteem'. It's when you have nothing to be proud of and you know it, when you leave the house with your head lowered because of the spots, wearing dark glasses because you think your eyes are too small and go to bed with anyone who asks you because (others say) your Darwinian sense of selection, your ambition to win an alpha male, has somehow been eroded. When other women say, *'Poor thing, such low self-esteem, she's anyone's.'* When you overhear some young man, rightly nervous about his sexual prowess, talk about *'a charity fuck'* and you realize he means you.

That wouldn't be too good for your self-esteem. Your argument – that you just like sex, that's why you do it – might sound a little weak, for a time. But it's just as likely to be true. You do it because you like it, nothing to do with low self-esteem.

Shout it to the rooftops and shame will gallop off into the night, with his rider self-doubt mumbling into his high collar as he goes, skeletal bones glimmering in the night, *'What I need is a people-carrier. I'm ashamed to be seen on this old nag.'*

But don't tell your fiancé too much about all this. You are a new improved person now.

More Irresponsible Advice

We are not pursuing happiness here, but survival. These actions require secrecy; you must never tell anyone. They are least-worst options, not good in themselves, but the best solution in the circumstances. For example I would say it was allowable to cheat on your husband/boyfriend when higher things were at stake. That is to say the preservation of your home/relationship/sanity.

I must warn you, in passing, that in my experience most significant secrets of a sexual nature are in the end revealed, but with any luck decades will pass before they are and perhaps then it won't matter so much.

But beware the deathbed confession:

He: 'Rita, I slept with Margie 30 years ago.'

When Rita's his wife and you're Margie. And the scandal gets round the retirement home. Well, at least you had a past.

Beware the brink-of-divorce disclosure:

She: 'And what is more I slept with Tom, Dick, Harry and Edward, and every single one of them was better in bed than you.'

It may be true, but twenty-four words can cost you a fortune in alimony.

Beware the impetuous desire to confess:

He: 'I have to tell you, Robert, it keeps me awake at night: I slept with your wife seven years back.'

Especially if you are Robert's wife. Some people can never just leave well alone.

Nevertheless, there are risks you may sometimes have to take.

On Not Having a Baby When You Want One

It hasn't happened naturally and all your friends seem to have one. You're in a bad situation: the solution is going to be least-worst. And it will not get better on its own. You have waited five years already.

(Sometimes waiting another ten works. So convinced was one of my friends after fifteen years that she was infertile, she took no precautions and suddenly, at 44, she was pregnant. Three cats had to go, and two dogs and a parrot. Psittacosis! And their pension scheme, and her job, and their three holidays a year . . . However. They went through with it. It is the most darling baby. But that's by the by.)

You may well blame yourself. '*I should have started earlier.*' Well, you didn't. Too bad. But that's in the past. And anyway, it might have nothing to do with you, it could be him. It might be his fertility that's in question.

You can start down the long gruelling road of treatment, surrender yourself and your partner to internal investigation, the humiliation of body and soul for an uncertain end – quite possibly ending up with neither partner nor child – or you can try another man, temporarily.

Choose a suitable evening and go where you will find others of your own kind, be it pub, club or old school reunion, choose the youngest, best looking and brightest available (and most like husband or partner, if you have any sense) and you do what you can to get yourself pregnant. I have known women do it and I have known it work.

'*We're pregnant!*' you say, full of pleasure and delight. And your husband's self-esteem is restored, he is spared the indignity of ejaculating into a jar and he loves the baby and never knows. And like as not you'll have another one, because you've relaxed (and because it's inconvenient: babies often come along at the worst possible time, as if nature were bent on challenging you to deny her. When you're ready for the baby, that's when it's least likely to arrive. Nature's little joke, as in the couple with the parrot).

My friend Clara did exactly this, had a boy by a drunken medical student and had three more babies within three years, with her husband, after the first. And now she has grandchildren, and her husband never found out. Just sometimes, when her son, now grown, tells a joke and makes her laugh, she thinks of the student, who might well now be a professor of medicine, and how drunk and funny he was, and wonders what became of him. They might have made something of it, because it was a pleasant encounter, but she didn't follow it up and she loved her husband, even though he never told a joke in his life.

Don't worry about it. Just do it. If you're planning fertility treatment, your need for a child will have overcome your love of your husband in any case.

You're Fertile Enough, But Where's the Man?
Anyone can find a man. It may not be the man you want, but there's a man to be found – at the Job Centre or down

the pub. Again, choose as good a genetic specimen as you can. It's a least-worst choice. Babies do not need 'proper' homes. What this baby needs most of all is life. It may say to you from time to time as it grows older, *'I wish I had never been born,'* but it's not likely to mean it. If you can afford a baby, have one.

(If the state has to support it, think again. Giving the child the state for a father is not on. You will need to be mother and father too. If you can do that, good for you.)

Once upon a time men did the hitting and running, planting the gene never to be seen again. Socialization had failed: the man was all-natural unimpeded male. Now you want to hit and run home with the baby. You're all instinct too, and no reason. All nature and no nurture. Socialization has failed but something has been gained: a living, squalling, riotous baby.

Let me tell you an historical tale, scarcely relevant to now, but illustrative of the point that what you don't know you don't grieve over. We live in an age of revelation. Manners and mores change fast. Science changes the way we think and feel. We know so much it's hardly possible to work out what's important and what's not. We can get things wrong. If I take you back into the past it's so I myself can get an overview.

This is a true story, set back in the mid-fifties, about a group of college girls seeking truth at a time when nice girls didn't have sex before marriage.

Good Lord, we were ignorant. We lived in a delicious fear that we might be pregnant and then our boyfriends would have to marry us. It wasn't that we lacked sexual experience, it's that the lights were always off and we never *looked*. Or if in the sunlight out of doors, on some grassy romantic sward, we kept our eyes squeezed shut. Men practised the withdrawal method – that is to say, they took their thing out (with any luck) before they finished. At least we thought they did. Our bodies were mysteries to us.

I was to get pregnant very soon and five years later knew pretty much everything about everything – too much for comfort.

Men had a 'thing' and we had 'down there'. We sat with our legs crossed as our mothers had taught us.

We were inorgasmic, and in retrospect our dedication to male sexual satisfaction was both absurd and noble. We wanted nothing in return. We were simply grateful to be the object of male attention, and 'dating' – going nearly all the way but not all the way – was exciting enough: the body could be suffused with so much pleasure it was nearly intolerable.

I have no doubt that in other circles in 1950s London there were others who knew about orgasms and even demanded them. There were women who knew everything there was to know. It was just that I and my friends did not.

The day that news of orgasms came to us we were drinking wine in an attic somewhere in Chelsea. None of us were virgins, Elsie, Rowena, Charlotte, Roxy, Brenda and me. We took no notice of our mothers, we loved sex, we wanted sex, we had one-night stands while looking for true love. We were humiliated and distressed when the true love so often left before dawn.

It wasn't much different from *Sex in the City*, come to that, except the face-saving ritual of the morning-after thank-you call had not yet arrived. Nor, indeed, had safe sex. And abortion was illegal and you went to prison if you had one. We were entranced by the pleasures of the flesh and, believing that sex and procreation were eternally linked, were the more awed by its power. Even if you had an illegitimate baby it was worth it, as I was to find out.

Now we are waiting for Penny to arrive. Penny is our friend, one of our circle. Unlike the rest of us she doesn't have a degree. She has a private income, however, and has gone to see a private doctor about birth control, as it's called. She can afford to. We can't. There's a new thing called a Dutch cap, something that can stop you getting pregnant, and Penny has the courage and means to enquire about it. This is 10 years before the pill and 15 years before the coil and 30 years before implants. No morning-after pills, abortion illegal – no wonder sex was exciting!

We wait impatiently. A Dutch cap! A rubber shield you put over your cervix. *'Where is it?' 'What's that?'* None of us has a clue. We think Penny is very brave to be prepared to face the embarrassment of an internal examination by a man. (Doctors were normally men.) I'd had one once when I had cystitis, and the doctor, discovering I was not a virgin, sent me off to hospital at once to be tested for venereal disease. My 18-year-old 'down there' was closely inspected by groups of students and declared to be disease-free and I was left to stumble home. It was traumatic but still uninformative.

Roxy, being from Texas, says it's no big deal. Texan girls spend a lot of time with men's hands up their insides as the doctor checks that they are 'developing normally'.

How strange we must have looked by the standards of today: hair in formal waves pulled back unflatteringly from the face, pencilled eyebrows, bright-blue eyeshadow, if any, a general desire to look 40 rather than 20, rubber girdles keeping in our tummies, preventing free movement. Little waists and full skirts. V-necked T-shirts which meant that if you show your shoulders you can't show your cleavage and vice versa.

But they make you feel sexy.

And then in comes Penny, back from the doctor's. She's smiling and she's excited. A revelation has been given to her.

'I had this rubber thing fitted,' says Penny. 'He says you have to stop everything and put it in, take it out after use and wash it and keep it in a tin. It isn't very romantic.'

The tin was large, flat, round and pink and she showed us the yellowy rubber contraption inside. We were fascinated and horrified.

'I had to lie there on my back with my legs open and he folded the rubber ring and pushed it inside me, where it bounced open. It felt quite nice.'

We were quite shocked. We did not normally go into sexual detail. Penny was less inhibited than the rest of us; she had had less education. She was a girl of the people.

'He was ever so good-looking,' she added, 'and quite young for a doctor. He asked me if I'd ever come. I said, "What's that?" and he said, "Like this." Then he twiddled this little lump in front of down there for a bit and I had this strange feeling, like shivers of electricity all over me, which kind of exploded, and he said, "That's what I mean. It's called an orgasm." "But only men have those," I said. "Women can too," he said. "Now you know, tell your friends."'

And so she did. And Elsie, Rowena, Charlotte, Roxy, Brenda and I pursued orgasms unrelentingly through the coming decades, with varying degrees of success.

Nowadays that doctor would be struck off. We just thought he was useful and a proselytizer for female happiness.

Those of you who can't stand too much attention being paid to the past may rejoin here.

You lot may think we have reached the pinnacle of right thinking, that history is bunk (as Henry Ford said, he who created the gridlocks of the future), that we now know all there is to be known about correct behaviour, but it is not so. Fear of history is denial of history, a burying of the head in the societal sand in case we have to come to terms with what we'd rather not: that everything changes and will forever go on changing, and we are not necessarily going from dark to light, from ignorance to knowledge, from barbarism to civilization.

The ostrich with its head in the sand is not happy, just fearful.

Now you shall have a final parable, the parable of Sylvia the housewife, who, when the four horsemen circled nearer, their nags champing and snorting, managed calmly and quietly to send them packing, while scarcely knowing she was doing it. She is the nearest person to a saint that I have ever met.

Mrs Blackbird

In the twenty-two years they had called the place home the suburbs had been raised around them. Now, when asked, Sylvia hardly knew whether to say 'I live in the country' or 'I live in the town.' Two years back, just before the divorce, Hugh had done a deal by which the acre field which went with the house had been sold off for development. Now Sylvia was overlooked by neighbours. They were pleasant enough and she could see she was lucky and what garden remained was large by their standards, but there were street lights all around and she missed the dark of a night which made the stars seem bright and important and her place in the universe, though humble, made clear. Namely, that she was needed in the great scheme of things, if only as an observer. Humanity, in Sylvia's opinion, existed to glorify its creator.

When she'd said this kind of thing to Hugh he'd been embarrassed, and she thought it was one of the reasons that he had left her – very amiably, and politely, and leaving her well enough provided for, and visiting quite often, but still he had left, for a nice bright rational young woman, Debbie, who saw no sub-text in life at all and never had irritating fits of whimsy. Sylvia liked to exchange ideas; other people, it seemed, including Hugh, preferred to trade information.

The new neighbours didn't go for Sylvia's kind of conversation either. They walked their dogs and said, 'Lovely evening,' and a few sat on riverbanks and pretended to be fishing, but mostly they talked about home improvements if they were men and diets if they were women, and the whys and wherefores of their existence didn't seem to worry them at all.

The new houses were little better than boxes, computer designed to make the best use of every square inch of space at the lowest possible price. Sylvia and Hugh's old farmhouse, with its lack of right angles and wandering corridors, was the one which now seemed out of place. And now Hugh was no longer there Sylvia could see herself increasingly cast as an oddity, a woman of a certain age, without a family, cut off from friends. Once she had been envied; now she was pitied.

Since Hugh had taken to property development he'd grown rich, spurred on by the realization that you could build a house for

214

£15,000 and sell it for £250,000. He'd grown rather fat and dull too, but was still quite a catch, apparently, for Debbie. Debbie could have babies, which Sylvia couldn't any more, having lost the one she'd had and messed up her insides, so Hugh was scarcely to be blamed for leaving. Why should her life's affliction become his, just because they were married? When he left she just felt blank. Now, a couple of years later, she could hardly think of a thing to say to him. She seldom had much to report.

Yes, she was fine, she had rejoined the library and was working on the garden, and no, she didn't want a holiday, and certainly not a cruise, not even if he and the pregnant Debbie came too. And then what was there to say? Hugh was not interested in the fate of the swallows which had gone elsewhere when their barn was destroyed to make way for the bungalow, or how the robin had weathered the winter. He did not care that Mrs Blackbird, who had fled when the ivy where she nested had been showered with lime and plaster dust, had returned after a season's absence and had set up home in the Virginia creeper outside Sylvia's bedroom window. She tried to tell him, but Hugh sounded puzzled and asked her how on earth she knew it was the same bird as before. When she came to think of it, of course she did not. She just hoped it was. So she shut up.

Sylvia was prone to wishful thinking: she knew she was. She had really believed that Hugh and Debbie were just good friends. All the same, she was home to a blackbird. She woke to her song every morning. She liked to think the bird knew the difference between her and the incomers, and preferred her, and included her in her singing. 'Oh, what a beautiful morning!'

She must not get too fond of Mrs Blackbird, though, the little boy in the new house next door pointed out, peering up at her with his plump, anxious, small-eyed little face, since the bird was marked for doom.

The boy's name was Darren. Sylvia supposed he was 9 or 10. She did not know much about children.

'What do you mean, marked out for doom?' Sylvia asked, crossly. She was snipping out extra buds from the roses – snip, snip, snip – to ensure extra good blooms later on. It was a wonderful sunny May that year.

'Our cat will get it,' Darren said.

'I certainly hope not,' she said.

'A cat's got to eat,' he said. 'That's nature, isn't it?'

'Then keep yours well fed,' she said, briskly, 'and don't let me see it in my garden.'

'You're weird,' he said and wandered off.

She felt she had exchanged Hugh for this grungy little boy called Darren Croxton. It had not been a good bargain. His eyes were too narrow and anxious, too close together, and his skin was grey:

a slum child by breeding. Her little girl, had she lived beyond two days, would have been on the side of the angels, and not spoken to her in that way. Yet she could see this wretched boy, by virtue of living in what had once been her orchard, was in some way her responsibility.

It was true there were now too many cats in the neighbourhood for the safety of Mrs Blackbird. There was a slinky Burmese called Khan, who prowled around meaningfully but fortunately did not seem to have the energy to pounce. There was an amazing creature called Catso by its owner, a good-looking young man with a Lamborghini and male friends – a Bengal cat who lived across the way, had tiger markings on its belly and was five generations down from a miniature Bengal tiger, bred for its good nature. So successfully had it been bred, indeed, that it seemed to love everyone and everything, gazing indulgently at flies and wishing even small birds like Mrs Blackbird well. It had cost £2,000 and was electronically tagged, like a criminal. It would come and sit by Sylvia's side down where the parsley and the sage grew, and they'd listen to Mrs Blackbird together, and Catso would even purr.

The cat Sylvia feared was the black-and-white tom Henry, from the Croxtons' house next door. Henry, as you might expect from such a household, was a miserable, uncared-for specimen, scrawny, with a savage gleam in his eye, whose pleasure was catching birds and laying them out on the garden path. He would sit and stare up at Mrs Blackbird's nest in the Virginia creeper. As Darren had observed, it was only natural for cats to want to kill birds, but Sylvia did not want it to happen.

The day after the Croxtons moved in Sylvia discovered Darren in her herb patch, picking parsley. He wanted his mother to make him a parsley omelette. It was evident from what the child said that he did not know the difference between a field, a common and a private garden, and also that his feckless mother scarcely owned a frying pan. They lived on takeaways. So Sylvia made him a parsley omelette and he said it tasted weird – his favourite word – but he ate most of it, spitting out the parsley into his hand. He hadn't realized it was so green. He did not like green food.

The Croxtons came from the inner city and had moved out, people said disapprovingly, not so much in search of fresh air as profit. Stay in one of the new developments for a year, make a few 'improvements' and you could sell on with a good mark-up, while in the meantime avoiding the pain of paid employment.

Now Darren seemed to be round at Sylvia's place all the time, his little anxious malnourished face appearing without warning, almost out from under her arm as it were, asking questions and making demands – a glass of water here, a plaster there, a piece of cake, would she look after his key in case he lost it? His parents never heard when he knocked. They smoked a lot of stuff, he explained, and kept the doors locked, but she wasn't to tell anyone. It was a question of the law.

'Do your parents mind me having the key?' she'd asked, ckecking.

'Nah,' he said. 'They say you're an old bat but you're okay.'

218

She took the key, not without reluctance, well aware that for every favour you granted more would be asked and less gratitude felt. The parents could barely be in their thirties. They must have started out in their teens with Darren. Of course they would think she was an old bat. If Sylvia had bothered to have the grey taken out of her hair and wore something other than flat shoes, elasticized skirts and old jumpers around the house she could have looked as good as Debbie, just older. She had better features than Debbie and a nicer nature than Debbie, which was why Hugh was always coming round, but she could see that to the outside world she could very well be an old bat. The barn had been converted to a nifty home for a Bengal cat and the real bats had fled, but that was the way of the new world. Perhaps they had left some of the spirit of battedness behind and it had lodged in her. That was okay by Sylvia.

No one thought much of the Croxtons. They let the side down, they didn't belong to this smart new development any more than Sylvia did. The father spent his time putting in patterned glass doors instead of plain, decking the garden and sticking pink plastic flamingos in what grass was left. Family rows could be heard down the street and the mother had been seen at the benefits office. She could see the blue-grey glow from the computer in Darren's bedroom late into the night, sometimes at three in the morning. She could take a broom and tap on his window and tell him to go to bed at once, but it was none of her business. In the morning he'd leave at a run for school, often late, eating some chocolate bar as he ran.

She took to leaving a plate of premium cat food for Henry under the apple tree to keep him well fed, smarten up his coat a bit and keep him away from Mrs Blackbird. Mr Blackbird, shiny and glossy and grand, appeared from time to time now that Mrs Blackbird had done all the work building a neat, well-hidden nest from twigs and moss, mud and leaves. He'd put his head on one side and add the odd well-placed twig. He reminded her of Hugh.

Mrs Blackbird laid her eggs and Henry prowled nearer and nearer.

'They won't make it,' Darren said. 'One in three fledgling thrushes don't.' He'd looked it up on the Internet. 'If it's not the cats, it's the rats and the squirrels. And the crows eat the eggs. And my mum says you're trying to steal her cat. She says if you don't stop feeding it she'll beat the shit out of you.'

Sylvia raised surprised eyebrows at Darren, who amended it to, weakly: 'Mum says would you please not do it.' She called round at Mrs Croxton's and though she was pretty sure the woman was in there, no one came to the door. So she went on putting food out for Henry under the apple tree. If Darren's mother had something to say to her, let her come round and say it.

Then Darren didn't come round for a time, until the fledglings had learned to fly and had left the nest. She imagined he was sulking about the cat food and punishing her. That was okay by her. Then she found him digging up her lawn with a spoon and putting in half-live worms he'd dug out of his own pitiful garden. He said he was providing extra food for Mrs Blackbird, but Sylvia suspected he was trying to lure the bird back onto the open lawn so Henry could do his pouncing. She said as much to Darren, who shouted and shrieked and swore, so she knew he was guilty. Really, he was a wretched child. He kept out of her way for a week or so. Good.

Then she saw a removal van draw up next door and the men load on the Croxtons' household belongings which were not up to much. Darren had gone off to school as usual. Into the van went a big plasma-screen TV, Darren's computer and a rather smart bath, amongst the barely serviceable rubbish of next door's everyday life.

Mrs Croxton came out and lured Henry into a cat box from under the apple tree, casting a snarling glance over towards Sylvia's house, while Mr Croxton removed all the light bulbs from the rooms and the fittings from the front door, and off they all went.

Later that day a bright-looking young couple turned up at the door and let themselves in and Sylvia heard cries of dismay and angry phone calls being made, and soon bin bag after bin bag of assorted debris and dirt started piling up at the gate. And Darren hadn't even called to say goodbye. She was more hurt than she had expected. A horrid lad, really.

But then there he was at her door again, in floods of tears, beside himself, and the new people next door were with him and asking her what to do, as if she were expected to know. The child had come home from school and found his parents gone.

'They took Henry,' he was saying, 'They left me!' And so it seemed the parents had. Flown the nest and left the fledgling.

'I know I'm bad,' he wept, 'but not as bad as all that.'

Social services said it did sometimes happen to children, just as it happened to dogs. The owners get fed up and scarper.

'I'm sorry about the worms,' said Darren. 'I didn't mean it. I really like Mrs Blackbird. I just wanted to know what happened next.'

'It's all right, all right,' she said, and found him an apple from Henry's tree, but when social services suggested that Darren stayed with her while they sorted things out and that she could even foster him if she passed the tests, she refused. She was too old, she had no intention of taking on a child, she knew nothing about children, she'd never had one, or one that lasted.

'You're just weird,' Darren shrieked at her. 'You are not too old, you just say you are. I hate you!' They dragged him off her, bribed him with a chocolate bar and took him away in their car to a fate in care.

The next day Sylvia was sitting in the garden when a mother crow alighted on the garden wall, followed by two fluttering baby crows. The three of them sat on the wall, the big bird impatient and cross, as crows always seem to be, the little ones unsleek and bumbling and rendered unnaturally large by virtue of having fluff rather than feather.

Mother Crow flew down from the wall to the garden. The babies were meant to follow. They wouldn't. They peered, they craned, they saw unimaginable depths below and refused to take the risk. They shook their heads. Up flew Mother Crow and tried again. Still they refused. Then Mrs Blackbird came and sat beside the three of them and watched. Crows and blackbirds do not normally get on. Blackbirds keep out of crows' way if they can. But Mrs Blackbird seemed to have forgotten caution.

Three more times Mother Crow gave her tutorial. 'This is the wall. This is the ground. Now fly from one to the other.' It was so simple for her. Three times more the babies looked at her and then at each other and shook their heads. Mother Crow, fed up, took off to a tall ash tree and sulked.

Mother Blackbird took on her job. She fluttered down from the wall to the garden. The babies looked on curiously. Two more times she did it and then one of the baby crows launched into space and joined her on the ground. The other one followed. Mrs Blackbird flew back up. The babies fluttered up after her. Mother Blackbird took a short flight, the baby crows followed. All returned to their wall and sat there, preening and proud. She'd taught, they'd learned, all had done as nature required.

Mother Crow flew back from her high ash branch. They were her children, after all. Mrs Blackbird prudently flew off. Mr Blackbird set up a terrible squawking.

And Sylvia, Sylvia went to the phone and called social services and said she'd look after Darren until other arrangements could be made, knowing full well that as long as she was on tap they'd probably not get round to 'other'. Darren would be with her for good. But a child is a child, and needs to be taught, and teaching the young is in the blood (unless you're the Croxtons), and anyone can do it. Crow, blackbird, human, so what? Hugh wouldn't think much of it, he'd squawk away, but he wasn't really much to do with Sylvia any more, and she'd have a new household.

Moral

If a blackbird can do it in the face of a
crow, so can you.

Something Here Inside

It's the reason most people go to therapists – something inside that torments them, a prisoner waiting be unlocked. You don't quite know where she is, you don't know quite what she's done, but she's there. *'Please, please, please,'* she's crying, *'let me out.'*

Desperate to help, you look for answers. You wonder, *'Is it my inner rage, my lack of self-assertiveness, something terrible that happened in my childhood? My father or my mother, current spouse, passing partner?'*

A therapist can steer you off in one direction or another and stop you washing your hands ten times in ten minutes, or losing all your friends by your cruel frankness (*'It's the truth, so you need to know it'*). But the feeling of something even less specific and more distressing that there is something terribly wrong can remain. You feel you have to get out of this relationship or die. The prisoner within is making too much racket. Not even the therapist can deafen you to her cries.

That's when a woman absconds from a perfectly good relationship, or throws out perfectly reasonable lovers and tries others. She's desperate. No-one understands but she'll have to put up with that.

Personally, I never had much difficulty in releasing the inner me, inasmuch as I cried copiously through my adolescence and early marriages without even the benefit of a therapist. I released all over the place and messed up my life, and that of others, self-esteem rock bottom, falling into the wrong beds, all that.

My problem was getting the prisoner back *inside*, locking her up, and I finally did it with the help of a stern and rigorous Freudian psychoanalyst. It only then became apparent that I'd got the wrong prisoner. There were two of them. The destructive one was in there, properly locked up, and just as well, at least for the time being, but actually there was someone in the next cell down, someone wholly innocent, not allowing me to live in peace.

My poor wretched bleeding soul was still waiting to be released, desperate for a little attention before she shrivelled up altogether. She didn't want to leave, she just wanted the door unlocked so she could wander round.

The very act of acknowledgement allowed the poor trapped thing out of there.

There are three parts of you. There is the body and its instincts (nature), there is the brain and its machinations (nurture) and there is the soul (God given).

Many, nervous of such a definition because it sounds so soppy and they are of a scientific bent, and where would you physically locate this thing anyway, link brain and soul together and refer to that as a third thing called 'mind'. That seems to me to be a cowardly approach.

Philosophers of the 'mind' do get as far as referring to the 'doxastic' state of the mind – that is, the awareness of 'belief' – and to 'non-doxastic' states – the awareness of information or emotion being processed – and separate out the two, and that's fine. Then what I had wrongly shut up inside was a doxastic state. It still needed to be released in order to make sense of the whole. *'Come on out, Doxastic! Welcome.'*

The marvel is that we are here on this Earth at all. Take a moment to think about it. A sense of wonder at our very existence, at the complexity and interaction of mind, body and soul is in itself healing. I know it's difficult. Depression can make you blind to the overall scheme of things, deaf to the music of the spheres. But small ridiculous things can open your eyes and ears. Pictures from Hubble, an aria by Mozart caught on the radio as you switch from one station to another, a landscape as you fight the traffic on the motorway – clues are given and are God sent. Personally, I go to church and sing old hymns. That does it.

The voice of the prisoner inside stops clamouring. She's okay. You are happy in yourself. You are no longer self-obsessed, trapped in your anxious, guilty, instinct-ridden body, looking for solace in transitory sensual solutions. You are a whole.

And that is why I say, *'Be good and you'll be happy. Be happy and you'll be good.'* These are the words that set the prisoner free.

Notes on the Soul

When I was a small child in New Zealand and going to a convent school, there was nothing but. Souls had to be kept pure and untarnished, and were always in danger from the devil, who tried to steal them. But they could be sold to him in an emergency. The body was the temple of the soul, which was why you had to keep it clean and in order and not mess about with it, in honour of what was inside you. (Which is why today I have a dislike of face painting on children, body piercing and so on, yet don't object to cosmetic surgery, that being building work on the temple, and decorative.)

I had the idea that our souls hovered over our heads like the proud milky little cloud in Pooh Bear, tethered by a golden cord and rather talkative. I asked the nuns and they said no, souls were inside us, and silent, and I asked where, and they pointed variously to the heart or just above the bridge of the nose.

I thought then perhaps souls were like the white inner sole of a slipper – they would have to be very thin and flexible to fit in. But I was told, no, every soul was different and none of this really mattered, the important thing was to treasure your soul and keep it from harm, or else you went to hell – or if you were me, and unchristened – to a place called Limbo. And if I didn't stop asking questions, such was the implication, I'd be there quicker than I imagined.

But I believed the nuns and I still do. The soul is the essential part of us, the inner recognizable core which stays the same while the body which ties us down changes. We blossom and flourish, like leaves on the tree, and wither and perish, but our souls go marching on, at least if we have in our lives allowed ourselves enough exhilaration, enough elation, enough wonder at the marvel of creation to keep ourselves spiritually sustained and the four horsemen at bay.

Twayne's English Authors Series

Sylvia E. Bowman, *Editor*

INDIANA UNIVERSITY

Sean O'Faolain

 70

Sean O'Faolain

By PAUL A. DOYLE

Nassau Community College,
State University of New York

Twayne Publishers, Inc.   ::   New York

70-2659

Preface

Although Sean O'Faolain is one of the most artistic and gifted writers Ireland has ever produced and is now the dean of Irish letters, his writing is not so well known in the United States as it deserves to be. In order to help remedy this neglect, this book presents a survey of his career, focusing on and examining his most important literary efforts—his short stories, his novels, and his work as essayist and editor in which he has probed the whole Irish historical, social, and cultural scene. Biographical details are added whenever they are particularly useful in understanding O'Faolain's development and viewpoints as a writer and man of letters. His critical and literary views are also incorporated.

This study does not consider the minor phases of his career, such as his work as biographer, translator, and author of travel books. His writing in these areas has little significance in comparison to that of his fiction and his polemical efforts in which he has been "for almost thirty years the keeper of [Ireland's] intellectual conscience." [1]

Several acknowledgments must be mentioned. I am deeply grateful to Sean O'Faolain who kindly answered my queries and allowed me to quote from his contributions to *The Bell*. I am especially indebted to Professor John V. Kelleher of Harvard who supplied biographical information and generously shared with me his valuable bibliography of O'Faolain's early writing. For some difficult-to-track-down biographical facts about O'Faolain, I am obliged to Daniel O'Keeffe and Tadhg Ó Ciardha of University College, Cork. I owe a considerable debt to the resources of the central reference collection of the New York Public Library, the Brooklyn Public Library at Grand Army Plaza, Princeton University Library, as well as to that part of the Reid Collection which deals with Irish history and literature and which was acquired by the library of Nassau Community College.

I also wish to thank two colleagues at Nassau Community College—Professors John J. Cadden and Michael J. Culhane, whose awareness of Erin's history and literature has been bolstered by first-hand acquaintance with Ireland. I further express gratitude to Matthew F. Keating, whose aid included research in the British Museum, and to Professor James J. Blake, Dr. Thomas L. Cahalan, Emanuel Finkel, Mrs. Edith Forbes, and Alan Walbank. Research for this book was begun before the acutely demoralizing and spirit-desolating death of my wife, Ann Keating Doyle. She shared with me an interest in O'Faolain's literary career and rendered assistance and encouragement before her sudden death. My gratitude to her for her help, her intense rareness of spirit, and for being *simpatico* is immeasurable.

P. A. DOYLE

Nassau Community College,
State University of New York,
Garden City, Long Island

Acknowledgments

I wish to express my gratitude to the following for permission to quote from copyrighted material:

To the *Atlantic Monthly* and to John V. Kelleher for permission to quote from Professor Kelleher's "Sean O'Faolain" (May, 1957), "Copyright © 1957, by the *Atlantic Monthly* Company, Boston, Mass."

To the *Commonweal* for permission to quote from O'Faolain's "Being an Irish Writer" (July 10, 1953).

To the Devin-Adair Company, New York, for permission to quote from O'Faolain's *The Irish: A Character Study*, published and copyrighted 1949; *A Summer in Italy*, published and copyrighted 1950; and *The Short Story*, published and copyrighted 1951.

To Atlantic–Little, Brown and Company for permission to quote from *I Remember! I Remember!* "Copyright © 1959, 1961 by Sean O'Faolain," and from *Vive Moi!* "Copyright © 1963, 1964 by Sean O'Faolain."

To The Macmillan Company for permission to quote lines from the poetry of William Butler Yeats: "Easter, 1916" (Reprinted with permission of The Macmillan Company from *Michael Robartes and the Dancer* by W. B. Yeats. Copyright 1924 by The Macmillan Company, Renewed 1952 by Bertha Georgie Yeats); "September, 1913" (Reprinted with permission of The Macmillan Company from *Responsibilities* by W. B. Yeats. Copyright 1916 by The Macmillan Company, Renewed 1944 by Bertha Georgie Yeats); "To Ireland in the Coming Times" (Reprinted with permission of The Macmillan Company from *The Collected Poems by W. B. Yeats*. Copyright 1906 by The Macmillan Company, Renewed 1934 by William Butler Yeats).

To the *New Republic* for permission to quote from "A Harvest of O'Faolain" (June 17, 1957), © 1957 Harrison-Blaine of New Jersey, Inc.

To *The New York Times* for permission to quote from "A Fine Novel Out of Ireland" (January 7, 1934), and "Talk with Mr. O'Faolain" (May 12, 1957).

To Oxford University Press for permission to quote from Donat O'Donnell's *Maria Cross* (1952).

To the *Saturday Review* for permission to quote from O'Faolain's "The Gamut of Irish Fiction" (August 1, 1936), and Horace Gregory for permission to quote from "Imaginative Tales" (May 25, 1957).

To the Viking Press, Inc., for permission to quote from O'Faolain's *Midsummer Night Madness* (1932), *A Nest of Simple Folk* (1934), *Bird Alone* (1936), *Come Back to Erin* (1940), and the *Portable James Joyce* (1947), ed. by Harry Levin.

To the *Virginia Quarterly Review* for permission to quote from O'Faolain's "Plea for a New Type of Novel" (April, 1934).

To H. W. Wilson Co. for permission to quote material from *Twentieth Century Authors* (1942), and the *Wilson Library Bulletin* (March, 1934).

To the *Yale Review* for permission to quote from O'Faolain's "The Emancipation of Irish Writers" (Spring, 1934), copyright Yale University Press.

Contents

Chronology

1900 Sean O'Faolain born John Francis Whelan in Cork, Ireland, on February 22; son of Denis Whelan and Bridget Murphy.

1918 Entered University College, Cork, a component of the National University of Ireland. In the same year he informally changed his name to its Gaelic form.

1918– Was a rank-and-filer in the Irish Volunteers and the Irish
1924 Republican Army. Served on the Republican side (the Irregulars) during the Irish Civil War. Acting "Censor" on the *Cork Examiner* for the Irregulars before they were driven out of Cork. Became a Publicity Director for the Irish Republican Army.

1921– Salesman for an Irish textbook firm.
1922

1922 Graduated from University College, Cork. Edited a political-literary journal *An Long* (The Ship) published in Cork; only three issues appeared, May–July, 1922.

1924 Received M.A. degree in Irish from University College, Cork.

1925– Taught school at Ennis, Ireland.
1926

1926 Returned to University College, Cork; received an M.A. degree in English and a Higher Diploma in Education.

1926– Commonwealth Fellow at Harvard; received M.A. degree.
1928

1928– John Harvard Fellow.
1929

1928 Married Eileen Gould in Boston on June 3.

1929 Lectured on Anglo-Irish literature at Boston College. Editor of *Lyrics and Satires from Tom Moore*.

1929– Lecturer in English, St. Mary's College, Middlesex, Eng-
1933 land.

1932   *Midsummer Night Madness and Other Stories*. Elected a member of the Irish Academy of Letters.

1933   *A Nest of Simple Folk. The Life Story of Eamon DeValera*. Contributed one chapter to *Consequences*, a complete story composed by nine different authors, Elizabeth Bowen, A. E. Coppard, John van Druten, *et al*.

1934   *Constance Markievicz; or The Average Revolutionary*.

1935   *There's a Birdie in the Cage*.

1936   *Bird Alone. The Born Genius*.

1937   Editor of the *Autobiography of Wolf Tone. A Purse of Coppers*. A play *She Had to Do Something* produced at the Abbey Theatre on December 27, 1937.

1938   *The Silver Branch* (translations of old Gaelic poems). *King of the Beggars: A Life of Daniel O'Connell. She Had to Do Something* published.

1939   *DeValera*.

1940   *An Irish Journey. Come Back to Erin*.

1940–   Editor of *The Bell*.
1946

1942   *The Great O'Neill: A Biography of Hugh O'Neill, Earl of Tyrone (1550–1616)*.

1943   *The Story of Ireland*.

1945   Editor of Samuel Lover's *Adventurers of Handy Andy*.

1947   *Teresa and Other Stories. The Irish: A Character Study*.

1948   *The Short Story. The Man Who Invented Sin and Other Stories*.

1949   *A Summer in Italy*.

1952   *Newman's Way*.

1953   *South to Sicily* (published in the United States under the title *An Autumn in Italy*). Lecturer at the Christian Gauss Seminars in Criticism at Princeton. Stirred wide controversy with his article "Love Among the Irish."

1956   *The Vanishing Hero*.

1957   *The Finest Stories of Sean O'Faolain*. Became a director of the Arts Council of Ireland.

1958   Visiting Lecturer in English literature at Northwestern University. Edited *Short Stories: A Study in Pleasure*.

1959–   Lecturer in Creative Writing at Princeton.
1961

1961   *I Remember! I Remember!*

1961– Phi Beta Kappa Lecturer at various American universities.
1962
1964 (Spring, 1964) Writer in Residence, Boston College. *Vive Moi!*
1965 (Spring, 1965) Writer in Residence, Boston College.
1966 (Spring, 1966) At Center for Advanced Study, Wesleyan University. *The Heat of the Sun: Stories and Tales.*

CHAPTER 1

In the Rebel Tradition

GIVEN John Whelan's home environment, nine out of ten native-born Irishmen would have become priests (as did one of his brothers) or civil service workers in England or Ireland (as did another brother). Reared in a narrow, puritanical and restricted milieu, Whelan's chances of breaking the mold appeared slight.[1]

His father, Denis Whelan, a constable in the Royal Irish Constabulary, was more English than the English. Denis, humble and scrupulously honest, loved the British Empire with a deep devotion. The officers in the constabulary were mostly members of the Anglican Church and were staunch supporters of Great Britain's imperialistic prestige and ambitions, and they had instilled this notion in Denis Whelan as well as in many other members of the force. So well did they succeed that, when the Irish rebellion occurred in 1916, the Irish Royal Constabulary overwhelmingly supported the British cause. Denis Whelan, infuriated to hear of the Easter Rising, condemned the rebels and boasted that the British troops would quickly annihilate such upstart rowdies.

John Whelan's mother, Bridget, was deeply pious, but her religious views were stultifying: "her religious melancholy withered everything it touched, like a sirocco,"[2] yet her ambition to have her sons educated and successful was fulfilled. Two of her children—in her terms—did achieve this success; but John's subsequent career was never understood or approved.

I *Formative Influences*

The attitudes of his parents tended to stifle his creative artistic impulses, but the first influence which enabled young John Whelan to break the pattern of repression was the Cork Opera House. The stage door of this theater, located on the same street as the Whelan home, was often open in the summertime; and then pirates, kings, soldiers, and other costumed performers moved about before a curious boy's eyes. Also observed were the castles, waterfalls, thrones, blue skies, and other stage props which were carried in and out of the stage door as plays came and left. On one occasion the youth observed Cinderella's carriage standing outside the theater, and he also saw local actors garbed as the Napoleonic army at the Battle of Waterloo come dashing out the stage door. These same "soldiers" then retired to the local pub. Young Whelan knew many of the local actors who played walk-on roles, and he was also acquainted with some of the stagehands who carried the exotic props in and out the rear door of the theater.

The wonderfully imaginative influence of the theater on the growing youth was further strengthened when his mother, in an effort to increase the family income, decided to take in traveling actors and actresses as lodgers. At his home, the young boy could talk to such as Long John Silver of *Treasure Island,* Mrs. Wiggs of Cabbage Patch fame, Simon Legree of *Uncle Tom's Cabin,* and even behold the ghost of Hamlet's father. As Whelan was to acknowledge later, these experiences and similar occurrences stirred his imagination, intrigued him with literature, and furnished the first awareness of a world to which he was ultimately to devote his artistry.

In January, 1915, when Whelan was fifteen years old, he went to the Opera House to see Lennox Robinson's *Patriots,* the first Abbey Theatre production he ever saw. On stage he observed the living room of a house in rural Ireland and recognized characters who could be his own relatives. The stage props—a flower pot, chenille tablecloth, padded furniture, pictures of the Pope and Robert Emmet—brought his own environment to his attention for the first time. With the hero of the play, a Fenian rebel who had been recently released from a British prison, John Whelan could make contact immediately. An uncle of John's had fled from the authorities after the Fenian Rebellion in 1867; John's father had often denounced the Fenians; and, of course, the lad had read about the Fenian movement. Now before his very eyes, he was witnessing life—not simply a dream world of fairies or a never-never land of pirates.

This new reality reached into the young man's imagination and began to shake the George Alfred Henty derring-do fantasies and his idealized notions of existence. While Lennox Robinson's play was an eye-opener for John Whelan, it did not at that time enable him to eliminate his romantic fantasies. His first literary production, a short story written for the *Cork Outlook* when he was sixteen years old, contained all the exaggerated romanticism which he had imbibed from his earlier contacts with the Cork Opera House. The narrative dealt with a British cavalry officer who was killed while courageously carrying an important message through enemy lines. As he now admits, the opening of his first story was borrowed from Henty and the conclusion was from R. M. Ballantyne.[3] Not until many years later did the reality of the Fenian rebel in Lennox Robinson's play actually appear in John Whelan's own style and manner as the protagonist of his first novel.

In addition to the theatrical release from a regimented existence, a second emancipation occurred regularly. John Whelan's mother and father were both born on farms, so each summer for approximately a month the Whelan children went to live with relatives in rural sections of Ireland. In Limerick, the Whelan boys stayed with their mother's sister; but, while in Kildare and County Dublin, they stayed with their father's sister. Away from the metropolis of Cork, John Whelan was now with the old ways, with tradition, with seeming permanence, and solidity. He could study the rural people and ponder local history. In the country he was free from parental pressure; he could daydream, enjoy nature, and come close to an awareness of it and its moods and compensations. Again his imagination and his recognition of reality were expanded, and countless scenes and people from these areas of Ireland later appeared in the author's short stories and novels.

Another influence that shaped John Whelan in his youth was a political one. Like his father, he was at first shocked by the Easter Rising against the British; but, as the resistance continued and the rebel leaders were captured and shot, John Whelan's feelings began to change. He decided that the British chauvinistic beliefs of his father and of G. A. Henty were not so sound as he had thought. Although a formal break did not come for some time, John Whelan's interests in political rebellion were quietly stirring, and they were connected with his absorption with the Gaelic language.

In high school he hero-worshiped a teacher named Padraig O'Domhnaill. O'Domhnaill, the one rebel on the faculty, was a member of the Irish Volunteers; and he spoke enthusiastically about western Ireland where the people spoke Gaelic as they went about their everyday duties of fishing and farming; and, all in all, O'Domhnaill gave the impression that this part of the west was the archetype of the Garden of Eden. O'Domhnaill wore an attractive pin in his lapel. When John Whelan questioned him as to its meaning, he learned that his teacher had the *An Fáinne* pin which meant that the wearer could speak Gaelic with any one else wearing the insignia. John Whelan's interest in learning Gaelic was aroused, and with O'Domhnaill's assistance Whelan won the right to wear the coveted pin.

By now, Gaelic was becoming associated with the rebel cause. In the summer of 1918 John attended a special summer school session for the study of Gaelic. Every student and teacher in this program was enthusiastic about learning the native language to perfection, and many enthusiasts changed their names to the original Gaelic forms; thus, John Whelan became Sean O'Faolain.[4]

O'Faolain won an entrance scholarship to University College, Cork, one of the divisions of the National University of Ireland; and in September, 1918, he began his college career. While he was attending University College, O'Faolain joined a group of Irish Volunteers, recruited from the school. O'Faolain vividly recalls his first military drill in a remote glen outside of Cork while some members of the group maintained sentinel duty so that the police or the military forces would not discover the secret training. On this occasion one of the college teachers addressed the group about the revolutionary struggle for liberty, and a feeling of purpose, devotion, and loyalty both for one another and for Ireland's cause swept through the ranks. Idealism, intense conviction, and camaraderie inspired these youths, and O'Faolain's exaltation dominated his life for several years.

As O'Faolain quite readily points out, he was not the gunman type; but he and the other rank-and-filers performed various duties. They did reconnaissance duty, delivered dispatches, cut down trees and dug trenches to block roads, served as honor guards at the public funerals of well-known patriots, and continued to train and drill. Even though these activities were minor, the rebel rank-and-filers were happy to be contributing in some measure to the Irish struggle for independence from Britain. Above all, there was a heartfelt belief among this group of young men that they were willing to die for Ireland. As O'Faolain was later to record, he now wishes he could believe in anything at all with the same conviction he then felt.[5]

"The Troubles," as the war with England came to be called, came to an official end on December 6, 1921, when some Irish envoys in London signed a treaty which created what was to be called with considerable hyperbole the "Irish Free State." This treaty provided dominion status for Ireland, required an oath of allegiance to the English monarch, and cut off the northern part of the country from the twenty-six southern counties.

In June, 1922, Civil War broke out between the supporters of the newly created government of the Irish Free State and the Irish Republican Army forces, who wanted a republic independent of British ties and based on a conception proclaimed during the 1916 Easter Rebellion. These Irish Republican Army units were called "Republicans" or "Irregulars," and O'Faolain chose this side. When O'Faolain presented himself for service at the Republican headquarters in Cork, he was assigned to the duty of bombmaker. As the Irregulars were constantly beaten in battle and forced to withdraw, the bomb factory had to be moved several times; eventually, it was located in a previously deserted cottage near Ballyvourney.

After the execution of one of the Republican leaders, the famous Erskine Childers, O'Faolain was ordered by the Irish Republican Army to leave the bomb shop, and he succeeded Childers as director of publicity for the First Southern Division. O'Faolain wrote an underground paper in Cork, and in time he was ordered to Dublin where he became acting director of publicity for the Republicans, and there for eight months he continued to write propaganda for the rebel cause. The Free State government, however, achieved victory; and in January, 1924, O'Faolain's Irish Republican Army duties ended. He left Dublin to return to Cork in order to re-enter University College. While there, he published his first really original short story, "Lilliput," in the February, 1926, issue of George W. Russell's *Irish Statesman*.[6]

At about the same time O'Faolain applied for a Commonwealth Fund grant; and, after obtaining recommendations from George Russell ("AE") and Lennox Robinson, O'Faolain went to London for his interview. Shortly thereafter he received a two-year scholarship to any approved American university. O'Faolain chose

Harvard. In September, 1926, O'Faolain left for the United States and soon settled into Harvard's linguistic and philological regimen. He studied assiduously, obtained "A"'s in his courses, and eventually received a master's degree in comparative philology.

But O'Faolain discovered that he really did not have the retentive memory necessary for specialization in philology. This fact, plus home thoughts of Ireland, love for his sweetheart, Eileen Gould, and a widening circle of social acquaintances, persuaded the artist in embryo that the scholarly life was not suitable to his temperament. Consequently, he resumed creative writing and revised "Fugue," which was to become one of his most effective short stories. "Fugue" was at first written in Gaelic; however, since O'Faolain's parents spoke only English, O'Faolain felt he did not have a natural and inherent knowledge of the old Irish language, and, therefore, he decided to write in English.[7] An additional factor involved in this decision was O'Faolain's realization that there were no Gaelic literary critics who could have helped a young writer with standards and analysis. In addition to reworking "Fugue," he began to formulate ideas for what was to become his first novel (not completed and published until 1933). He asked Eileen Gould to leave Ireland and join him in America; when she did so, they were married in Boston on June 3, 1928.

While his wife taught school, O'Faolain continued both his studies and his creative work, edited a collection of the poems of Tom Moore, and began to translate old Irish verses which he in time gathered in an anthology. When "Fugue" was published in *Hound and Horn,* O'Faolain sent a copy of the magazine to the English critic Edward Garnett, who approved the story enthusiastically and requested further creative work. O'Faolain and his wife had already decided to return to Ireland, for the lure of the old country was persistent and enticing. O'Faolain realized that his vocation was to be that of a writer and his topic was to be Ireland. His fascination with his homeland had increased and become obsessive during his three years in the United States. His years in this country helped alleviate some of the intense disillusionment which he had felt over the Irish Civil War. The chaos of the Republican cause as the war progressed and the reality of brother fighting against brother had been a shattering experience. O'Faolain's years of study at Harvard, therefore, gave him an opportunity to settle on a vocation as well as time to think out problems about Ireland and let the bitterness heal.

Rather than return to the uninspiring routine of secondary school teaching in Ireland, O'Faolain and his wife decided to seek temporary positions in England which would give more time for writing. They would also be closer to the thriving London literary scene and have more direct contact with Edward Garnett. The young author obtained a job at a teacher's training college while his wife was also able to find a teaching position at a nearby school. He contacted Edward Garnett who encouraged him and served as critical guide. O'Faolain recalls that in writing his early stories he would rewrite each sentence about twelve times before he was satisfied with the style and the arrangement of the thoughts. Finally in 1932 the firm of Jonathan Cape published his first collection of short stories, stories begun in the 1920's, some of which were started while O'Faolain was in America. This volume was called *Midsummer Night Madness and Other Stories*.

II Ireland—"Broken and Bleeding"

Prefaced by an enthusiastic introduction by Edward Garnett, O'Faolain's first book of short stories was well received by the critics. Pundits such as J. B. Priestley were enthusiastic about the book,[8] and one American critic insisted that this was the best volume of Irish short stories since Joyce's *Dubliners*.[9] *Midsummer Night Madness* is indeed a most exciting compilation; yet, at the same time, it is the kind of book that O'Faolain was never again willing to write.

All seven stories which comprise the volume are set in the time of the Troubles and treat both the rebels' struggle against the British and the Civil War turmoil between the Republicans and the Free State forces. Certainly no group of twentieth-century short stories is more saturated with the aura of a particular time and place. William York Tindall's comment is that "Nowhere has the spirit of place been caught more happily than in this excellent book".[10] The stories are pervaded by a Conradian attention to atmosphere, and Conrad's famous dictum about making the reader hear, feel, but, above all, "to make you *see*" is carried out in an obsessive manner. We can especially feel O'Faolain himself in these stories: things he has participated in, experienced, or heard.

The title story immediately plunges us into Ireland during the Black and Tan period. The narrator, called only by the name of John, is a young revolutionist who travels from Cork city to visit the area of Farrane and Kilcrea to see why the rebel unit there had been inactive for several months. John was assigned to interview Stevey Long, the local commandant; and the contact with Long was supposed to be made at Henn Hall. This large country home was owned and dominated by Alexander Henn, a wealthy Englishman who had never married but who always had fashionable women about his large estate.

With the passing of time Henn Hall has fallen into decay, and Henn himself is unkempt and drinks heavily. So complete is Henn's decline that the only women who would now condescend to stay with him were girls from impoverished families of tinkers. At present Gypsy Gammle, a rough, aggressive, and voluptuous young tinker woman, is keeping house for Henn. Henn's condition is underscored when he is forced to allow Stevey Long to use his house at Gypsy's insistence.

Henn belongs to his adopted country, and yet he does not belong. The local farmers and townsfolk are suspicious and hostile, and now that he has allowed himself to deteriorate and his estate to decay, the nearby English gentry also dislike him and avoid his company. Henn's position is an example of the situation of many Anglo-Irish gentlemen who can never be completely assimilated in Ireland because the ordinary people are antagonistic to their power and wealth. At the same time such individuals are, as O'Faolain explains in one of his biographies, never completely accepted by the English who live on the home island.[11] The Anglo-Irish have connections in both England and Ireland, but they are not really perfectly at ease among either the English or the Irish.

Stevey Long and a group of his rebel followers march to Henn's domain and threaten to burn down Henn Hall unless Henn agrees to marry the pregnant Gypsy. Stevey claims that Henn is the father of Gypsy's soon-to-be-born child, but John surmises that Long is the real father and that this is his way of avoiding responsibilty for his conduct. Under threat of burning the house, Henn agrees to marry Gypsy. He has pity and some genuine affection for her, and she is all he now has and can hope to have. Gypsy is really in love with Long but realizes he is not the marrying type, that he would never be more than a roving lover. She marries

Henn because she wants a father for her child, and she accepts the fact that no one else would marry her in her present condition. The story ends on a note of de Maupassant incongruity where Henn and Gypsy marry and go to live in Paris. The contrast of the old, withered and weary English gentleman and his young over-dressed, gauche tinker wife moving about the fashionable boulevards of Paris is grotesque and incredibly ironic.

The themes of "Midsummer Night Madness" are many: the disorganization and irresponsibility of the Irish Republican Army; its often foolish and immature leadership; the terror foisted on the country by the Black and Tans; the extreme poverty of the ordinary people contrasted with the elegance of the aristocratic country homes, many of which, however, have now fallen into decay; and the general chaos and confusion of a time of dissension, warfare, and rebellion.

Contrast between the present and the past is repeatedly emphasized. Years before, Henn's power and prestige was a byword in the area. He was feared and avoided whenever possible by the local residents; now he is in such a pitiable plight that the likes of Stevey Long can frequent his estate, and Long and his men can force Henn into a marriage he does not really want. An effective scene of Henn's singing drunkenly to a record of *Don Giovanni* while at the same time kicking his chamber pot underscores past grandeur with present decay, and the highest aspirations of the spirit mixing with the most basic of bodily functions. Fifty years before, the handsome and well-groomed Henn had entertained sophisticated women in grandeur and elegance as his butler hovered about; now Henn entertains the two faded Blake women and their father (they have just been burnt out of their home) amid soiled and tarnished surroundings while the pregnant Gypsy hovers about.

It is especially noticeable that in handling his artistic materials O'Faolain does not choose sides. The faults, weaknesses, and blunders of all are recorded. At one time John sees Alexander Henn as one of the Anglo-Irish aristocracy who had crushed the poor while enjoying the fruits of the good life. Yet later, Henn is allowed to expound his own point of view: how he had offered loans to the neighboring farmers; how he had suggested improved farming methods and more up-to-date selling of eggs and produce. But the people did not cooperate; and, as a result, no improvements were

accomplished. Henn hates the local peasants for their backwardness and inertia. He wanted a prosperous country; and he blames
the natives for not achieving his goal. They, in turn, wanted a
prosperous country; and they blame the colonizers. For the first
time John realized that the hatred was mutual and intense on both
sides. Each group held the other responsible, and each worked
against the common good of the country; consequently, the country was torn apart, and only decline, decay, and irresponsibility
remained.

Overall, the story is effective and arresting, yet defects are present. The ending is too manipulated, too consciously clever and O.
Henry-like to be credible. It intrudes an artficial and literary exercise note in the narrative which weakens the effect of verisimilitude so pervasive in the previous parts of the tale. The story's
ending is a blunder that only a writer seeking a too calculated and
ingenious ending would be guilty of.

Further, in parts of the story there are materials which seem
unduly incongruous. Henn, for example, rationalizes his marriage
to Gypsy by remarking that her child, if it is a boy, will at least
keep the family name alive. At this point, O'Faolain inserts an
authorial comment to the effect that one would think Henn was a
Hapsburg or a Bourbon. This remark—while conveying the notion that Henn, no matter how degraded, has not lost some sense
of family obligation and pride—is in manner of presentation too
high-flown and artfical. The comment is not out of place; the
way it is self-consciously inserted is. In his early stories O'Faolain
is not always able to blend various kinds of material together;
consequently, some of his material does not seem to flow logically
and appropriately out of the story but appears to be an after-
thought and a later insertion.

The story "Fugue" depicts two rebels on the run from the relentless pursuit of the Black and Tans. The two refugees, Rory
and an unnamed narrator, flee among the hills and valleys of the
countryside. They are sheltered by sympathetic farm families, and
the narrator meets at one home a young woman who is obviously
attracted to him. The two soldiers, however, must constantly
move on as lorries filled with Black and Tans and scouting patrols
press about the area. Eventually, Rory and the narrator are forced
to stay at separate billets. At his shelter the narrator again meets
the farm girl he had seen earlier. When he is alone with her for a

time, they embrace each other and engage in romantic endearments. But a fearful knock on the door interrupts their idyllic respite, and a little child appears and announces in terror that Rory has been killed and that the Black and Tans are now coming for the other rebel soldier. The narrator dashes into the night and continues his flight. Hopes of love are shattered; little rest or solace can be found in these troubled times; but the fugitive passes onward, still enjoying the beauty of nature and hopeful of love and a better life.

A reading of O'Faolain's autobiography demonstrates that some elements in this story actually occurred to him while he was on the run.[12] O'Faolain also explains his choice of title by remarking that he was much influenced by the fugue musical form while writing this particular story and he notes that the motifs recur and interact,[13] that the piece moves *da capo*.[14]

While constant danger and continual flight are stressed, the two principal recurring movements are the beauty and solace of nature and the comfort of love personified by the young woman who first meets Rory and the narrator at a farmhouse door. Even when he does not see the girl in person, her image haunts the narrator as he tramps on through the mountainous terrain. As he repeatedly daydreams about her, he even imagines her being married in a year or two and thinks of her and her husband on their wedding night as they retire to bed. Later, when he wonders where he will sleep on a particular night during his flight, he chooses a peasant's marriage bed. When he again meets her in another house twelve miles from their original scene of meeting (this is the only improbable note in the story), he fondles her, and she returns his affection. But love in such troubled times must be more of a dream than a reality, and the startling knock at the door and the cry of warning (handled with wonderful narrative virtuosity) sends the unfulfilled lover racing out into the rainy night; but he again carries the girl with him in his dreams as he thinks of her in her warm bed while he wanders on through the drenching rain.

The image of the girl, which occurs early in the story, and is reiterated frequently to the very end and is complimented with scenes of natural beauty in the region around Inchigeela. The story commences with the arrival of dawn (the night before the unnamed girl had been met). Nature in its various forms is constantly impressed on the two weary guerrillas. Even in flight there is the solace of a rippling stream, the beauty of birch and rowan trees, the comfort offered by the sight of some farmers in nearby fields trying to finish their threshing before the onset of rain. The rain, when it comes, brings security, protection, and cleansing; and finally the dawn is again observed moving along the mountaintops bringing another day of continued danger and flight, yet offering the two compensations which the narrator has found meaningful. The tonal control displayed in "Fugue" is expertly handled. The story's emphasis on present trouble counterbalanced with the beauty of the countryside and the eternal verity of love, operating even under the most trying circumstances, beautifully epitomizes one aspect of these disturbing years in Ireland.

Another superior story is "The Bombshop." This narrative involves three Irish Republican Army members, Leo, Sean, and Caesar, who make bombs for the revolutionary cause in a building in Cork city. An elderly woman who keeps a clothes shop on the first floor and lives on the second allows the rebels to use the third floor. Since the bombmakers are not allowed to leave their workshop for fear of discovery and arrest, they are frequently edgy and restless in their cramped quarters. Eventually, their pent-up frustration and the monotony and confinement which they endure break out into a violent quarrel. Sean draws his revolver; and, as he scuffles with Caesar, two shots are discharged before the men realize their foolishness. Except for the two bullet holes in the floor, no damage appears to be done, and the group settles down into more reasonable attitudes. But Norah, their courier, discovers that the two bullets have penetrated through the floor and have killed kind Mother Dale as she sat in her armchair in the room below. After the death of Mother Dale, the group finds it difficult to concentrate on bombmaking. Leo is very young, and his aims and ideas are unsettled. At one moment he is extolling the rebel cause and insisting that freedom is essentially beauty, and he proclaims the "God of Freedom. He freed men because He knew that in Freedom all beauty has its source." [15] Yet in his state of emotional turmoil Leo can later turn and denounce Ireland.

Leo and Norah go separately to a religious service in a nearby church. A funeral service is in progress with the body of the deceased resting in state in a coffin. When the two revolutonaries leave the church and return stealthily to the workshop, Leo becomes extremely panicky when someone knocks on the street door. He decides to pack up some of the bombmaking materials and flee. Norah accuses him of cowardice and tries to calm Leo's distress. But she herself later believes that she sees the ghost of Mother Dale, who still sits in her chair on the second floor staring at the fire "fixedly into its flames—her eyes big with Death." [16]

The narrative concludes with this quotation and appropriately so. Death becomes the pervasive symbol. Mother Dale is a symbol for Ireland, a place of death. There is the physical death of May Dale, the spiritual death of the quarreling and nerve-shattered revolutionaries, death at the church service (death and religion now especially allied in Eire), death in the streets of Cork, death being prepared in the house itself—not only affecting others through the bombmaking for war use but even causing death inside the house. Death triumphs. The eerie, sinister, and ominous atmosphere of death sits and broods over the house and its inhabitants, just as it pervades the country itself and the population. The prevailing mood and characteristics of the Troubles—death, decadence, disillusion, disorganization, terror, and flight furnish the leitmotifs for this story; but it is death in all shapes and forms which hangs over Ireland, victimizing the innocent as well as the guilty, the young and the old. The hollow eyes of death peer at and dominate the country.

The story of "The Patriot" centers on two characters: Bernie, a member of the Irregulars during the Irish Civil War, and a former teacher of his, Edward Bradley, who is a fiery political orator. In seven months of guerrilla life Bernie travels from place to place, constantly on the move, and finally comes to a small hotel in the mountains. This hostel is the headquarters of his rebel division. Bernie is depressed with the constant flight, the poverty, the hunger, and the terror under which the guerrillas labor. He hopes to see Bradley again so that he may be reinspired about what seems to be more and more a hopeless cause.

At the hotel a picture of complete chaos presents itself. This portrait is a historically accurate one of the dissolution of the Irregulars in the last days of the war against the Free State forces. Now little or no discipline exists among the Irregular troops; the men are ill-clothed and ill-fed; and they are weary and disillusioned. This was a period of frightful disillusion for O'Faolain and for most of those who were fighting on the left side in the Irish Civil War. O'Faolain has remarked that he has drawn this time faithfully in "The Patriot," and in one of his prose statements he has noted the characterstics of the period:"men unwilling to fight and without the character to throw in their guns, much cruelty and brutality, politicians maneuvering for position while young boys and young men were being executed or murdered for murdering one another by the score." [17]

Edward Bradley appears at the rebel hostel, although he is a political figure and not an army man. Bradley delivers an impassioned speech urging the men to continue fighting for the cause; but, speaking privately to Bernie, Bradley admits the sad state of the Republican cause. Not having the wherewithal or the proper leadership to mount a potential attack, the rebels can only hit and run whenever Free State troops come near. A short time later Bernie and two of his buddies are taken prisoner and jailed. Bernie spends a year in prison before he is released.

Peace has now been established. The Irregulars have been defeated, and political amnesty has been granted to the Republicans. Bernie is now married and can look back at previous years. He and his wife see a notice that Edward Bradley is still the patriot; he is still campaigning. They attend a Sinn Fein Abu meeting which he addresses. Bradley, the orator, although now more elderly, still uses his impassioned delivery; but the young husband and wife are no longer interested. They had been disillusioned by the handling and failure of the cause. Now they turn to their love and the enjoyment of life.

Later that night they see Bradley from their hotel room window. He is driving out of the town, still working for the goal—relentless and implacable, giving his whole life and devotion to the "God of Freedom," just as the young couple now give themselves to the God of Love. No choice between the obsession with freedom and the obsession with love is made, although love seems to be more satisfying anl rewarding. But the old patriot cannot be gainsaid. Everyone must choose his way: Bradley and Bernie pursue separate roads, each fulfilling the dominant demands of his particular nature.

Critic John Kelleher cites this story as an outstanding example of O'Faolain's objectivity and compassion.[18] From his prose works it can be concluded that O'Faolain dislikes and distrusts a man like Bradley, the abstract idealist, who in his fanaticism and unconcern for common humanity is willing to sacrifice men's lives in a hopeless cause and to bring about more tragedy. Yet so understanding is O'Faolain's usual approach in writing fiction that the reader can sympathize with Bradley even while noticing his weaknesses and shortcomings.

The shortest selection in O'Faolain's first book is "Lilliput." This primarily descriptive episode is hardly more than a cameo, but is an extremely vivid sketch. The scene is Cork city during the Black and Tan days. Lorries containing the Tans prowl after the ten o'clock curfew while a grimy and slovenly tinker woman lives in her wagon which is disabled in one of the Cork streets. Her three small daughters are with her, her husband is in jail, and the donkey which pulled the wagon has been killed. The people in the neighborhood become frantic because they are afraid she and her disabled wagon will attract the attention of the Tans to their quiet street. After the first night passes, the people, amazed that she has survived without being disturbed, can only reflect that "the devil takes care of her own." Policemen come and order her to remove the cart, and later a British patrol discovers the situation, but no one makes any serious effort to harm her or to move her wagon out of the street.

The story "Lilliput" suggests more than a revelation of the bizarreness of the times and the stoic endurance and resilience of the very poor. O'Faolain tells us that this sketch is based on an actual occurrence that he witnessed.[19] While the city people of Cork were terrified of the ravages of the Black and Tans, O'Faolain was impressed that a rural wanderer without fear could defy in her small way the forces of power and violence. O'Faolain regarded this episode as having mythic implications, and, hence, he chose the story's title with this in mind.

He conceived of the tinker woman as a female Gulliver—a Gulliver among the frightened pygmy-like city dwellers. She symbolized the west of Ireland where the people were more natural and free, an image to impress more ordinary creatures. She receives the respect of the soldiers, a gift of food as a sort of ritual offering, and a surprised reaction from a priest who does not understand this quasi-pagan. She is the primitive surviving in a more regimented, constricted, and unnatural society.

Two other stories in O'Faolain's first collection of fiction—"The Small Lady" and "The Death of Stevey Long"—are not so artistically handled as the narratives just considered. These two stories

are much more melodramatic, contrived, and self-conscious. They
do not naturally flow out of historical events; they seem artificially
invented and imposed on the time, rather than being an integral
part of the period and setting.

Mrs. Sydney Browne, the title figure in "The Small Lady," is
one of the well-to-do English women living in Ireland. She informs on six young Irish rebels who are caught by the British
authorities, brought to trial, found guilty of treasonable activity,
and summarily executed. In reprisal she is kidnaped and taken to
the Trappist monastery at Mount Melleray, where she spends the
night on account of the guestmaster's connivance with the Irish
Republican Army group. Mrs. Browne is placed in a room in the
wing of the monastery reserved for visitors and guests. Only her
rebel captors; Brother John, the guestmaster; and a drunkard,
who is staying at the monastery in an attempt to rehabilitate himself, are aware of her presence. Mrs. Browne is guarded by Denis,
a young rebel from the city; and she is attracted to him. She is a
vibrant, pleasure-loving, passionate woman; and she and Denis
have sexual relations in her cell. Denis has great pangs of remorse.

The basic theme of the story is the motif of eternity and its
relationship to life and death. In each of the rooms of the monastery there is a sign stressing that life is transient and that improper
pleasures and lusts should be avoided because one risks an eternity of punishment for such deeds. The sign stresses the pains of
hellfire and cautions that, although a person is now alive, death is
ever imminent. But Mrs. Browne is not really disturbed by this
sign. She has had an enjoyable life, participating in all of the sensual pleasures of existence. This was the only life she ever knew;
she cannot conceive of eternity; she has only brief regret that her
life is apparently going to be terminated, but she resolves to continue to enjoy life to the very end.

Although she has met only one monk, the guestmaster, she is
conscious that the monastery and the monks themselves are pervaded by the notion of eternity. Yet she and the monks are on
different levels. Again O'Faolain's objectivity is striking: no judgment is made as to which attitude is correct. It is simply a matter
of different experiences, of different ways of looking at things. As
the wife of a British Army officer, Mrs. Browne supports English
rule in Ireland just as her captors represent the opposite viewpoint of rebellion.

In the context of Ireland itself, the looming role of eternity impinges on the pleasures of the present time. Just after Denis and Mrs. Browne have had sexual relations, the drunkard who has reread the sign about eternity runs wildly through the halls screaming about his own sins and his punishment for all eternity. When Denis's father learns that his son and Mrs. Browne had been intimate, he prays that his son may be preserved from death, that Christ may have mercy on Denis. He invokes the memory of Christ's bitter death. As a Catholic, he accepts the doctrine that Denis's act of adultery with Mrs. Browne is a mortal sin which, unless repented, means that the soul is dead eternally—damned forever. It is this concept of eternal death which so disturbs Denis himself after his interlude with Mrs. Browne.

Because of his background and religious conditioning, Denis cannot be at ease with life until he has confessed his sexual relationship with Mrs. Browne. By confessing and repenting Denis believes that he has avoided eternal death. Now, unencumbered by the fear of losing eternity, he can again bathe in the physical joy of present existence. Mrs. Browne, not accepting the notion of eternity, strips in her room and bathes naked at the window, reveling in both the beauty of the moon and all the other elements of night's grandeur. A pagan goddess moves among men who have deliberately restrained—or in some cases attempted to restrain—sensual appetites and pleasures by using a religious creed which puts greater emphasis on a spiritual life in the hereafter.

Despite O'Faolain's objectivity, a reader senses throughout this volume of stories that the author's sympathies are with the values of physical love, the beauty of nature, and the freer, more natural pleasures and aspects of life. Garden of Eden pleasures are contrasted with a less healthy, repressive, and death-dominated type of existence.

"The Death of Stevey Long" concerns the same Irish Republican Army revolutionary who appeared in the story "Midsummer Night Madness." Stevey has been captured by the British and is as treacherous and unprincipled as ever. Stevey becomes friendly with a disillusioned and homesick Black and Tan prison guard who assists Stevey to escape after the rebel promises to help the Tan get back to England. But, when he and the Tan manage to flee the prison safely, Stevey betrays his liberator, leads him to a rebel trap, and has one of the revolutionaries kill him.

Stevey travels to Cork city; and, since he has been out in the rural areas for some time, he is unaware that a curfew is in effect. In fleeing from a Tan patrol, he pushes into a doorway and accidentally stumbles into the abandoned bomb shop after Leo and Norah have left it. He spends the night there, discovers the dead Mother Dale but assumes she has died of natural causes. When he attempts to leave the shop, he is caught by a raiding patrol, accused of killing the dead woman, found guilty, and executed.

As is true of all the stories in O'Faolain's first collection, this last story is heavily ironic. If, for example, Stevey Long had not violated his pledge to the Black and Tan guard, he would not have gone into Cork city and, doubtless, would have avoided death. He is condemned for a crime he did not commit; yet he is given a patriot's funeral by members of the Sinn Fein liberation party since they knew him as a rebel. Thus one of the most unscrupulous, dishonorable, and thoroughly unprincipled members of the revolutionary group is buried with full honors. The most prosaic irony of all is the lament of Stevey's father. By trade Stevey was a plumber; a fine plumber, his old father maintains, and his true vocation has been ruined because of his participation in the rebel movement. A life that might be useful under normal conditions is wasted in a time of militaristic turmoil. The many ironies which arise out of less effective stories like "The Death of Stevey Long" are not so subtle and as well blended into the narrative as is the case with "The Bombshop" and other more accomplished narratives in this volume.

III *Romanticism*

In recent years O'Faolain tends to be somewhat apologetic for the stories in the *Midsummer Night Madness* collection.[20] He finds them overly romantic, and his present artistic credo eschews such romanticism. O'Faolain is now distressed by such purple passages as "Fallen hawthorn blossoms splashed with their lime the dust of the road, and so narrow were the boreens in places that the lilac and the dog-rose, hung with wisps of hay, reached down as if to be plucked, and under the overhanging trees I could smell the pungent smell of the laurel sweating in the damp night-air";[21] or again: "A light fog had crept up the valley of the Lee from the harbour mouth and the lamps on the bridges had gathered from it a rich and reddish hue, while their dagger-like reflections trembled but slightly in the cold and glassy river-water." [22]

O'Faolain now deplores the weighted and romantic words, the overuse of metaphor, and the repetition of "and's" and "but's." [23] He decries the ripe lushness and rococo lavishness found even in the description of city housetops "on whose purples and greens and blues the summer night was falling as gently as dust." [24] But he realizes that he cannot now rewrite these stories, and he admits that he still likes the best of them, despite their romantic excesses. [25] One can understand O'Faolain's negative comments about the *Midsummer Night Madness* stories and yet observe that they relate perfectly to their time and place. The period of "the Troubles" was a realistic period, but it was an era impregnated with youthful idealism, patriotic fervor, and, in the Wordsworthian phrase, "Bliss was it in that dawn to be alive/ But to be young was very Heaven!" The style of these early stories is redolent with much of this particular fervor and bliss. The writing is a vivid recording of the sights and sounds of Ireland under revolutionary passion.

Almost every critic who had commented on the *Midsummer Night Madness* volume has praised the beauty of the writing and lauded these stories for being so effectively "rich in atmosphere," to use a phrase by "AE." [26] This success with atmosphere reinforces the "we-are-there-with-the-people" feeling which is one of the strongest impressions received from the book. When Edward Garnett praised *Midsummer Night Madness* for its poetry, its accuracy of characterization, and its rendering of atmosphere, he noted that it also captured the poetic quality of the Irish spirit. [27] Robert Cantwell extolled the book's poetry, but he became too zealous in defending what he believed was the intrinsic appropriateness of O'Faolain's style and imagery. Cantwell erred in arguing that no episode or occurrence in these stories is present simply for its picturesqueness. [28]

Without denigrating the beauty of O'Faolain's prose and his success with atmosphere, one can agree with O'Faolain himself that he has—in these particular stories—too often romanticized his anger and disillusionment. [29] It is true that, when O'Faolain deals with actual combat scenes or with the effects of demoralization on the Irish Republican Army supporters, the writing becomes more stern and sparse as it catalogues different attitudes, reactions, and events; but, in general, a poetic Romanticism hangs too heavily over these stories. Once, in discussing Chekhov, O'Faolain spoke of "romantic atmosphere . . . a quality of *mind* that is always in Chekhov, controlling his emotions, so that he does not bathe in the thing, but contemns it all while he writes of it so sensitively." [30] This comment may be used in connection with O'Faolain's first book of short stories: Too often in the *Midsummer Night Madness* volume O'Faolain bathes in the romantic atmosphere and does not condemn it "while he writes of it so sensitively."

In thinking about his first collection in retrospect, O'Faolain, who tends to be an overly harsh judge of his own work, also censures himself for having put too many of his personal thoughts and sensations into the stories rather than thoughts which would more normally originate in the characters themselves. Again this self-criticism is only partially true. In several instances the accusation is valid; in other situations the author is obviously so much an integral part of the narrator or the other characters that the similarity of observation or viewpoint is apropos. O'Faolain is certainly John in "Midsummer Night Madness"; he is the unnamed narrator in "Fugue"; he is Leo in "The Bombshop"; he is Bernie in "The Patriot." And in these—the best stories—the verisimilitude and vividness of the material is established, enhanced, and reinforced by the author's similarity to his characters. In these stories there is almost no feeling of authorial-character dissociation which O'Faolain later came to observe. His point is very valid, however, for the less successful narratives; for example, in "The Small Lady," or in "The Death of Stevey Long," the weakness of authorial intrusion is pronounced. It is indeed true that most of these stories are characterized by too much expository analysis. Instead of letting basic ideas appear through dialogue and action, O'Faolain relates too baldly the feelings of Mrs. Browne and Denis, for example. Or again the reader is informed unnecessarily that Stevey Long is cruel, cunning, and fearless.

If romantic excesses and too much bald exposition are present in O'Faolain's first book, these weaknesses should not cause anyone to slight the collection's finer points. In addition to its success in conveying atmosphere and a decidedly laudable penetration in handling characters and ideas, the book demonstrates much organizational ability which enhances the overall effect. The stories, for example, are arranged so that the first narrative takes place early in "the Troubles" when the Irish Republican Army still has much local power and when the Black and Tans have not yet come to be a fearsome band. The later stories progress historically; they deal with the strife itself—first the struggle against England, then the Civil War. "The Patriot" ends the book and portrays the end of effective Republican resistance although some individual rebels continue to struggle for freedom.

O'Faolain also demonstrates considerable narrative ability. He handles the basic hunter and hunted, chase and flight formula with mastery. The tension of discovery and capture, with all of the sinister suspense associated with this kind of narrative material, is well maintained. This raw narrative proficiency can be seen in the use made of special artistic techniques within individual stories. For example, in "The Small Lady," he saves much time and a laborious introduction by presenting the necessary background material in the form of a ballad lamenting the death of six rebels who have been captured and shot because of Mrs. Browne's treachery. This ballad, effectively appropriate to time and place, not only serves as a clever narrative opening, but also sets the death and eternity motif of the whole story. In "The Death of Stevey Long" O'Faolain neatly uses the closed-door device so much favored by writers like Robert Louis Stevenson. Stevey's accidental opening of the door into Mother Dale's shop, so similar to Stevenson's use of the same device in "The Sire de Malétroit's Door," is handled with a narrative facility that makes something farfetched extremely credible.

When its strengths and weaknesses are listed, the balance supports the belief that *Midsummer Night Madness and Other Stories* was a notable beginning for a creative writing career. The rebel spirit and the stirring emotions of Gaelic nationalism which convinced John Francis Whelan to change his name to Sean O'Faolain, then to join the Irish Volunteers and the Irish Republican Army, and to fight on the idealistic but underdog Republican side in the Civil War, uniquely qualified him to produce an accurate and impressive account of the Irish Rebellion in which the sights and sounds of Ireland under duress and the attitudes and reactions of its people are convincingly displayed.

As he remarks in his autobiography, O'Faolain was early in his life a natural rebel.[31] Many years later, when O'Faolain was to have a play produced at the Abbey Theatre, the first performance aroused howls of protest from the audience.[32] Recalling the 1907 Abbey Theatre riots when John M. Synge's *Playboy of the Western World* was shown and the wild turmoil caused by Sean O'Casey's *The Plough and the Stars*, O'Faolain wryly remarked to an interviewer who asked about the reception his play received: "I'm very pleased to say, it was soundly booed. One likes to be in the tradition." [33] O'Faolain was definitely in the tradition, and *Midsummer Night Madness* was an early proof of this status, as well as of the fact that O'Faolain was particularly gifted to be a perceptive, sensitive chronicler of the Irish revolt.

CHAPTER 2

Novels About
"The Most Distressful Country"

TWENTIETH-CENTURY Irish literature has achieved emi-
nence in the areas of drama and the short story. But one of
the most noticeable aspects of contemporary Irish writing is the
lack of significant novels. Apart from Joyce's *Portrait of the Artist
as a Young Man* and *Ulysses,* relatively few novels of first rank
have appeared. Some of the novels of Liam O'Flaherty and Elizabeth Bowen are of considerable importance, but most of the other
work in this genre lacks distinction.

It has been argued that the lack of a clearly defined class structure with established patterns is primarily responsible for the
dearth of important Irish novels. Unifying elements in Ireland—
such as Catholicism and nationalism—which might have furnished established social patterns have been so narrow and repressive that they do not give an artist the necessary freedom to
write expansively about his material.[1] Frank O'Connor believes
that since the Revolution, Irish material is too uninspiring, provincial, and empty to provide the proper climate for novelists.[2]
O'Faolain, who also offers some explanations of why great Irish
novels are rare, maintains that since the revolutionary struggle has
ended, Ireland has lost its one great theme for a large and very
dramatic presentation. Contemporary Irish society tends to be
rigid, conservative, and unstimulating; and, while such a society
can offer suitable portraits for short stories, it does not offer the
variety or *dramatis personae* necessary for exceptional novels.[3]

After the *succès d'estimè* of his first collection of stories, O'Faolain and his wife, supported by a subsidy from his publisher, returned to take up residence in Ireland. O'Faolain devoted himself
wholly to the life of a man of letters, and within seven years produced three novels of the Irish scene: *A Nest of Simple Folk*
(1933), *Bird Alone* (1936), and *Come Back to Erin* (1940).[4]
With characteristic understatement and modesty, O'Faolain calls

these efforts merely "honourable." In actuality, *A Nest of Simple Folk*, despite some flaws, is one of the most sensitive and richest works of fiction to come out of Ireland in the last thirty-five years. The other two novels, while possessing defects and limitations, contain so much good writing, so much acute characterzation, and so much astute commentary on twentieth-century Ireland's political, social, and religious difficulties that they make rewarding reading and furnish valuable insights into the basic themes in the literature of modern Eire—rebellion, isolation, and exile.

I   *"O'Donnell Aboo"*

A Nest of Simple Folk, so named as a mark of homage to Turgenev and his novel *A Nest of Gentle Folk*, is a long *roman de fleuve* centering primarily on the life of Leo O'Donnell. The story begins in 1854 in a rural section of County Limerick and follows O'Donnell as he eventually moves to the small town of Rathkeale and thence to the city of Cork. (This movement is indicative of the ever-expanding shift in Ireland from the countryside to the towns and cities.) The novel concludes in 1916 at the crucial political climax of the Easter Rising.

Leo, the tenth and last child born to Long John O'Donnell, a hard-working and dictatorial farmer, and Judith Foxe, the daughter of Protestant gentry, was, after his father's death, reared by his maternal aunts at the ancestral estate of Foxehall. His aunts, with the approval of his mother, had his name legally changed so that he could possess gentry status. One "l" was dropped from his last name, and his mother's family name was affixed; thus Leo O'Donnell became Leo Foxe-Donnel.

For part of each year, Leo was sent to the city of Limerick in order to have the social and educational advantages of associating with the Wilcoxes, relatives on the Foxe side of the family. Yet when Leo first reached Limerick city in the company of his Uncle Nicholas, he was taken to his Uncle Frankie O'Donnell's combined store and tavern, where a meeting of the Tenants' League was in progress. Leo was enthusiastically received and was made to feel much more at home among this group than he was with his aunts. When he reached the home of his cousin Dr. Wilcox, Leo's clumsiness, unpolished rural ways, and lack of manners made a poor impression. As often as he could, Leo returned to Frankie O'Donnell's pub in the Irishtown section of the city.

Although Leo spent many days in Limerick city for several years, the drawing room aura of the Wilcoxes had little influence on his development. On the other hand, he was deeply impressed by two things: first, by the beauty of the countryside outside the city "that sighing land, wet above and wet underfoot" and, second, by "the damp and dusty and always rancid taprooms of Clare Street and Pennywell, their drovers and buyers and farmers that packed them as they packed his brain, men full of talk and argument" and always ready for a song about a landlord or an agent.[5]

After the death of his aunts and through the help of his mother, Leo managed to take full possession of Foxehall. But he became a loafer and a ne'er-do-well. He spent a good bit of his time drinking and dallying with girls, finally getting a servant girl pregnant. Leo and his mother had frequent disagreements about his failure to do anything useful. Yet the old woman was still attached to her youngest son; he and she would frequently walk arm in arm in the fields, and she defended her son thus: "And my son Leo is a gentleman, and he have the breeding of a gentleman, and he have the education of a gentleman. . . . He's a credit to me." [6]

But Leo required a purpose in life; he needed to be motivated in some direction; otherwise, his lackadaisical existence would continue. This motivation came in the form of a fiery speech by James Stephens, the Fenian leader, who not only spoke of injustice but was also bitterly anti-clerical. Leo's dislike for priests became crystallized, and Stephen's words equated with information, facts, and ideas Leo had heard for years in various taverns in Irishtown. Deeply stirred and emotionally influenced, Leo for the first time could give his life a central focus.

At Leo's invitation, James Stephens spent the night at Foxehall, and Stephens "set the heart and mind" of Leo Donnel, as he was now commonly called, "crackling like a fiery furze." Not so long after Stephens' visit, Leo and his uncle Nicholas led a group of Fenians against a police station at Ballingarry. The police were warned by an informer—Julie Keene, a cousin of Leo's who was later to become his wife—and both Nicholas and Leo were captured. Leo spent ten years in prison, and the long incarceration drained much of his pride and spirit. While he was in prison, his mother died, disapproving of Leo's Fenianism and of "the Cause," never understanding why Leo was involved in rebel activities. She never understood or accepted the fact that his love of the Irish countryside and his attraction for the ways of men who supported Irish independence outweighed his training in the homes of English gentry.

After he and his Uncle Nicholas were released from prison, they both supported the organization of the Land League. After a time Leo was again arrested, but this time he was released after only a few months of detention. Leo's own personal business affairs were near bankruptcy, and foreclosure on Foxehall was expected momentarily. When Leo sought to have the Land League support his case, he found no help. The League Committee respected him as an old Fenian and as a supporter of Irish freedom; but his wild carrying on with girls, especially now with Julie Keene, and his undisciplined, prodigal way of life had alienated them. His anticlericalism, too, was a feature that few cared to identify themselves with.

Eventually the local priest, hearing that Julie Keene was pregnant and wishing to avoid public scandal, promised Leo twenty-five pounds if he would marry Julie and use the money to open a small store in Rathkeale selling newspapers and sundries. Leo was homeless and on the verge of starvation; hence, the priest's proposal seemed the only feasible course at that moment. Although, on the surface, married life with Julie in Rathkeale appeared to be ordinary and uneventful, Leo was still quietly involved in rebel activities; and the police were aware of Leo's involvement. Johnny Hussey, a member of the Royal Irish Constabulary and the husband of one of Julie Keene's sisters, was alerted by his superiors to spy on Leo. Johnny Hussey served as an informer and implicated Leo in a gun-smuggling plot for the revolutionaries. In the ensuing action, Leo was caught after wounding a policeman and was again imprisoned, this time for a period of five years. After his release, Leo went to live in Cork city and opened a tiny tobacco store. Again as the years passed, Leo appeared to have mellowed, but in reality he was quietly attending secret meetings and was involved in unknown plots and plans. The 1916 Easter uprising was at hand. Leo participated in the Dublin fighting and met death in the concomitant carnage.

In almost every way Leo Donnel's life exemplifies failure and defeat. Given material advantages and the prestige of an estate and social position, Leo squanders his whole life in wild, irresponsible living and meets death on a flaming Dublin barricade. Although in worldly matters his life must be counted a failure, he has had the same effect as many more illustrious and real life Irish names—Wolfe Tone, Robert Emmet, Charles Stewart Parnell, to mention a few. Granted that such figures had a much greater impact on Irish thinking and had wide and varied influence, Leo's life has reached into the mind and spirit of his grandnephew Denis Hussey. Leo has not simply added his name to the roles of the dead supporters of Irish freedom, he has managed to pass on the flame of rebellion to at least one member of a new genration. This struggle will continue into future years, and, although Leo Donnel will not be alive to see this continuance, his personal influence has planted a seed which will grow and be developed by one of his own family and by other rebels.

This torch-passed-on-and-carried-by-a-new-generation theme appears in a précis of the novel to be very emotional, melodramatic, and rousingly partisan; but only at the end of the book does such feeling come through. Until the very last pages the material is presented with almost complete dispassion. A coldly neutral and objective tone reigns, and the main impression—at least until Denis's conversion to "the Cause"—is that the omniscient narrator is neutral: he is neither for nor against Leo; he is simply recording Irish life and history year by year. The wave of emotion in the final pages—while out of keeping with the general tone of the story—may be justified by noting that this is the way Denis would react under the circumstances of his life. His feelings are intensified by the patriotic fervor of the period; the connotative appeal of the Easter 1916 image, when in Yeatsian terms "A terrible beauty is born," adds inevitably to the sweep of emotion typical of that time.

Before he completed this novel, O'Faolain, discussed the book's main theme: "In America I had leisure to think back to my own people, the simple middle-class people of the towns whose lives are a slow tale of pathetic endeavor; that is a story worth telling, —how a nation lives within itself a double life, each life in that duality thwarting the other, the instinct to strive violently, to erupt volcanically on the idealistic plane, the instinct, as deep and terrible of self-preservation." [7]

The balance between conformity and rebellion is sharply depicted in the contrast between Leo O'Donnel and Denis Hussey's father, a policeman who supported the British rule and the status quo. Part of the last section of the novel is presented from Denis's viewpoint. When Denis hears himself denounced as the son of a British spy, he quarrels with his father, and, as the Easter Rising continues, the acrimony between the two reveals their totally opposing attitudes. Johnny Hussey, who had served twenty-five years on the police force, apostrophizes: "May God bless England! . . . England has only to withdraw her hand from this country in the morning, and we'd be crawling to her on our bended knees in a week." [8] In response, his son can think only of his brave uncle and the continued struggle in Dublin: "Dublin in flames, fiery with its own murder, and that old man fighting there under the crumbling roofs." [9] Out loud, however, he responds with typical rebel vehemence. He proclaims that England has done nothing but "bleed us to death." Denis recalls the "hard and cruel" lives led by his relatives in the rural areas (the novel has called attention to this life), and he denounces the British landlords for sending Leo Donnel to prison when all Leo sought for the people was fair treatment and improved living conditions.

Johnny Hussey responds that Donnel is nothing but "a common criminal" and that he sent him to jail previously and will do it again. Denis is amazed by this revelation. He thought the spy's-son charge was merely an allusion to his father's position as a policeman. Now Denis excitedly upbraids his father and is turned out of the house by his enraged elder. Another rebel has been formed, and Leo Donnel's death in the Easter Rising illustrates again—in a different way—the old Gaelic proverb: "The dead man's grip is stronger than Samson alive."

Again one can see both autobiographical and historical materials at work which render the characters and history genuine. In discussing the influence of Lennox Robinson's play *Patriots*, O'Faolain recalls being told about one of his uncles, Uncle Paudh —who like, Leo Donnel, came from County Limerick but was forced to flee the country because of his participation in the Fenian uprising of 1867. [10] When he wrote *A Nest of Simple Folk*, O'Faolain remarks that therein he found the Fenian of Robinson's play as well as his parents and his relatives from Limerick. [11] Family genealogy and local and family history related by elders also passed into the novel. There is considerable material from venerable figures like Theo, the patriarch of *A Nest of Simple*

Folk, whose "bottomless memory, linked with these in their turn bottomless memories, reached back so far that in that one decaying brain one might see, though entangled beyond all hope of unravelling, the story (as well as the picture) of his country's decay." [12]

The aged Theo is a folk-figure symbol of tradition going back countless years. He traveled with the poets of the Maigue, recalls Grattan's Irish Volunteers, was flogged in 1798, marched with O'Connell, voted in 1828, and his wife and several children died in the Famine of 1845. He links old Ireland with the Tenants League, the Fenian movement, and other developments carrying Ireland to the pivotal date of 1916. If "The dead man's grip is stronger than Samson alive," which is true of the past in England's grip on Ireland, it is also true of all of the steps—taken bit by bit, year by year—which finally culminated in eventual independence. History of past, present, and future is all tightly interlinked, generation after generation after generation. On the day of Long John O'Donnell's burial, Leo saw his granduncle's fallen tombstone in the cemetery. Uncle Owen was killed during the Famine of 1847 while pleading for food for his starving children from a ship's captain who was taking away grain to England. [13] The officer who killed Owen was a granduncle of Leo on his mother's side of the family.

O'Faolain's autobiography confirms that he has put many aspects of his own family into *A Nest of Simple Folk*. Johnny Hussey bears many characteristics of O'Faolain's own father, and much of the life of the O'Faolain family in Cork has been transposed into the lives of the Husseys. As a youth, O'Faolain visited relatives in various parts of Ireland, particularly in his mother's home county of Limerick; and personal acquaintances with uncles, aunts, and cousins, plus family reminiscences, establish the verisimilitude which is convincingly felt and witnessed in the story. The portrayals of life in both Limerick and Cork reflect a genuine feeling for both areas.

In one of his historical biographies, O'Faolain recalls the continuous rebel spirit working in Ireland from the Young Ireland period, the Fenian tradition, the rebellions in 1848 and 1867, up to the time of Parnell, and then on to the Irish Citizen Army, the Volunteers, the Easter Rising, and beyond. [14] Often these movements worked underground with considerable secrecy and pa-

tience. This perseverance and persistence is conveyed effectively
in *A Nest of Simple Folk*, and the inexorable movement toward
freedom marches relentlessly despite indifference or hostility from
many of the people, and arrests and imprisonments of men who
were frequently mistreated and who were released weary and
broken.[15]

Leo Donnel's opening a tobacco shop in Cork is reminiscent of
the real life Fenian Tom Clarke who, after spending fifteen and a
half years in jail for Republican activities, eventually opened such
a shop in Dublin which became a center of the rebel movement.
Clarke later participated in the Easter Rising and was eventually
executed with two other signers of the Proclamation of the Irish
Republic posted on the walls of the General Post Office in Dublin's O'Connell Street. Leo Donnel is actually a fictional counterpart of Tom Clarke, an old Fenian who also had plotted against
England for almost sixty years.[16]

O'Faolain has used an especially appropriate name for his principal character. The O'Donnells were famous clan chiefs in the
sixteenth century, and the famous song "O'Donnell Aboo"
("Aboo" is Gaelic for "Onward") was commonly used for rousing
rebel sentiments. The name O'Donnell is immediately recognizable as a freedom symbol to readers with a knowledge of Irish
history; and Leo becomes O'Faolain's symbol of the Irish rebellion over the years—a rebellion always thinking, planning, watching, and waiting for an opportunity.

These rebels and their activities possessed the virtues and defects of any rebel group: they were often stubborn, misfitted, ignorant, foolish and foolhardy, wild, frequently isolated and alone,
stupid yet heroic, often misunderstood by the people, rejected by
their own relatives, frowned upon by the clergy, scorned, betrayed, persecuted, imprisoned, yet persevering, indomitable,
beaten but never crushed. In Leo's case, a certain foolhardy ignorance is stressed. Leo, for example, is not intelligent enough to
pass examinations which would qualify him to become either a
medical doctor or a veterinarian. Leo also evinces a single-minded
brutish nature which is more animalistic than human. Such qualities are necessary components in any rebellious activity. The very
ordinariness of Leo Donnel and his lackluster character also reinforce the basically stoic endurance and relentlessness of the rebellion. He also enables O'Faolain to demonstrate how rebel activity

existed side-by-side with everyday life, the life of "self-preservation."

The novel's principal weakness is several rather dry and overly
detailed sections which unduly slow the narrative movement and
cast a quiescent somnolence over parts of the book. This undulat-
ing movement of high and low points of interest and narrative
intensity, more or less understandable and inevitable in any *roman de fleuve*, is too pronounced. The first sixty-three pages of the
novel centering on the dying Long John O'Donnell and his last
will and testament are masterful in characterization, suspense,
and conflict. The gathering of relatives and friends for the death
watch; the appearance of Norry-all-night, whose vocation consisted of visiting wakes; the distrust and quarreling between Long
John's relatives and his wife; the sharp contrast between continuous praying while arguments and intrigue are taking place; the
grasping and hard-hearted concern only for the inheritance of the
land—these and similar occurrences sear into the mind. O'Faolain
knows these people, as J. Donald Adams once remarked, "to the
marrow of their bones." [17] Although their life on the land is hard
and cruel and their existence meaningless unless there is an afterlife, they must grasp for the land—it is all they have, and every
other consideration is of secondary importance.

Other sections too obviously mark time and present historical
filler material. This material would be more dynamic if it were
condensed. Leo's contacts with his aunts and much of the third
section dealing with Johnny Hussey and Bid Keene and day-to-
day life in Cork, for example, illustrate this aspect of the book.
Narrative interest lags as the story introduces new characters, and
the gaps between generations are difficult to bridge in an interesting manner.

This approach does serve to reveal the "middle-class people of
the towns whose lives are a slow tale of pathetic endeavor," and
this portrayal is one of O'Faolain's avowed purposes in writing his
first novel. As one critic observes, O'Faolain shows the people of
Ireland—both the farmers and the townsfolk—in the "daily business of living" with "its exaltations, its dullness, its despair. He
writes with a feeling as sensitive for the subtleties of human
mood, with a psychology at once acute and profound, as he writes
of the natural aspects of his world." [18]

In style, *A Nest of Simple Folk* has lost much of the passion and vitality displayed in *Midsummer Night Madness and Other Stories*. Except in certain highlight sections of the novel, the material does not pulse vigorously. The nature of the material and the chronicle approach do not lend to the same sort of exuberance found in the short stories. The romantic lushness of the earlier volume has also been deliberately toned down. An ardent feeling for the countryside persists, but even that has been subdued. O'Faolain's artistry has advanced in his control of dialogue and in his ability to record the various dialectal words and picturesque sayings which are especially characteristic of Irish speech.

But a caveat must be recorded. The reader is jarred by two occurrences. First, it is surprising that Leo Donnel would court and marry the girl who informed on him and caused him to spend ten years in a British prison; and, second, it is incredible that Donnel would become intimate with his niece's policeman husband, Johnny Hussey, who also informed on him and brought him to imprisonment. Both of these choices on Donnel's part seem to be not only incredibly stupid but also inconsistent with narrative logic. Such treachery did happen in Ireland during the nineteenth and twentieth centuries—relative informed on relative, friend on friend; for example, in the famous Irish rebel song "The Croppy Boy," the rebel is captured and eventually hanged by the British through the treachery of his first cousin. Nevertheless, these examples of Leo's willingness to forgive informers seem improbable in the context of the novel. O'Faolain's aim is clearly to show the perpetual loyalist-rebel struggle sentiments, the one "duality thwarting the other," and the conflict of "the instinct to strive violently" with the instinct of "self-preservation." O'Faolain is also trying to keep as many of the main characters as close together as possible for more compact and easier handling; however, the result here is incongruous and causes disbelief.

In toto O'Faolain has chronicled more than three-score years of Irish life so credibly that everything he has presented is vividly seen and felt. Farmers, townsfolk, the conformists, and the rebels are all presented with an insistent awareness of Irish history. In the background are the emigrants to other countries. One member of the O'Donnell family went to Boston and was killed in a railway accident, one went to Australia, and others who left the country were never heard from again. They depart continuously and find their separate ways.

At the end of the novel, Mag Keene, ninety-eight years of age and the family patriarch since the passing of Uncle Theo many years before, cannot blame Leo for his participation in the rebellion of 1867 or in the 1916 Rising; but she thinks his conduct is folly. She can only pray and hope for the best, for life is too complicated and too unpredictable to be explained satisfactorily. Mag Keene emits a sigh, and the author too sighs over Ireland and its people—the mystery and the wonder of it all.

II *Non Serviam*

Bird Alone, O'Faolain's second novel, considers the life and times of Cornelius Crone, who was born in Cork in 1873. This novel is narrated by Crone when he is an old man, and the narrative focuses practically all of its attention on the first thirty years of Crone's biography. Corney—as he is usually called—was a carpenter and house builder by profession, who grew up in a home controlled by a strict, funereal father "miserable with piety." Although the father was very upright and conscientious, he did not have a friend in Cork and was nicknamed "Christ-on-the-Cross" Crone.

But, as far as Corney is concerned, the dominating figure in the household is his grandfather, old Phil Crone, who lives in a spacious attic room. Grander Crone, a likable extrovert, is a storytelling codger who had been an active Fenian in his youthful days. Grander read books to the children of the household, told them stories, let them snuggle into his bed. Corney was his favorite grandchild. Later, when Corney was older, he would follow Grander about the pubs of Cork; and every month on the third Sunday he would be with his Grander and Arty and Christy Tinsley as Arty and Grander would decorate the graves of Fenians. In the pubs Corney listened to favorable comments about the various rebel movements and to criticism of the British.

Grander continually manages to stir young Corney's imagination. He is able to bring the past to life, and Corney comes to appreciate former Irish history and the struggle against oppression. Corney's grandfather is a born rebel; and, since he does not practice Catholicism and is strongly anti-clerical, he is frowned upon by Corney's parents and by several other people in Cork; but he has his old Fenian cronies such as Arty Tinsley to chat with and go drinking with. Grander's nonconformity evokes a kindred spirit in Corney, and both consciously and unconsciously Corney adopts many of his grandfather's attitudes and viewpoints. Grander's sympathetic conviviality and his ability to show affection for Corney contrast poignantly with Corney's father's harshness and aloof righteousness; and they draw Corney even more into the old man's orbit.

One incident particularly impresses itself indelibly on Corney's memory. He vividly recalls Grander's reaction when his old Fenian comrade, Arty Tinsley, dies. At first, Grander is in charge of the funeral arrangements; however, he refuses to fill in the word "Catholic" on the cemetary registry for Tinsley's burial. Since the Church had banned Fenianism in Ireland and had condemned anyone who took the Fenian oath, Grander does not believe that Tinsley should be buried as a Catholic. He knew that Tinsley would never have repudiated the Fenian oath and argues that, since the Church did not want to accept Tinsley when he was alive, why should it accept him in death? Eventually, the immediate issue of Tinsley's burial is resolved by having the funeral arrangements taken out of Grander's hands; but Grander's defiance and his Fenian staunchness have made a deep impression on his grandson and help to solidify their close relationship.

Corney and his uncle are staunch supporters of Charles Stewart Parnell, perhaps the most colorful of the Irish independence movement leaders. Just as James Joyce's father supported Parnell and influenced his son on this question, so does Grander Crone influence Corney. At a family dinner scene, obviously modeled on the Christmas episode in Joyce's *A Portrait of the Artist As a Young Man,* a heated discussion develops over Parnell's adulterous conduct with Mrs. O'Shea. Grander and Corney's Aunt Virginia are among the staunch defenders of Parnell, while some of the others reprove his behavior. Virginia argues that "We must stand true to our leader. We must stand by him." [19] Because of her kindly behavior and her Parnellite convictions she wins Corney's support, so that the two people who are identified as staunch patriots are also lax in moral behavior and religious conviction.

This identification of political and sexual emancipation, as found in the outlooks of both Grander Crone and Virginia, is the quality that Donat O'Donnell considers to be O'Faolain's own personal "parnellism" (as distinct from Parnellism as a political element); and he finds this attitude to be the key theme in O'Faolain's work.[20] This "parnellism" is designed to overthrow British oppression and puritanical religious notions which have predominated in Ireland. The "parnellism" theme is unquestionably present in some of O'Faolain's work—very much so in his novels. (*Bird Alone* especially is the "parnellite" novel). However this "parnellism," as Benedict Kiely points out,[21] is only one characteristic of O'Faolain's writing, and it does not take into account other aspects and later developments in his work.

Corney's tendencies to rebellion are spurred more pointedly when he is accused of participating in a Republican Brotherhood raid at a police barracks. As it happens, Corney is innocent, although he and Grander help to harbor one of the fugitives and Corney assists the rebel to escape. Corney is arrested and brought to trial; and, although he is acquitted of sedition, he becomes more staunch in both his personal nonconformity and in his realization that he, like his grandfather, is a loner. Because of the scandal of the arrest and trial and because of the publicized knowledge that Corney has been alone with a girl in the woods at midnight, Corney is ostracized by many of his friends and acquaintances. Corney, embittered by this situation, attributes it to the same reactionary tendencies demonstrated in the case of the Fenians and Parnell. The post-Parnell years entrench both Grander and Corney in their defiance of the herd and its attempts at uniformity and thought control. Corney "realized suddenly that in those dead years in which I lived, the years after Parnell, the shore of Ireland was empty, too, and would remain empty for a long time, and that I was merely one of many left stranded after the storm." [22]

Another event plays a prominent role in helping the reader to understand Corney's process of development and his frame of mind. For some time Corney has been dating attractive Elsie Sherlock, who eventually becomes pregnant by him. Corney does not believe that their love relationship was evil or sinful because he loves Elsie and wishes to marry her. Her father refuses to grant permission because Corney does not earn enough money to support Elsie adequately. Undoubtedly, Elsie's father would agree to the match if he knew that Elsie was pregnant. She does not wish him to find this out, however, since he is an extremely pious widower with several priests and nuns in his family. In desperation Elsie tries to commit suicide; although she does not succeed, the complications resulting from her attempt finally kill her. Corney comes to believe that their love affair was a sin for Elsie because her religious upbringing and beliefs led her to this conclusion. Corney has come to respect her beliefs because of his deep love for her and because of the zeal of her convictions. As far as he personally is concerned, however, he does not regard their love and their relationship as evil, and he adheres to this conviction.[23]

Public reaction against Corney in the matter of Elsie Sherlock's pregnancy and death makes him even more of an outcast. His father and mother will not speak to him, and they lock him out of the house. People shun him. Even Grander is not around, having died just a short time previously. Corney now becomes truly a bird alone, a lonely spirit moving quietly among alien people. O'Faolain quotes a line from Psalm LXXXVII to illustrate Corney's state: *"Factus sum sicut homo sine adjutoria inter mortuos liber."* (I am a man without help—a free man among the dead.) This statement is used as the motto of the novel.

The temptation is strong within him to give up his independence and to join the security of the group, but he cannot accept Roman Catholicism—at least not the puritanical type found in Ireland. Like Joyce and Stephen Dedalus—the comparison is irresistible, and O'Faolain unquestionably has modeled Corney on Joyce—Corney "will not serve," his pride and strength of mind will not allow him to subordinate himself to herd instincts and to group patterns of conformity. Just as Stephen Dedalus must sacrifice his family and friends, even his country and his religion, to the demands of his intellectual convictions and, especially, to the goddess of Art, so too must Corney Crone sacrifice family, friends, and religion to the demands of freedom and personal beliefs.

Corney is not an intellectual, like Dedalus, although he is a well-read man and a deep thinker; but he possesses some of the same Joycean tendencies toward rebellion and nonconformity. This evolution of Corney's views and the strands which explain and cause them are presented with a marvelous perspicacity and verisimilitude. In this presentation lies much of the power of the novel. The total and compelling portrait of Corney Crone which strikes the reader at the finish of the narrative is sharply memorable. A lonely, but courageous, man stands revealed. The reader knows Corney and understands the ideas and events in his life which have made him the way he is.

The portrait drawn of Grander Crone is even more effective, becoming one of the most fully realized creations in Irish fiction. If *Bird Alone* had been a stage production or a movie, Grander could have been played to perfection by Barry Fitzgerald or Cyril Cusack. Grander is a "character" in the colloquial sense of the word. He has his crotchets, his quirks, his vanities. He is filled with a lifelike vigor, and he possesses a lovable roguishness which has affinities with Falstaff, Parson Adams, and several Dickensian characters. Grander's excitement and distress over the burial arrangements for Arty Tinsley;[24] his running war with and ambivalent reaction toward Pidgie Flynn, Corney's mother; his anguish over the fact that one of his sons eloped with a young carnival actress he wanted for himself (Grander was always "weak in the carnalaties"); and his encounter with an aged Parnellite priest who attempts to hear his confession—these situations are richly rewarding in character penetration and insight.

Yet despite O'Faolain's success in portraying Corney and Grander Crone, *Bird Alone* is not a successful novel. The principal reason for its failure is that there are two divergent themes which are not unified enough to leave a totality of impression. It is possible to read *Bird Alone* on a Joycean *"non serviam"* level. Corney becomes the traditional rebel, both political and religious, and his suffering as a "loner" is carefully recorded. If this had been the novel's central theme, its energies and its overall impact would not have been dissipated by the intrusion of the Elsie Sherlock material.

In his autobiography O'Faolain states that he was actually writing a type of Irish *Scarlet Letter: Bird Alone* is really a novel of "sin and salvation in an Irish setting";[25] it treats of "a young man's and a young woman's passion in a community as merciless and alien to passion as Hawthorne's Salem. . . . The total destruction of those two young people is as true, honest and inevitable as the destruction of Hester Prynne and Arthur Dimmesdale in *The Scarlet Letter*."[26] This element in the novel clashes with the "loner" theme, with the rugged-individualist notion which Corney has exemplified. Corney is presented as a sympathetic and essentially admirable person, true to himself and true to the rebel spirit; however, his behavior towards Elsie jars with the sympathetic portrait the author has been careful to paint. This contradiction in character is particularly evident when Elsie becomes pregnant and Corney becomes confused, indecisive, and almost cloddish. He cannot think; he wants to marry Elsie but he is deterred by explanations which are flimsy and appear to be more the result of authorial manufacturing than the result of logical character behavior. In this section of the novel Corney appears to be a weakling, and his conduct lacks the backbone which the reader has come to associate with him.

O'Faolain is so motivated to develop the effects of Elsie and Corney's fornication that he neglects, therefore, the consistent characterization of Corney. Because of his preoccupation with the effects of sin, O'Faolain mixes incongruously a novel which exists on a level of political and social rebellion with a novel of sin and retribution. The two ingredients do not blend—at least not in this novel—because of the way they are handled.

O'Faolain also incorporates a Faustian theme in *Bird Alone*. When Corney was a little boy, his grandfather used to relate the Faust story (in a version by George W. M. Reynolds);[27] the young lad could particularly remember the end of the narrative when Mephistopheles came to claim Faust and Faust begged for the time to say an Act of Contrition. This request was refused, and Faust was immediately thrust down into the pit of hell.

If Corney is Faust, then Elsie Sherlock is Marguerite. She is the religious and innocent girl who attracts Corney, but, because of her religious scruples, she at first resists his advances. Later in the novel Corney meets Elsie in London, where she is visiting her priest brother, and he takes her to a tavern owned by Corney's uncle. At this pub, the young couple find happiness, drink, and good song, and the Auerbach Cellar episode of *Faust* is paralleled explicitly. After the visit to the pub tavern, Corney manages to seduce Elsie, she becomes pregnant, and he then becomes inept. His conduct becomes absurd and is much more culpable for Elsie's fate than the puritanical environment which O'Faolain wishes above all to blame. When Elsie tries to commit suicide, she induces premature labor; in her dying condition, she asks for a priest to whom she can confess her sin. She dies, however, before the priest can arrive. Like Marguerite, she is carried to death without being shriven—at least by mortals.

The stress on Elsie's sexual behavior with Corney and her subsequent death cause Corney to be completely isolated from society. He is the "bird alone" of the title. Corney is isolated from a society which does not look with favor on sexual aberration or indeed on any public deviation from the rules of the Church. It is the case of Parnell all over again, both sexually and politically.

It is clear that O'Faolain wants to demonstrate how a person suffers unless he follows religious and social conformity in Ireland. Corney's loss of faith initially hinges primarily on the influence of his grandfather, and then on the Church's opposition to Parnell. At first, then, Corney's deviation is politically motivated: the basic opposition of the Church to Fenianism, to Parnell, to the struggle for independence. As Corney's understanding of the power and influence of the Church in Irish society grows, he sees Catholicism as a formal ritualistic organization, an organization built on authoritarianism, rigorism, and Jehovah-like prohibition. This Church that Corney beholds is cold, aloof, and forbidding; it is not content to condemn the sin; it is also excessively uncharitable toward the sinner. It looks not for the mote in its own eye and is (barring a few of its number such as the individual priests who would hear Fenian confessions) without compassion, understanding, and humanitarianism. Love does not dominate in such a church; formalism and prohibitions are its principal characteristics.

Corney comes to hate the society in which he finds himself, and yet, paradoxically, he favors the people; "it was not that I did not believe in men, but that I could not believe in what men believed." [28] The people believe in a harsh and oppressive church; they are priest-ridden and overly concerned about what other people will say about them if they do not strictly conform. In their lack of freedom, human understanding, and compassion and in their regimented daily activity, they are filled with hypocrisy, timidity, and fear. Metaphorically, they are dead.

At this point some readers will recall the scene in Joyce's "Clay," where the laundress Maria, a symbol of Ireland, blindfolded in a Halloween game, selects clay (death) and the prayer book (religion in Ireland), which Joyce equates with Ireland's condition of pious sterility. Corney's position, however, is even more frustrating and defeating than Maria's. He resists both clay and the prayer book and retains his freedom, but this freedom is frightfully bitter since it is a lone gesture among people who are either moribund or dead. "I have kept my barren freedom, but only . . . a free man among the dead."

Donat O'Donnell censures O'Faolain for his viewpoint of believing in the people while refusing to accept what they believe. O'Donnell remarks, "The clear-cut attitude of Mr. Frank O'Connor, who can laugh both at the people and at what they believe is not for him, since he believes in the people." [29] Yet O'Faolain's presentation of this dilemma, which is a Joycean soul-probing and questioning analysis of a basic problem of Irish life, is more meaningful in this form than if it were handled in a flippant, satiric manner.

Rather than being a novel of "sin and salvation" as O'Faolain maintains, *Bird Alone* is essentially a novel of *"non serviam,"* a novel expressive of the guts and courage necessary to continue to live in a Rhinoceros-like (to borrow a term from Ionesco) society where everyone must conform or suffer the consequences. This situation was particularly true of Ireland—at least at the time of which O'Faolain writes; for Catholic Ireland is and was a fairly close-knit unit. On the Irishman who does not practice his religion —or at least does not follow its outward forms by attending Sunday Mass—much family, business, and social pressure is exerted. Furthermore, since the nonconformist has been reared from childhood in Catholicism, his religion early takes a firm hold on him; and these beliefs become extremely difficult to give up completely. One recalls Julia Flyte's comments in Evelyn Waugh's *Brideshead Revisited* about how difficult it is to give up Catholic tenets if one is indoctrinated early enough. The seed planted in childhood frequently roots deeply.

In resisting this pressure Corney Crone is a fictional counterpart of the James Joyce-type rebel. Corney's rebellion is a heroic choice since it means he must suffer intensely and be isolated. Corney is true to his beliefs; he is consistent in his rejection. As Donat O'Donnell remarks, "The fact that he said 'No' seems to me to put the book on a much higher plane . . . the level of truth. . . . The reality of the character emerges in the stubborn rejection. *Bird Alone* is about human fate, which is harder than fiction." [30]

It is important to record that O'Faolain himself in his autobiography takes a different tack. He deprecates the first part of the novel which deals with Corney's development under the influence of his grandfather. He says he did not actually know the prototypes of Corney and Grander, that he was too romantic and not realistic enough in dealing with them, and that Corney's development should have been constructed in a slower, quieter, and objective manner. On the other hand, he finds that the latter part of the novel which deals with Elsie and Corney's fornication is well-handled and that the effect of sin in a community as harsh as Hawthorne's Salem is depicted with accuracy and inevitability. He regrets that he did not eliminate the earlier part of the novel and concentrate more on the sin theme in an Irish setting. If he had written a dark, poetic, and oppressive novel stressing guilt and punishment, he feels that he would have written a story similar to *The Scarlet Letter*.

The style of *Bird Alone* is excessively romantic. It possesses the exuberance and emotional fervor found in the *Midsummer Night Madness* volume, but O'Faolain's other comments about the novel appear inaccurate. False notes dominate Corney's relationship with Elsie Sherlock. Too much manipulation on O'Faolain's part occurs in bringing his lovers together, in separating them at certain times and places, and in the insertion of marking-time material during Elsie's pregnancy. On page 185 of *Bird Alone*, O'Faolain introduces two new characters, Marion and Stella. Much time is wasted in describing these two girls whose only function is to furnish a cottage where Elsie can find a refuge and keep her pregnancy a secret from her father. Marion and Stella intrude upon the story; their appearance is digressive and artificial, and they reduce the narrative drive.

The plot also becomes artificial at this point. One easily concludes that Corney and Elsie do not marry primarily because the author is manipulating his materials so that Elsie must attempt suicide and then die without having the opportunity to go to confession. All of this simply does not ring true; it is merely contrived.

The first part of the novel, however, possesses much verisimilitude. O'Faolain may claim that Grander Crone was created out of his imagination and is not a real person; nevertheless, Grander's reality is attested by the fact that he is the type of individual many people have actually met. If they have not met him in real life, they can visualize him as existing because he contains the Falstaffian quality of being immediately recognizable. He is not a caricature; he pulsates with the breath of human life.

O'Faolain's attempt to denigrate Corney's political and social authenticity may be challenged on the basis of an awareness of James Joyce's life as well as by the historical fact that concern

over the treatment accorded Parnell was not limited to Joyce's
personal feelings. This matter aroused vehement motions
throughout Ireland and caused much soul-searching among the
people. Frank O'Connor in his autobiography, *An Only Child,* recalls the attitude of a neighbor named Ellen Farrell. When the
priests canvassed their parishes forbidding people to vote for Parnell because of his conduct with Kitty O'Shea they found a portrait of Parnell on Ellen Farrell's front door. When a priest attempted to take the picture down, the old woman beat him off
with a stick and vowed never to go to church again. And, as
O'Connor observes, she kept her vow.[31] Life in general supports
the credibility of such a creation as Corney Crone and attests to
the truth of the portrait given by O'Faolain. It is unfortunate that
O'Faolain weakened the total impact of his novel by the "sin and
salvation" material when, despite an overly romantic approach in
his style, he succeeded in conveying the depth of feeling that the
question of Charles Stewart Parnell aroused in many an Irish citizen.

III   *The Ache of Exile*

Come Back to Erin analyzes the Hogan-Hannafey family, most
of whom live in Cork. Mrs. Hogan-Hannafey's first husband was a
storekeeper named John Hogan who was eventually killed by
overwork due—according to Hogan's relatives—to his wife's ambitions and social-climbing aspirations. Five children, St. John,
Leonard, Clara, Michael, and Eolie resulted from this marriage.
Mrs. Hogan's second marriage to Philip Hannafey, a Cork stock-
broker, produced three children, Frankie, Natalie, and Claude.
Phil Hannafey was a great ladies' man and his conduct distressed
his wife. Disturbed by her husband's behavior and worried over
Frankie's involvement with the Irish Republican Army, Mrs.
Hogan-Hannafey (she now uses both names) becomes demented
after her second husband's death. For a short time she is placed in
an asylum, but then the family loyally agrees to care for her at
home.

Of the eight children, only St. John has married. He early left
the family home and emigrated to New York; he has become a
success as the owner of the Hogan-Hannafey shoe-store chain.
Leonard is a priest in New York City; Clara, a nun in Ireland.
Michael is the principal breadwinner of the family; Eolie is the

housekeeper; Natalie teaches. Claude, the youngest of the children, is still attending school. The family represents, therefore, a cross-section of Irish life—priest, nun, housekeeper, rebel, mechant, teacher. The two most important characters are, however, Frankie Hannafey, who is on the run, and St. John Hogan-Hannafey, the wealthy American businessman who has been away from Ireland for thirty-four years.

The main events of the novel take place in 1936, although, as always in O'Faolain's stories, history is pervasive since much of the past is recalled and is observed to be pertinent to the present moment. Frankie, now thirty-three years old, had, at the age of sixteen, joined the Irish Volunteers; from that moment he has spent all his time serving the Republican Army. Most of these years have been spent wandering about the country, although he has also been jailed several times. He is presently sought by the authorities in connection with the murder in Waterford of General Blennerhasset. At the moment Frankie is hiding in the upper story of the Hogan-Hannafey family home in Cork. He has long experienced the pressures on the Irish rebel: "the slow attrition, the wearing of the spirit, the despair of the heart, the stripping of the nerves." [32]

Frankie is a heroic figure but also a pathetic one because he is an anomaly. He is out of touch with his time and place. After the Civil War many of the old revolutionaries gave up the struggle. They sought regular jobs, lost their idealistic goals, and began to conform. The dream of the Republic began to fade under the lure of conformity and materialistic security.

When Frankie eventually escapes to America, he meets Shawn Kearney, an old rebel comrade. Frankie taxes Kearney for not returning to Ireland to help the revolutionary cause. Kearney reveals that he did return, but that most of the Irish people were now content to accept easy government jobs. The old days and the old dreams are finished, Kearney argues; but Frankie is a diehard. He still wants to fight for a Republic; indeed, he refuses to admit that times have changed.

It is Frankie's philosophy that, despite the appearance of an Irish Free State, Ireland is still laboring under a slave mentality and is actually under the financial control of English bankers. Ireland is being exploited by commercial and governmental groups, while the ordinary farmers and laboring men are suffering economically, and over one million people are out of work. He maintains that absentee landowners still control Irish mineral and fishing resources and that even the Irish ports are still controlled by British financial interests.

When Frankie is asked how this situation can be improved, he insists that cooperatives must be introduced into the country and that there must be cooperative ownership of financial resources of the country. When he is called a "Communist," a "Red," or a "Fascist" for advocating such ideas, he responds that he's a Collectivist not a Communist; but on other occasions he regards himself as more or less a Communist. Frankie, who wants the conditions of the workers and the poor improved in Ireland, feels that a revolution against the vested interests is necessary. Frankie's position is closest to that of the Saor Eire (Free Ireland) organization (prominent in the 1930's) which wanted political power in the hands of the farmers and the laboring class. This notion of a workers' state also advocated the elimination of British control in Ireland. Saor Eire, whose best-known proponent was Peadar O'Donnell, was very critical of the economic injustices tolerated by the Free State government.[33]

But, as Frankie moves from Irish tavern to tavern and from social club to social club after fleeing to New York City, Frankie discovers that he is unable to communicate with his listeners. As some of his New York City friends explain, his audience wants a romantic Ireland; they want the Lakes of Killarney or the Blarney Stone; they want an idealized picture of the "old sod"; for them Yeats' lines do not apply: "Romantic Ireland's dead and gone;/'Tis with O'Leary in the grave";[34] or, as was later added by a wag, " 'Tis with O'Leary in New York, Boston, and Chicago."

Frankie's faith in his cause is shaken. He begins to feel the hopelessness of the struggle and the little that can be accomplished when the overwhelming majority in both America and Ireland is not really interested in improving conditions. Frankie does not fit in America since his heart and spirit are in Ireland; yet he comes to realize that, if he goes back to Ireland, he would not be adjusted to life there either. And, near the end of the novel, after Frankie is cleared of the charge of participating in the killing of the British general, he does return to Ireland. He sadly accepts the fact that all he is really qualified to be is a rebel; but, like most of his fellow-countrymen, he makes a compromise. He obtains a job as an inspector of diseased cattle. The symbolic implication of Frankie's new position is clear. The Ireland of the mid-1930's is a drab, conforming, diseased country; it has lost its glamor, its heroism, its idealism. The glorious aspirations of the 1916–1924 period have come to little.

For many years Frankie Hannafey had lived hopefully: "numbers never counted in Ireland. It was always a few men who did everything. Anything can suddenly create a fermentation in the minds of the people. Then all it needs is a few men to keep it on the boil. There's great power in the people here." [35] After twenty years of adhering to this belief, of suffering every privation for the dream of a free and enlightened Ireland, Frankie now gives up his belief in the people and resigns himself to complacency, mediocrity, and conformity. Thus, Frankie's own life symbolizes the change from the Ireland of Pearse, Connolly, Clarke, and the other patriots to the drab, stultifying Ireland of the 1930's.

In addition to the portrait of the honored rebel in rebel days contrasted with the picture of him in later years, the character of Frankie Hannafey also involves important religious characteristics. In conversing with his half-brother Leonard, a New York City priest, Frankie says he is a "bad Catholic"; but he is not concerned about his own religious condition. When he is asked about the attitude of the priests toward his collectivist ideas, he admits that the clergy are opposed; but, since they were opposed to the Fenians, Parnell, and Sinn Fein, this opposition does not trouble Frankie. His anti-clericalism is stressed, and he regards the Church as one of the vested instruments in Ireland which is still keeping Ireland subordinate to England: "The way they told us we were heretics because we fought for Ireland. . . . They simply grabbed God and sold him to the British Empire." [36] Frankie has been excommunicated from the Catholic Church for fighting on the side of the Republicans during the Irish Civil War.

Frankie's religious problems are complicated by his falling in love with his brother St. John's wife, Bee Hannafey. Bee, an Episcopalian, is a forty-one-year-old matron whose beauty is fading but who still possesses considerable appeal.[37] Frustrated and lonely, she frequently finds solace in affairs with younger men. Bee is attracted to Frankie and he, in turn, finds her appealing and desirable. But, when it comes to sexual relations, Frankie is cautious. Although in his early thirties, he has never had inter-

course. The strong influence of Jansenism and Puritanism common in Ireland and his dedication to political rebellion have
forced him to be chaste. The peculiar nature of Irish theology
tends to equate sexual abstinence with virtue; hence, although an
individual may be given to drink, gambling, dishonest practices,
the only real evils in the minds of many Irishmen are fornication
and adultery.

Although Frankie is not practicing his religion and although he
is in political opposition to the Church and its clergy, he can still
consider himself a Catholic as long as he does not violate the
Church's sexual taboos. Frankie attempts, therefore, to avoid the
inevitable contact with Bee. When staying at her home, he locks
his bedroom door, and he writes a long romantic letter to Josephine Hogan in Ireland in order to distract himself. Bee herself
notes the limitations in the Irish concept of love. Puritanism and
the engrained religious indoctrination against sex hangs heavily
about, and one recalls the old witticism to the effect that the Irish
are the only race who believe that chastity is possible.

Nevertheless, the time comes when Frankie can no longer restrain his desire for Bee. He possesses her and knows the happiness of sexual love, but at the same time he suffers guilt and regret. Bee had been correct in her analysis of Frankie's love; it was
fiercely passionate, but mentally it was incomplete and suffered
restraints. This aspect of his love and his religious attitudes, as
well as his homesickness for Ireland, result in Frankie's ultimate
rejection of Bee.

Next to Frankie Hannafey the most complex and intriguing
character in *Come Back to Erin* is St. John, who had emigrated to
America from Cork in 1902. Through hard work and with the help
of the financial advantages received by marrying into Bee's well-
to-do family, St. John becomes the owner of a shoe manufacturing
concern. He achieves business success and wealth; but, since he
has given up his Catholicism in order to marry Bee, he is funda-
mentally troubled and unhappy about his spiritual condition.
When St. John returns to Ireland for a visit, he represents the
romantic and sentimental viewpoint toward Ireland on the part of
American emigrants. He is entranced with the beauty and picturesqueness of the Irish countryside, loves the people, and finds
everything perfect. He is the tourist type who waxes eloquent
over the Blarney Stone, the Lakes of Killarney, and all the other

symbols of Irish homesickness and nostalgia for the "old sod," the old country, the homeland.

Although his birthplace in Ireland was nothing but a rural shack, St. John is thrilled over this "little spot of heaven." He is ecstatic; he is delighted to commune with his ancestors. The return-to-Ireland strain expressed in a thousand songs from "I'll Take You Home Again, Kathleen" to "Where the River Shannon Flows" is deeply meaningful to the sentimental St. John. He is especially mesmerized by the song "Come Back to Erin," which is played by passenger ships entering and leaving Cork harbor. At this point in his life St. John's most obsessive desire is to "Come Back to Erin," but he feels he cannot come back permanently because, like Frankie—although for different reasons—he too is an exile.

When St. John was establishing his business and his children were growing up, he was distracted from his spiritual problems. Now that his company is established on a solid basis and the children fully grown, he becomes more and more troubled by his break with the Catholic Church. Although on the surface he appears to have discarded Catholicism through the years, he has never been able to escape its early indoctrination. Now the pressure of this indoctrination is returning, and St. John feels that all he needs are the soothing roots of Ireland; but Frankie shrewdly conjectures that he really needs a priest. And even if St. John wants and needs Ireland, Frankie reflects, he cannot have Ireland without being a practicing Catholic. St. John is not strong or hard enough to adopt the *"non serviam"* philosophy of James Joyce or Corney Crone; he is not politically motivated or an idealistic rebel, and he cannot adopt the attitude of Leo Donnel or Frankie Hannafey. The only solution for St. John is to reconcile himself to the Church, to become typically Irish, to pay Ireland her price—religious orthodoxy and conformity.

St. John begins to drink more and more heavily; he goes into violent rages; he resumes the mistreatment of his wife. He is also disturbed by the fact that his daughter has been reared as an Episcopalian (at his father-in-law's insistence—and St. John was not at the time financially able to resist his father-in-law's wishes). St. John's other child, a son named Randall, has been reared as a Catholic, but he had little conviction or inclination to practice this religion. Acting on the advice of his brother Leonard, St. John

decides to ask for a legal separation from Bee, acknowledge to
Randall that he has given him a bad example and that his marriage was wrong, and claim his daughter. With these matters accomplished St. John hopes to return to Ireland and settle there.

In this whole matter Bee's position is indicated in juxtaposition
and complicates the issue. Ten years previously Bee demanded a
divorce from St. John, and he had refused. She points out that his
refusal to grant her request was motivated primarily by his desire
not to lose her father's money. Now, she contends, he wants to
wipe out the marriage with a separation and demonstrate to Randall that he has lived in sin all the years of his marriage; and, from
Bee's point of view, this makes her appear as simply St. John's
mistress. Bee is again willing to obtain a divorce, but St. John,
who does not believe in divorce, will not agree. Bee refuses to
consider handing her daughter over to St. John's control. Here the
stalemate rests with both sides presenting understandable and
compelling arguments for their respective positions.

Under the circumstances St. John cannot receive the sacraments
of Catholicism, and he cannot undo the damage he feels has been
done to his children by a marriage which is invalid according to
the tenets of a religion he cannot escape. St. John suffers also because he feels that God has deserted him. He seeks relief in another visit to Ireland. The brief vacation that he spent there earlier in the year he regards as the happiest period in his life. But on
the trip over to Ireland St. John is reported missing, lost at sea.
Returning to Ireland without the solace of Catholicism which Ireland requires from such as St. John, his acute depression brings
him to suicide, although O'Faolain deliberately leaves the matter
—accident or suicide—in doubt. St. John finally discovers that
"you can't go home again"—at least not to Ireland unless one carries credentials of orthodoxy.[38]

Another compelling character study in the novel is the analysis
of Michael Hannafey. The partially crippled Mick is a post-office
clerk in Cork and a commonplace type in Ireland—the unmarried
basic support of the family who sacrifices himself for its requirements (or, perhaps more accurately, surrenders quietly to others).
Mick lives a compressed life although he finds distraction in fre-
quenting the pubs, reading de Maupassant and Balzac, and playing Dvorak on the gramophone. While Frankie dreams of Ireland
as a workers' state free from British domination and while St.

John dreams of a return to Catholicism and a quiet retirement in nostalgic Eire, Michael dreams of Paris, although on occasion he has also dreamed of New York City. St. John invites Michael to come to New York for a visit, but Mick offers the usual excuses of his life: he has to help take care of his mother, he receives only two weeks' vacation from the post office, he really does not have enough money to go. The mother obligation is uppermost, however; taking care of mother is an obsession in matriarchal Ireland where many sons and daughters never marry because of excessive devotion to their mothers.

Twenty-five years previously Mick had been dating a girl, but his mother had disapproved of the possibility that this son might leave her for another woman and Mick terminated the relationship. He was since regretted that he did not marry, and for a time, when Frankie and Josephine Hogan's friendship seems to be ended because of Frankie's affair with Bee, Mick pathetically considers asking Josephine to marry him. But he has no confidence in himself, and he denigrates any aspects of his character which might attract a wife. He mentions on one occasion that, since St. John is the only one of the children who has managed to marry, he was perhaps the only member of the family with enough worthy qualities to attract a woman.

Under these pathetic circumstances, it is a poignant episode to observe Mick visit a house of prostitution. Irish society and its matriarchal character have driven Mick to this recourse. Yet, ironically, St. John later writes Mick a letter in which he reveals how his own marriage has worked out so badly and how unhappy he is. St. John exclaims that he envies Michael's happiness and urges him to remain single. St. John knows so little about his brother that he assumes Mick is happy because he has not married. Yet Mick had secretly envied St. John because of his marriage.

The verisimilitude of the picture of Josephine Hogan is likewise deeply affecting. Josephine had been active in the revolutionary cause. She recalls that her family's farmhouse was a refuge for the rebels and that many a night she stayed up and baked bread for the men. But she is now tired of "the Cause" since she sees that its time has passed and that it can now accomplish nothing. Josephine, deeply devoted to Frankie, wants love, marriage, and children; but she must wait until Frankie overcomes his main interest and wholehearted obsession—"the Cause." In helping him to flee to the United States and in later warning him that a policeman is observing his return to Ireland, Josephine risks her life for her loved one. She is friend, confidant, helpmate—but never lover or wife, the things she most desires to be for him.

With all this devotion and companionship she is completely crushed when she learns that Frankie is having an affair with Bee. So emotionally involved is she with Frankie that she never could come to love anyone else, and so deeply has she been distressed by his ingratitude and betrayal that it is doubtful if she could ever forgive him and achieve the state of marriage and child-rearing of which she has long dreamed. Even religious consolation is unavailing. After confessing her almost nonexistent sins to a priest, she is not eased mentally: "All she really knew was that she was suffering in body and mind . . . and that there was no form of words that could get anywhere near the inmost truth of her life, or near the life of anyone at all." [39] Another unhappy life reveals itself, and another spinster is created in a country overflowing with women in this category.

The last character in *Come Back to Erin* who is probed in depth is Leonard Hannafey, the priest, who is almost fifty years of age. He possesses a hard-boiled, cold, and forbidding nature and the distinctive aloofness and separateness which the priestly office often confers. Leonard, a bright, intelligent man, has no softening quality of love, kindness, or gentleness. Leonard was born in Ireland and received his theological training there. He is aware of defects in Ireland—Irish inertia, for example. But since he has lived in America, he frequently suffers nostalgia for Eire, and, for a long time, he was homesick for the old country. Leonard is particularly bitter about his stepfather because of the latter's extramarital affairs and the anguish brought to his wife. For years Leonard could not forgive his stepfather, and he wonders if he really has forgiven him yet. Ironically, forgiveness is one of the touchstones of the religion in which Leonard professes to believe.

Other contradictions are found in Leonard's character. He can urge Frankie to marry Josephine Hogan since only one of the family has married and he regards this situation as unfortunate. (Leonard does not consider St. John's union with Bee a legitimate marriage.) Yet at the same time, Leonard reveals the strong strain of puritanism found in the Irish character. Leonard relates that he really has no confidence or joy in considering the idea of marriage.

He realizes that such an attitude is a defect on his part: "It's a sin against the spirit, against life itself, and I try to crush it down—would you believe it, I rarely, very rarely, perform any marriage ceremony with the slightest sense of pleasure? . . . I sometimes feel the sin of the Manichees inside in me." [40]

Leonard, a typical Irish cleric, is more interested in the letter of the law than in the spirit of the law. He can be ruthless and overbearing, even heartless in his obsession with rules and regulations. For him, everything exists for the greater honor and glory of God; unless an issue fits into his interpretation of what is for the power and the glory, he becomes aggressive and nasty. His browbeating of Bee, for example, is both uncharitable and ill-advised. He represents a form of inquisitorial spirit where every matter is black or white and where each individual's problem is either an open or shut case.

In *Come Back to Erin* the major characters and the other figures who are probed less completely are imbued with a fundamental restlessness and sense of exile. Everyone is, first of all, an exile from his youth or from days that were happier. Everyone is exiled from that which they would like to obtain: Michael wants to live in Paris; St. John wants to live happily in Ireland; Josephine wants to get married and rear children; Frankie wants Ireland to be the way he and the other Irish Republican Army men dreamed it would be while they were involved in the Troubles. Since their aspirations are not realized, people must compromise and settle for less—each in his own way (Michael, with weary semicomplacency) and with those personal qualities (Frankie's idealism, St. John's sentimentalism) which form the basic element of the individual's character. In one of his more perceptive moments, St. John realizes that he cannot really "Come Back to Erin" since it is too late to renew the past in the same way that one remembers it. Frankie, who reads passages from Joyce's *Exiles,* feels his physical exile from Ireland after living in America for a while. But he also realizes that in his revolutionary fervor, he is also an exile from the majority of his fellow Irish in his native country.

An additional sense of exile is also present in each of the characters, whether it is openly acknowledged or not. This final exile is from God, from the Garden of Eden. St. John feels this displacement most acutely; but Frankie, Michael, and Josephine exem-

plify it, and Leonard discusses it in a direct way when he speaks
of those who attempt to live only for money or sensual pleasures.
Leonard believes that down deep the materialists and hedonists
feel a longing for God or even for mumbo-jumbo—something
mysterious, something that is present but cannot be grasped fully
or understood completely. Since in the varying degree of ways
each man is cut off from the Godhead and from fulfillment, his lot
must be frustration, loneliness, and exile. Because of the fact that
the Irish are so God-obsessed from their religious orientation and
the influence of the Church in their daily life, they are especially
prone to the results of being ostracized from the Biblical Eden.

In *Bird Alone* one of the non-Irish characters speaks of the
"prisons" which obsess the Irish and which force them to live in
sadness. According to this speaker the Irish are unaware of the
prisons they can break out of and the ones they cannot break out
of. The sense of religious exile and the pull of religious orthodoxy
are prisons from which the Irish cannot really escape. Individuals
may do so—James Joyce, Corney Crone, Frankie Hannafey—but
the people as a whole are held in the grip of religious influences,
and perhaps by character and temperament this grip upon them is
something the people accept sadly but willfully. Not that the notion of religious influence is necessarily wrong—people feel the
need of God awareness—but in Ireland it has tended to become
narrow-minded, puritanical, and distorted.

Donat O'Donnell, in discussing Frankie Hannafey's Catholicism, points out that Frankie admits that he is a bad Catholic, yet
his Catholicism is not frowned upon even by his brother, the
priest, who tends to be severe. O'Donnell quotes O'Faolain to the
effect that there are two kinds of Catholicism in Ireland: one held
by the simple people, the other by the well educated. The second
group accepts Catholicism with qualifications so as to render it a
different religion from that in which the ordinary persons believe.[41]

A final element of mystery occurs when inexplicable ironies of
life are probed. In *Bird Alone* one of the characters speaks of life's
stamping each person in a particular manner, and then each person follows his mold.[42] For a moment in *Come Back to Erin*
Frankie speaks of his determinism. Frankie thinks that, if he had
never been acquainted with rural Ireland, he would not have
joined the Irish Republican Army. This teasing quality of "the

road not taken," or of why a person took the road he took, or of the element of chance and coincidence having such an important influence in each person's life is never far away in O'Faolain's work. This quality, which reflects a brooding concern with the haphazard nature of human destiny, casts a special melancholy and perplexity over the scenes and characters. No matter how thoroughly O'Faolain penetrates into the Irish mind one comes again and again to the realization that no words "could get anywhere near the utmost truth of . . . life, or near the life of anyone at all." This is the ultimate reason for the sense of exile and loneliness which is in existence itself.

Again, as in the other novels, *Come Back to Erin* is saturated by the influence of past history and the traditional rural ways of Ireland which seem changeless. In his flight from the police Frankie spends time in his aunt's house in Kilfinnane, County Limerick. In the main room is a picture of Daniel O'Connell, large photographs of dead relatives, and on the table rests the huge family album in which ancestors and the past continue to live. The house and the little hamlet itself reflect this same rooted continuity.

In another part of rural Ireland where the Hogan people originated, Manus Hogan can quote the history of most of the families thereabouts. He has a book which tells the immigration patterns of the people and their racial characteristics. He knows, for example, that the Hannafeys were from the O hainfeain tribe, that they tend to have light-colored hair, are short in stature, and are usually energetic. He is an authority on the local traditions and folklore, while the aged Aunt Nell speaks of the Famine, of O'Connell, the cruelty of the landlords, and of the Rebellion of '98. It is difficult, as Frankie observes, to know where the memory of these old country people stops and their grandparents' memories begin. This emphasis on the past not only gives the novel solidity but also helps explain the characters more fully—the life of the farmer with all its values and deficiencies lies deep in the Irish consciousness no matter how sophisticated or urbanized many a modern Irishman has become.

Come Back to Erin is such a comprehensive "Inside Ireland" survey that it is regrettable that the book does not achieve its potential. The first part of the novel, which takes place in Ireland, is suspenseful, creates interesting people, and displays a convincing feeling for locale. The contrast of Frankie as a gunman on the run with St. John's sentimental nostalgia is sharply focused and forms a thoughtful study of two different views of life in Ireland. The second part of the novel—set in New York and Connecticut and told primarily from Frankie's point of view—and the third part—with the locale again returning to Ireland and told primarily from Josephine's point of view—tend to dissipate the novel's early suspense and energy. Too much description in these sections clogs the narrative; the material becomes uneven in both its appeal and its pertinence. The second and third units of the novel should have been cut to sharpen the focus on the central conflict. Individual scenes and episodes stand out movingly, but too much of the material appears to be mere padding to lengthen the narrative and the going becomes dry and laborious.

Further, the characters become jumbled as O'Faolain rambles and meanders about somewhat aimlessly in several sections of the book. There is a distinct feeling that often O'Faolain himself is not certain where the story or characters are going next. So much detail is incorporated and so many elements included that the central emphasis on Frankie and St. John blurs. So wandering and so scattered does the narrative become that one can only gather all the accumulated impressions by putting them together in a jigsaw-puzzle fashion. In order to analyze the novel thoroughly, the reader must record each character's name on separate sheets of paper and then enumerate every fact about each character until a total picture is complete. While this procedure is a rewarding intellectual exercise, it would not be within the time and patience of most readers.

Despite all the memorable sections which can be recalled from the three novels—the struggle over the dying Long John O'Donnell's will, Denis Hussey's quarrel with his father, the burial arrangements for Arty Tinsley, the despair over Parnell's death, the suspense as Frankie Hannafey hides in the family house while the police lurk outside, the discussion over who is to carry Aunt Nell's coffin, the arrangements with plumber Cassidy to put a sink in an Irish farmhouse, the validity of the characterizations, the perceptive descriptions of place, and the intellectual probing of Ireland's history—it should be noted that all of the novels possess some flaws. They suffer principally because O'Faolain is at heart a short-story writer rather than a novelist. He himself has admitted that he can perfect and control the smaller canvas of the short story better than the more sprawling panorama of the novel.[43]

Another reason why O'Faolain's novels—although worthy and important efforts—are not so great as they could have been involves the limitations imposed by the subject matter itself. As John V. Kelleher has astutely observed: "[O'Faolain] was not satisfied with either of the two obvious solutions to conflict in an Irish novel, frustration or the emigrant ship. . . . In other words, as a novelist he was beaten not by lack of talent—he has always had talent to spare and fling away—but by his too great demand upon a society intimate, homely, compact and too rigidly narrow." [44]

It can be said without fear of contradiction that no other Irish novelist has yet portrayed the years from the time of the Troubles to the mid-1930's with more thoroughness, accuracy, and intellectual understanding. Especially memorable is O'Faolain's repeated questioning and searching for the "meaning of it all." In O'Faolain's probing of existence we find a Greek fate concept, a Hamlet-like "more things in heaven and earth . . . than are dreamt of in your philosophy." As his sad and unhappy characters are caught in and puzzled by life's ironies, contradictions, inexplicable happenings, coincidences, and accidents of fate, the essential mystery of living is scrutinized closely but never solved. Readers are reminded of this state of man with Conradian phrases—"the sense of mystery surrounding our lives," "the loneliness of innumerable hearts," man's "uncertain fate," and life "obscured by mists."

O'Faolain once wrote that "Literature teaches nothing. It merely confirms Life, which leads, lures, pushes, drags us mindlessly into our own hopeless heartburning longings or frustrations." [45] If, as O'Faolain claims, we esteem what we recognize as true in literature,[46] then his novels must be granted much praise because of the truth and depth of his portrayals of life and because his characterizations have a validity that, while on occasion peculiar to the Irish scene, generally transcends the limits of one locale and reaches a universality which cannot only be recognized in the mind but also cherished in the heart. Furthermore, one respects O'Faolain's reverence for life and his avoidance of facile answers.

CHAPTER 3

Developments in O'Faolain's Fiction

I *Literary Viewpoints*

TO understand and evaluate O'Faolain's short stories and novels accurately, it is advantageous to know his critical attitudes about literature. In his comments about fiction, O'Faolain finds fault with Naturalism, escapism, and Romanticism in the modern novel because he believes that writers under the influence of such attitudes do not present life as it really is. They reject contemporary existence by lamenting the passing of bygone times, or by examining a limited and narrow aspect of life and restricting themselves to negativism.[1] Indeed, O'Faolain insists that most of the weaknesses which characterize the modern novel come from Naturalism. The traditional novel from Henry Fielding to the latter half of the nineteenth century acknowledged the zest and wonder of life. Naturalistic writers eliminate this element of wonder; they oversimplify life and, therefore, furnish a picture of existence that does not square with life itself.

In discussing the proletarian novel, however, O'Faolain notes that the Communist writer contributes an important aspect to any consideration of modern fiction since any novelist of importance must exhibit moral feeling and that at the present time (he is speaking of the 1930's) this moral feeling can be legitimately aroused only by the consideration of subject matter which is of importance to the community. But the genuine novelist must part company with the Communist writer when the latter fails to move beyond the revelation of social truths.[2] The Communist writer ignores the sense of awe found in life as well as the inexplicable and the impenetrable. The really great writers, O'Faolain maintains, present "a greater sense of the poetry of life, an acknowledgment that life is a thin ice where one goes with tiptoe, and one's heart as one goes an impalpable, undefinable, uncontrollable, vain and unstable show." [3]

O'Faolain asserts that a good novelist must be a Realist. An effective author must work with concrete materials since fiction must force the reader to "see" the scene presented. O'Faolain argues that George Meredith's novels are defective because they "starve" the sight. Really successful fiction must stress the visual. Some vivid passages appear in Meredith's works, but O'Faolain rightly questions if a reader can really "see" Diana's Crossways, or Renée de Croisnel?[4]

O'Faolain is especially concerned about Anglo-Irish fiction; he believes that the Irish novelist by his nature possesses a strong pull toward the lures of the imagination. He admits that his own stories have their origins in the Russian tradition[5] and are especially influenced by Chekhov and Turgenev.[6] He maintains that modern Irish prose writers are most allied to the Russians;[7] and, of all the Russian writers, Chekhov has the most appeal.[8] Chekhov mingles several qualities that Irish writers find particularly desirable: poetry, realism, mood, brutality, tenderness, and atmosphere.[9]

The Irish people in general, O'Faolain believes, possess a basic lackadaisicalness and likeableness which makes them entertaining, quaint, and picturesque. It is the duty of Irish writers to convey these characteristics which, to some degree, are admirable. Yet, while Irish writers may esteem such qualities and like the people, these same writers must also censure the people for their lack of progress, for their tendencies toward undisciplined routine, and for their habit of deemphasizing intelligence. Instead of intelligence, the Irish stress the imagination. The Irish novelist must, therefore, combine a love of the people with an awareness of their follies. He must make judgments on his characters the way Chekhov did, although not judgment in the sense of didactic preachments.

In his own novels O'Faolain has attempted to follow the critical viewpoints he stresses. However, he did not succeed in writing a perfectly satisfying novel, primarily because his talents, while able to handle short episodes effectively, faltered in dealing with the long, consistently sustained narrative requirements demanded by the novel. In one of his essays O'Faolain remarked that the short-story writer is a sprinter while the novelist is a long-distance runner.[10] Although he could theorize intelligently and convincingly about the characteristics of a successful novel, his own aptitude

was for the short story. O'Faolain found that he was by talent and
training a sprinter.

Most of O'Faolain's critical comments about writing are concerned with the short story.[11] He asserts that a plot is the least
important part of a short story, but he also admits that the absence of a plot does not mean that a story will be effective; some
sort of plot is present even if it might be called a plot of character.[12] In discussing the matter of plot, O'Faolain notes that such
ideas as invention, suspense, surprise, contrivance, action, and climax are usually associated with plot; and then he asks if modern
short-story writers have eliminated these elements:

By what do they replace surprise, invention, fancy, climax, contrivance,
suspense, narrative, action, adventure, and so forth? Or . . . 'What
comes instead of plot?' I think the truth is that the short-story has not
dispensed with any of these things. I think that if we read a dozen
stories by acknowledged masters of the short-story we will find them
all there: but that *their nature has been completely changed.* There is
adventure, but it is now an adventure of the mind. There is suspense,
but it is less a nervous suspense than an emotional or even intellectual
suspense. There is surprise, and plenty of it; but it is no longer the surprise of the man who opens a door and finds that a corpse falls out, but
the surprise of a man who opens a cupboard and finds that a skeleton
falls out. There is climax, but it is not the climax of the woman who
discovers her lost jewels in the hat-box but the climax of the woman
who discovers her lost happiness in a memory. There is contrivance
but it is not the contrivance of the gangster who deceives his enemy,
but of the citizen who deceives his friend. A great stock-scene in the
old-fashioned stories of adventure is when the hero unmasks the villain.
It has become a stock-scene in the modern short-story when the author
unmasks the hero: or it is one of the commonest themes of Tchekov
when the hero unmasks himself.[13]

O'Faolain believes that Chekhov's "Gooseberries" is the finest
short story ever written:[14] "So much irony: so much humour: so
kind and understanding: and wrapped up in the most delicate
poetic mood." [15] O'Faolain delights in acknowledging the power
of Chekhov's stories and in praising their artistry, but he admits
that younger readers today do not find Chekhov appealing since
they seem to prefer more flashy sky-rocket effects. O'Faolain does
not maintain that Chekhov's writing is flawless or that the short
story as a form "has come to absolute perfection in his hands. . . .
I would not even agree that what perfection he has achieved is

the only kind of perfection; or deny that others have not written on other lines as finely as he did on his. His countryman, Gogol, for example; or Maupassant; or Robert Louis Stevenson." [16] It is, nevertheless, important that a good story should not be merely plot or a story "whose comment is too heavily scored in black-and-white for the reader who has become too tired to look beneath the surface of life for himself." [17]

In the best modern short stories the writer does not directly relate information; he implies his most important insights and ideas.[18] Data is to be conveyed "in the most indirect manner possible." [19] On this point O'Faolain cites a comment once made by Chekhov while finding fault with the work of a friend who described the moonlight in a long poetic passage. "Not that way," Chekhov remarked. "If you want to describe the moon just mention that the old broken bottle on the side of the mill-dam was glinting in the moonlight." [20] The mere telling of information is an unsophisticated and ponderous method. Such a technique does not, O'Faolain argues, "tickle our imagination, hold our attention so firmly as when we get a subtle hint. Above all, telling never dilates the mind with suggestion so much as implication does." [21] The use of realistic detail is closely allied with the "general revelation by suggestion;" [22] realistic detail is not used just to give verisimilitude. Everything in the story is directed to the implication; therefore, in reading good short stories one must always read between the lines. Further, O'Faolain declares that the purpose of the writer is to pose questions, not answer them.[23]

Another feature of the good modern short story is the convention that the narrative may begin without an elaborate preamble, a long leading up to the introduction of the subject. A modern writer plunges right into his story with direction; he moves immediately into the heart of the matter. Compression is essential, and O'Faolain maintains that "Tchekov's advice to young writers is so much to the point:—'You can always cut the beginning.' (And to that one might very well add, that one can also cut some of the middle. And it is generally no harm to cut some of the end as well.)" [24] In such cutting, relevance of detail is a vital consideration.

In regard to style, O'Faolain favors the technique of uniting suggestion and compression. He uses the words "engrossed" and "alert" in reference to good style. The beginning of the narrative

must at once establish the mood of the story and then the writer
works carefully word by word, sentence by sentence, toward the
total effect—the innermost illumination which is really the story
which lies behind the story.[25] In this connection O'Faolain observes that, by its compressed and suggestive nature, the short
story "cannot really develop character: it generally reveals it by
some incident which peels off the purely social mask or outer
skin." [26] Again, any story by Chekhov would illustrate this ac-
complishment, but "what the [protagonist in a short story] was in
the beginning he is at the end, and even if he has seen into himself
one may be sure that he will revert to his chosen role very quickly
—at most with some added understanding or sensibility as to
what he or Life is. Time is the Tyrant in the short-story; it is so
precious that every word makes every second of it count." [27]

The writer of the short story should be detached and objective.[28] He should not become an advocate for his characters. Cen-
suring a short story submitted to *The Bell* by a beginning writer,
O'Faolain asserts: "the weakness of the story . . . is that the author has sold himself to his characters. You must never do that.
Keep apart from your characters, and however fond of them you
are, preserve some sense of irony." [29]

Finally, he maintains that a *je ne sais quoi* element is involved
in the composition of a good short story. This quality involves an
intuitive or psychic process which is present apart from the rational or conscious process of writing. O'Faolain asserts that intuition plays the most important part in artistic creation. From his
own experience he finds that he frequently cannot recall how elements and aspects of his stories came about. When he looks back
over a story, he is amazed at much of the material. He often cannot remember the origin or the manner of creation of many of his
narratives.[30] He insists that there is much about the accomplished
short story that is indefinable,[31] and that all great art in general is
based more on genius or mystery than on skill.[32]

II   *A Broken World*

In surveying O'Faolain's career, one observes that his theories
about writing became more crystalized in his fiction about the
time of his second collection of short stories, *A Purse of Coppers*
(1937), which deals with the Ireland of the late 1920's and early
1930's. The years of "the Troubles" and Civil War have ended,

and the period under consideration in this volume is, in contrast to the turmoil described in *Midsummer Night Madness,* a quiet, almost sleepy era in which Eire is recuperating, taking stock of itself, and facing economic and governmental decisions.

"A Broken World," the initial study in the *Coppers* collection, could serve as an epitome title for the whole post-1924 era. Only three characters appear in "A Broken World," and they are seated on a train traveling through the lonely countryside during a snowstorm: a priest, a farmer, and the narrator whose occupation is unstated but who obviously represents the intellectual class.

The priest, no longer young, recalls his first clerical assignment in a remote parish in County Wicklow. The people in his mountainous area were very poor, and the land they farmed was not particularly fertile. The poor farmers in Father X's parish were struggling to exist on unsuitable land, while productive valley ground nearby was abandoned but still owned by absentee landlords in England. In addition, many of the farmers in the mountainous area were either emigrating or leaving to work in the cities.

The world of the Irish countryside lacks a moral unity. It is a world of the prosperous on one side and the very poor on the other side. The narrator reflects that, since the majority of the aristocrats have left, why could not the poor now make a unified successful world for themselves. The priest answers negatively that no solution presents itself, and he nods slyly, indicating the farmer seated nearby. Shortly thereafter, at the next station, the clergyman leaves the train. After the priest departs, the narrator questions the farmer. He is told that the priest has been silenced for his political activity. This political activity consisted of attempting to have the poor farmers obtain and use the good land deserted by the English aristocrats. The priest attempted to start a farmers' league to help improve knowledge and techniques of cooperative farming and to help in distributing and marketing the produce of the land.

Oddly enough the farmers—as the priest had silently indicated —are the principal obstacle to this sort of highly desirable improvement. The farmers have been conditioned by frustration and past history; they are indifferent, unprogressive, somewhat lazy. The very opportunity for rural improvement is being thwarted by that group which stands to derive the most benefit from amelioration. The welfare of Eire itself also suffers from such a reactionary attitude. The farmer on the train will not even defend his conservatism before the mounting anger of the narrator. The old countryman is soon asleep; his lot and his condition have made him "no more human than a rock."

The narrator is left to reflect on the alienation among the various groups in Ireland—the clerical, the agricultural, and the intelligentsia. The Irish Free State of the years from 1924 on into the 1930's is a "broken world"—a world of considerable poverty, of the indifference and cloddishness of the old farmers, of emigration to the cities or to foreign countries, of the Big Houses of the gentry in decay—their land, for the most part, unproductive and useless. This is a time when even kindly, progressive, and well-intentioned clergymen, who seek the improvement of the people's lot, meet resentment and opposition—not only from their clerical superiors but from the very people whom they seek to benefit.

The Ireland of this period is "broken," confused, disorganized. Ireland is caught symbolically in a snowstorm of blindness, of depression, of obfuscation. The country is still living, but it is in a comatose state and badly battered: "under that white shroud, covering the whole of Ireland, life was lying broken and hardly breathing." [33] Nevertheless, as O'Faolain was to point out elsewhere, the country "is not dead but sleeping." [34] O'Faolain, the intellectual, still has hopes for Ireland's recovery; but the forces aligned against such improvement are presently covering the land like snow; and the implications of "A Broken World" are that this snow will hang over and oppress the land for a long time to come.

In relatively few pages, "A Broken World" capsules expertly and thoroughly the Irish scene at the time O'Faolain was writing this narrative. The tempo is quiet, dreamy, trance-like, and this makes the contrast with the excitement and enthusiasm of the time of "the Troubles" even more startling. The exuberant style of *Midsummer Night Madness* has been toned down to a low key perfectly evocative of a barren, depressing, and unheroic period of Irish history when the harsh realities of a bleak time had stunted the colors of a former, seemingly resplendent dawn.

"The Old Master," the second story in *A Purse of Coppers*, attacks—although in a tranquilly ironic fashion—the Irish obsession with sexual impropriety. Irish puritanism, derived in part from the French concept of Jansenism,[35] is so rampant that an unofficial

Anti-Sex League has been established and prevents a mature viewpoint on sexual matters on the part of many influential elements in the country.

"The Old Master" commences with the visit of a touring Russian ballet company to Cork. The protagonist of the story, a non-practicing lawyer named John O'Sullivan, is in charge of a small law library which is rarely used. Consequently, O'Sullivan's position amounts to a political sinecure, and he has time to read and develop himself as an enthusiastic exponent of culture. He extolls the old days of complete British control when the Lord Chief Justice entered the local courthouse with much pomp and ceremony. Now in the days of the Free State his esthetic sense is offended because plainness and dullness have replaced the previous pageantry. O'Sullivan also vociferously stresses that his cultural qualities are a throwback to the old days of color; in his own words, he is "an old master, lying forgotten" in the present "deserted mansion" that is Ireland.[36]

In the light of his continually self-proclaimed advocacy of beauty, art, and culture, O'Sullivan is delighted when the Russian ballet troupe comes to Cork city. But, when he goes to the theater, he encounters two men outside the building. One of the two holds a notebook in his hand, and he writes down O'Sullivan's name. O'Sullivan is informed that if he enters the theater, his name will not be removed from the writing tablet. When the librarian inquires about the purpose of this name taking, he is told that the ballet is considered indecent and attendance at its performance is being discouraged.

O'Sullivan leaves the front of the theater, quietly walks to the rear of the building, and unobtrusively enters the stage door. He presents himself to several members of the ballet company and apologizes for the conduct of his fellow countrymen. After O'Sullivan has promised the troupe that he will take legal action to prevent the continued harassment of the artists, he returns to the front of the playhouse, where a huge crowd has now gathered. Encountering the priest who brought about the demonstration, O'Sullivan protests very weakly and feebly against the gathering. Soon, however, he is swept into the now hymn-singing group of protesters who begin to parade through the city. O'Sullivan desires to stand out and denounce the group, but his job has to be renewed every year by the local council, and if he opposes the priest on this present issue, he almost certainly will not be rehired. As the procession parades by the theater, the ballet performers see O'Sullivan and wave to him, but he cannot acknowledge their pleas.

When the procession arrives at a public square, it is decided to hold a protest meeting, and the priest expects O'Sullivan, as a respected and educated Cork figure, to give a speech. To avoid this request, O'Sullivan flees to a nearby public lavatory. For a long time O'Sullivan takes refuge there; later he leaves the building and sneaks quietly home. He rationalizes his position and notes that he did at least make a gesture—feeble though it was—of protest; in a very tiny way he had defended beauty and culture and art against the philistines. To boost his self-esteem he exaggeratedly thinks of himself as "the only man left in Ireland with a sense of beauty . . . the old master deserted in the abandoned house." [37]

Free State Ireland is not only a "broken world," it is also a world without beauty, a world oppressed not only socially and economically but also oppressed artistically—books are censored, ballets and movies are condemned, and artists in general suffer. O'Sullivan's long wait in the lavatory brings on pneumonia, and within two weeks he is dead. The lengthy tarrying in the lavatory and the resulting death are obvious symbols of the condition of art, artists, and the cultural minded in Ireland.

Free State Ireland of this period is driving artists and their supporters to actual death or to spiritual death (exile or the fear of expressing their feelings for art and beauty). Ireland is driving out the Sean O'Casey types, and the glorious period of the Irish Renaissance around the turn of the century is, by comparison with the present time, the era of the "old masters." The present finds Ireland a land deserted by its artists because of repressive governmental measures such as a rigorist censorship and the dominance of puritanical clerical interests. Even the period of the British control was superior to this condition because there was at least pageantry and an appreciation for beauty; and, since the Church was not then so powerful, a climate could develop in which Lady Gregory, Synge, Yeats, and others could flourish. In this sense the Free State is not the improvement it should be. The people are now quite willing to sacrifice their artists with relatively little thought or concern. Conformity with the State and the Church means relative security both economically and socially, and few of the Irish are now willing to give up such security to support artistic endeavors.

The central theme of "Discord," another of the superior stories in *A Purse of Coppers*, is built around a young married couple who are honeymooning in Dublin. The newly wed pair visit the room of a priest friend who calls their attention to the historical associations of this particular place. In this room James Clarence Mangan wrote many of his poems, while John Mitchel and the writers of the *Nation* gathered and attended meetings here. Nearby in this area of Dublin, Wolfe Tone had been born, and Robert Emmet was also associated with this part of the city.

Father Peter, the host, invites his friends to see the crypt underneath the church. As they enter the church, they see an unkempt man praying ostentatiously; Father Peter explains that he is an ex-soldier who is not mentally sound. Down in the depths of the crypt the priest and his guests observe the large number of coffins of dead parishioners. One of the coffins contains the remains of Leonard McNally who pretended to be a friend of Emmet. But after McNally's death, it was revealed that MacNally had actually participated in betraying Emmet.

After their visit to the gloomy and decaying charnel house, the young couple eventually part company with the priest, hurry to their hotel, and make love to each other with great intensity—their reaction to the "putrefaction" which they have witnessed. Shades of the past are all about, for eighteenth- and nineteenth-century Dublin still has a grip on the people. Associations with political issues and with the struggle for freedom from British control are ubiquitous and pervasive but, at the same time, deadening. Ireland is engulfed by and, to some degree, paralyzed by its past. In contrast to such worn-out and now useless political and rebel manifestations, there is at least the sensual glow and delight of romantic love.

It is not until the young couple completely close the windows and window blinds in their hotel room that they are at ease, free from both political and religious pressures of Ireland's past and present. The desire to venerate the metaphorical and literal coffins of political endeavor, religious narrowness, and puritanism conflicts with a newer and more liberal spirit where love reigns untrammeled and unstifled by sentimentalism and unquestioned conventions.[38] Ireland can never mend its "broken world" unless a new spirit of genuine freedom, love, and enlightened thinking sweeps away the dead thoughts of the past which are too much with the people. The present is the all-important time, but Ireland clings to the old and outworn.

Pat Lenihan, the title character of "A Born Genius," is a gifted individual, and yet he is never able to reach fulfillment. Everything he turns his hand to seems to end badly; he is thwarted in part by a lack of perseverance and an inability to deal with life's imperfections. His greatest potential rests in the fact that he possesses a marvelous tenor voice. He appears in amateur theatrical productions as the male singing lead opposite an accomplished girl named Trixie Flynn, but he needs further study and training under a professional teacher. The opportunity for singing lessons occurs when Lenihan's father (who deserted his family and emigrated to America twelve years previously) asks his son to come to New York City to take lessons for which he will pay. Pat Lenihan, who gladly accepts this offer, envisions the day when he can return to Ireland with his father, who will then presumably be reconciled to his mother.

When Lenihan arrives in New York, he studies singing and progresses well in his musical training. But Pat learns that his father has married again and has apparently not told his second wife that his first wife is still living. Pat's disillusionment with his father's treatment of his mother causes him to give up his training and to return to Ireland; his last chance for success in a singing career is, therefore, cast aside because of religious intolerance, and a refusal to adjust to life's tragedies, disappointments, and imperfections. Like many of his race the world over, Pat remains hurt by life and by its cruelties the rest of his days.

"A Born Genius" loses much of its focus as a story, however, simply because of O'Faolain's attempts to cover too much territory. The story tends to digress and wander about; its loose threads are not pulled together compactly. O'Faolain allows Pat Lenihan to take up contact with Trixie Flynn. In contrast to Pat's abortive ambitions, Trixie has had a successful singing career. She has given concerts at Paris and Milan and been well received. Eventually, she returns to Cork city and becomes Mrs. John Delaney, the wife of a building contractor. Lenihan agrees to sing with Trixie at a Cork charity concert.

Delaney, Trixie's husband, builds mainly for religious institutions, and at the present time he is bidding for the opportunity to get the building contract for a new cathedral. When Lenihan makes several social visits to the Delaney home, he arouses the suspicions of Father Shanahan, who is the bishop's secretary. A close, social friendship develops between Lenihan and Trixie, who is disillusioned with her crass, materialistic husband. At the charity concert, which the bishop and Father Shanahan both attend, Lenihan and Trixie sing their love duets with such passion that the two puritanical clergymen are scandalized, and, as a result, Trixie's husband does not obtain the building contract.

Given a more positive, more realistic nature, Lenihan could have married Trixie long before she met Delaney; now he has lost not only success in his career but also his one opportunity for a meaningful romantic relationship. The "born genius" comes to heartbreak as well as disillusionment; he will spend the rest of his empty life as an inept clerk in a vinegar factory. The work in the vinegar factory symbolizes the vinegar and gall characteristic of Lenihan's existence.

The born genius is essentially Ireland, "a broken world" in discord; it is out of tune. Possessing considerable potential, it has not (like Lenihan) succeeded in fulfilling its potentialities. A refusal to compromise, a basic inertia, and lack of perseverence, a stress on unrealistic ideals, and an unwillingness to forgive have scarred Irish history. So much greatness was blighted or realized only in part (the lives of Emmet or Tone, for example) because of conditions in Ireland. A refusal to forgive any sort of transgression is part and parcel of this environment. Pat Lenihan's disillusionment with, and harsh treatment of, his father when he learns of the father's second marriage may be equated with Ireland's reaction to Parnell's involvement with Kitty O'Shea. The traditional Irish puritanism is also indicated in Father Shanahan's and the bishop's reaction to the friendship between Lenihan and Trixie.

Other traditional characteristics of Ireland are also seen. Pat's brother, Flyer, spends most of his time "boozing in the pub," while Pat's mother spends much time in the chapel with her confraternity. On one hand (as is remarked in "Discord"), Ireland is "girt around by pubs"; on the other, it is "girt around by prayer." Both of these qualities have been carried to extremes in Ireland, and, as a result, they have unnecessarily restricted and hampered the people and prevented maturity and development of potential resources. The Irish are too often either drunk with religion or else drunk with liquor.

While in structure and content "A Born Genius" is too rambling and its impact is scattered, in theme the story presents a vivid panorama of Ireland by contrasting the potential of a people with their frustration—thwarted by defects which could be controlled and corrected.

The remaining stories in *A Purse of Coppers* possess less implication and depth. Constructed on a smaller scale, they are vignettes and cameos of the Irish scene. For example, "A Meeting" contrasts the activity and excitement of the rebel days with the present dullness of life in a small Irish community. "My Son Austin" paints a portrait of Dinny Fagan who has always idolized his son Austin and supported him in every manner; eventually Austin Fagan deserts his needy and aged father and emigrates to America. "Kitty the Wren" presents the life of Kitty Canavan, who lives in a lonely glen ostracized by the nearby puritanical villagers because she bore an illegitimate child.

In "Sullivan's Trousers," one of O'Faolain's few attempts at rowdy, robust satire, Roger Sullivan is a pig salesman who is opposed to the new economic policies of the Free State government. New government regulations call for self-sufficiency, with an emphasis on rural living, essential products and no luxuries, and very little exporting of goods. Roger Sullivan feels that this is a return to the primitive past, and in wild protest tears his clothes off and goes about naked until he is prevailed upon to at least wear kilts. His reasoning is that the forefathers of the country wore little or no clothes at all, so if the present government scheme is to be logical it should also adopt a trouser-less mode of living. "Sinners" relates an amusing conflict between a young domestic who tends to be a chronic prevaricator and an aged, crotchety priest who attempts to hear her confession. In this tale an effective contrast is drawn between the ill-tempered pastor and his young, patient and understanding curate. The tendency of time to dull idealism is stressed.

The differences between *A Purse of Coppers* and *Midsummer Night Madness* are striking. Objecting to the Romantic style, the passion, fire, and subjectivity characteristic of his first collection of short stories, O'Faolain has deliberately subdued the tone and style of the stories in *A Purse of Coppers*.[39] Purple patches are avoided, description for its own sake is not used, and objective detachment is sought. O'Faolain is now attempting to follow the theories of Chekhov, and in some of these stories—notably in "A Broken World," "Discord," and "Sinners"—he succeeds in achieving his goal.

In most of the other stories, defects of one kind or another can be seen. Verbosity and an attempt to cover too much material weaken stories like "A Born Genius" and "There's a Birdie in the Cage"; improbability and authorial manipulation mar stories like "Kitty the Wren" and "Egotists"; a lack of subtlety exists in "My Son Austin" and "Sullivan's Trousers," while a story like "Confessional" is a mere anecdote. In most of these stories O'Faolain has still not reached the ideal of Chekhovian irony, and he also tends to state too much of his material baldly rather than to suggest and imply.

The subdued tone which is evident throughout the collection is particularly apropos for the unheroic period being described. A deadness, a dullness, a snowy paralysis has descended over Ireland, and the period of a "terrible beauty" has moved into a period where the world is broken and in discord. Brokenness and discordance had not been absent from the time of "the Troubles," but at least this period had made men's hearts pulse vigorously both in hopes and fears. After this time of passion, fervor, and excitement, Ireland now is in a deadening period when the artists are oppressed, beauty and culture disregarded, and frustration and repression have become the dominant characteristics. The power of the Church and the Free State government is being used to reinforce these particular aspects of everyday life. A narrow-minded puritanical outlook is in the ascendency, and a desirable spirit of freedom, enthusiasm, and zest has vanished. The remaining rebels are isolated and disillusioned, and exile in various forms either beckons or is an accomplished fact.

Although most of the individual stories in this collection are not without some artistic flaws, the stories, as a whole, expertly carry out the overall motif of the volume. Again, as in *Midsummer Night Madness and Other Stories* (with the appropriate differences enumerated), one book epitomizes a particular period of Irish history with a profound awareness of character and environment.

III   *The Man Who Invented Sin and Other Stories*

O'Faolain's third collection of short stories was published in America under the title of *The Man Who Invented Sin and Other Stories*; but the European edition, minus two stories, was called *Teresa and Other Stories*.[40] The title story in the American edition ranks as one of O'Faolain's best literary productions. The scene is rural Ireland in 1920 during the period (from about 1915–1920) when students and young priests, nuns, and brothers used to summer in the country in order to study and become proficient in Gaelic. The narrator boarded in a house with two monks, Brother Virgilius and Brother Majellan, and two nuns, Sister Chrysostom and Sister Magdalen. Ordinarily, the nuns and brothers stayed at separate hotels, but these lodging places were so overcrowded that some nuns and brothers were assigned to stay overnight at nearby farmers' houses. The religious had their main meals at their hostels and studied throughout the day. At night, however there was free time—for more study, for conversation, for relaxation. As the summer progressed the group became more friendly, used nicknames for one another, and even played an occasional game of pitch-and-toss. They also gathered around the piano and sang songs.

On the night before the end of summer school, the four religious joined a large boating party, and singing rang out for several hours. When they were returning to shore about midnight, the large boat became stuck about twelve feet from land. There on shore they saw the local curate whom they called Lispeen, the Gaelic name for frog. Lispeen complained about how they were keeping the whole town awake with their singing. The two nuns and two brothers hid in the crowd on the boat so that Lispeen did not know they were on board. He proposed, however, not to let the boat land until he had written down the names of everyone on it.

The boat was rowed back to the center of the lake and a conference held. The problem was to try to prevent the four religious from being observed. When the two brothers took off their collars and black hats, they could pass as ordinary laymen. With the nuns, however, the matter was more difficult. They had to pin up their skirts, remove their cowls and gimps, and place kerchiefs around their heads. The boat now headed for the shore. When it arrived, the men ringed Lispeen and started to argue violently while the women, the nuns, and the brothers ran. Soon everyone dashed off into the darkness, and the tricked Lispeen was alone. Nevertheless, he had discovered evidence of irregularity—a nun's gimp on the ground. Lispeen would have caused considerable trouble for the nuns had he not been forced to travel three and a half miles to answer a sick call. The call was a hoax. In his absence the narrator climbed into Lispeen's room and retrieved the missing gimp.

The narrator saw Brother Majellan twenty-three years later in a large city in Ireland. When the old summer outing was recalled, Majellan was quick to point out that he did not approve of young folks spending summers in that particular manner. He now felt that the carefree attitudes of that summer were improper and wrong. The narrator also encountered Lispeen later the same day, and they recalled the events of that summer so many years ago. Lispeen remembered the situation with amusement; he admitted that the religious involved were "only children. Such innocents!" But he insisted that he "*had* to frighten them!" As the conversation ended and as Lispeen moved off down the street, the narrator noticed that Lispeen's "elongated shadow waved behind him like a tail."

In this story Lispeen is linked with the Devil, the principle of evil, the Serpent in the Garden of Eden: "The Serpent had come into the garden with the most wily of temptations. He had said, 'How dare you eat this apple?' And straightaway they began to eat it." [41] The tragedy here is that no distinction is made between innocence and evil. Innocuous pleasures and enjoyments are frowned upon as evil and these innocent activities are often the cause of guilt feelings and the beginning of puritanical notions.

While this situation applies in particular to Ireland, where puritanism has been such a dominant streak in recent times and where such harmless pleasures as dancing and a free mingling between the sexes have been accounted evil in themselves, the story has a general validity for all times and places. Instilling false notions of evil, sin, or prejudice into the innocent young warps them and leaves them with erroneous views and beliefs. A basic element of joy and of fundamental goodness is constantly threatened and scarred by the purveyors of evil—especially by the purveyors of fancied evil. Enough genuine evil exists in the world without adding guilt complexes and without denouncing as evil intrinsically innocent and harmless joys and activities.

The story builds into a sharp contrast between a quasi-Garden of Eden state where goodness and innocence reign and a later contaminated, negative, and rigidly conservative viewpoint caused by the machinations of the Serpent. In this later development even innocence is beheld with a jaundiced eye. In fact, certain influential individuals are looking for imaginary motes in the eye. These individuals, symbolically of the Serpent's following, are eager to blacken goodness and innocence and to drag them down to an alleged dirty level. The universal implications of this story are noteworthy in their indictment of rash judgment (considering only appearances), character assassination, and movements like McCarthyism.

The irony of the story is particularly biting when Lispeen who, after causing harm and instilling evil interpretations, can laugh about his conduct and be completely unconcerned about the folly and false concepts he has helped to propagate. To his victims, however, *joie de vivre* is magnified into complexes which will help these same nuns and brothers propagate puritanical attitudes in the school children and parishioners who will be under their charge. Thus are false notions of evil spread to do their harm in future generations, not only in Ireland but in other countries.

"The Man Who Invented Sin" is felt intensely. In his autobiography O'Faolain indicates that this story came out of the period of youthful enthusiasm for Gaelic study, a period when English names were being changed to Gaelic.[42] The visualization of the characters and setting is recaptured with fidelity to the vigor of the period, indicating a belief in an older period of time when innocence and a Garden of Eden grandeur prevailed. In the study of the ancient Irish language we can detect a longing for a more natural, innocent existence when both the people and the countryside were uncorrupted. At such a period one could, without blame, climb a mountain "to bathe naked in some tiny loch." Now, however, attempts to recapture such elements of the past are tainted by overzealous searchers for evil who impose puritanism on a former world of natural goodness. In one form or another evil triumphs, but the supreme Devil of all—sweeping over Ireland especially—is the tyranny of evil, persuading that even good is evil.

The story "Teresa" has as its central character a young novice of that name who is taking a trip from Dublin to the French shrine of St. Theresa at Lisieux in order to discover if she has a genuine vocation for the religious life. The young girl is accompanied by Sister Patrick, an older nun. They visit the convent at Lisieux where Sister Patrick's aunt is stationed. When Teresa observes the discipline and austerity of the Carmelite sisters, she announces that she cannot really be a nun because the life would be too difficult for her. She believed that, if she were a nun, it would be easier to become a saint but now she feels that attempting sainthood would be too arduous.

The two sisters leave Lisieux and visit Saint-Malo. At Saint-Malo Teresa suddenly begins to abstain from food and to engage in very strict religious practices. She claims to be doing penance for the sins of the world. She wants to join the Carmelites as she finds the religious order in which she is now enrolled too worldly and too undisciplined. When they eventually return to their home convent in Dublin, the novice Teresa stealthily leaves the building early the next morning. But Teresa did not carry out her intention of joining the very strict and cloistered Carmelite order. When we next hear of her, she is happily married, and she and her husband make a brief visit to her old convent in Dublin. After Teresa and her husband leave the convent, she tells him that he "will never know what [she] gave up to marry" him.

Teresa is used as a symbol of those who wish perfection in the world but who do not have the discipline or single-minded dedication to reach close to spiritual perfection. Teresa is repelled by the order she joins; it is too easy. Its representative is Sister Patrick, a frivolous, finicky, superficial nun who eats too much and who is imperfect in many ways although she is a member of a calling that demands strict control and the highest perfection. Teresa cannot have halfway measures; she is not content to become another Sister Patrick. On the other hand, she feels that she cannot reach the heights demanded by the cloistered Carmelite order. If she cannot be a saint, she at least will not be a mediocre nun.

When she informs her husband that she has given up so much to marry him, she means that she has given up the desire for perfection, for sainthood. She has felt its fascination. In her visit to the Carmelite convent and in her subsequent rigorous religious

practices at Saint-Malo, she came under its spell, but this challenge is beyond her. She can, of course, remain in the easier order
and become another Patrick, but she refuses to do so. She refuses
to settle for the second-rate. By implication O'Faolain agrees she
has made the correct decision. How many nuns—and priests for
that matter—are truly worthy of their occupation? They are
called to a state of highest religious perfection; yet they are on
occasion unjust, unkind, cruel, mean, petty, and intensely worldly:
qualities which by the very nature of their position they should
earnestly try to avoid. Teresa is more worthwhile as a happily
married person (even though she is tinged with some sorrow
because she has seen the glow of sainthood and realized that she
has not the resources to aspire to this ideal state) than she would
have been as an ordinary, uninspiring nun.

"The Silence of the Valley," one of the most remarkable stories
in *The Man Who Invented Sin,* is set in a lonely but scenic section
of Ireland (about forty miles from Cork) that some tourists are
visiting.[43] As the tourists have a drink at the bar of the small local
hotel, they hear that the cobbler, an honored and useful man, is
near death. His occupation, his old-style tools and methods of
working, and the fact that he was a great storyteller and gossip all
added to his popularity. The cobbler soon passes into death and is
buried in the churchyard nearby. Since he was considered a
throwback to the old days of rural Ireland, another bit of the old
Ireland departs with his burial.

The area where the cobbler lived and died was bucolic and
tranquil: "Everything was still—the sparkling lake, the towering
mountains, the flawless sky. 'It is as still . . . as the world before
life began.'"[44] But the visitors want to impose logic, sound organization, and modern ways. They want a regular meal schedule
announced in the local inn; they want special dinners served and
advertised to attract crowds from Cork and the surrounding vicin-
ity. Some of the visitors envision a thriving modern, industrial Ireland with the latest comforts of an up-to-date civilization. They no
longer want "backwardness and inefficiency," the ways of the old
cobbler, the quaint and picturesque and beauty of old rural,
scenic, and pastoral Ireland. The cobbler's death represents,
therefore, another step in this transition. The valley's silence will
eventually be stilled by the roar of modern cars and the hum of
new industry. The predominant symbol in the story is autumn,

although the time is May. A visiting American soldier explains to an Irish priest that in America autumn is called "fall," and several of the figures in the story quietly acknowledge the appropriateness of the word "fall" for the present scene and place.

As Robert H. Hopkins points out in an analysis of this story, "The Silence of the Valley" reflects a struggle between primitivism and the old ways as opposed to the demands of progress, urbanization, and technology.[45] The old folk-world and pastoral life in the Western world are slowly vanishing; bucolic existence must yield to the requirements and techniques of modern civilization. The emphasis on the death and funeral of the cobbler, Hopkins notes, stresses the passing of the old Gaelic world since the cobbler was a shanachie, the traditional storyteller found in Celtic culture.[46] The beauty and silence of the old life yields to modernity, and, consequently, man loses his state of paradise, his Garden of Eden. In exchange for the gains of civilization and progress, man suffers the loss of primal joys, peace, and harmony.

A clear recognition exists on O'Faolain's part for the need of unity between the old ways and the new. A balance which would retain some of the best features of the traditional rural beauty with some of the most advanced features of modern civilization is desirable. Yet while an amalgam of some of the finest features of both worlds would be beneficial, the stress on autumn indicates that it is too late to attain such a condition of equilibrium. The old ways must fall. The sadness which this inevitability brings about is juxtaposed with realistic awareness that, no matter how desirable, one simply cannot have the best of two different worlds.

"Up the Bare Stairs" uses as its motto two lines from one of Yeats' poems: "A pity beyond all telling/ Is hid in the heart of love." [47] The narrator strikes up an acquaintance with a train passenger on the way to Cork. The gentleman, aged about sixty, who is now returning to Cork, is Francis Nugent. He has just received the title of baronet in the British Honors List. As the conversation continues, Nugent reveals that he was determined to succeed and to become prominent. He could also pinpoint the time when this determination entered his mind. When he was about fourteen or fifteen years of age, he was very fond of Brother Angelo, one of his teachers at the West Abbey School. Angelo was partial to Nugent, especially because they were both vehement supporters of the Molly Maguires, a political party at that period.

Angelo would divide his class into two opposing groups—the Molly Maguires and the All for Irelanders and then have competitions between the two factions in all areas of study. On one occasion when a mathematics competition was taking place between the two groups, Nugent missed a problem which would have tied the contest between the Mollies and the All for Irelanders. Nugent's blunder lost the game for the Molly Maguire group, and, as a result, Brother Angelo kept Nugent after school. The teacher knew that this act would cause his pupil considerable embarrassment and trouble at home.

Nugent's father, a tailor, and his mother, a seamstress, worked at home and were exceedingly industrious. They never stopped laboring, and their one goal was that their son should get on in the world. When Nugent arrived home from school, they were furious. Nugent's father whipped him, and his mother's tears were copious. Between them they drained their son, but they made him promise to work more diligently. It was at this moment that Nugent resolved to be an important man in the world.

The next day in school Brother Angelo insisted that Francis Nugent do the problem he had missed the day before. From the way this matter was handled, it was obvious that the teacher was attempting to renew their friendship. But, remembering his humiliation at home, Nugent was not going to accept Angelo's overture. He did the problem correctly, and then he announced that he could have done the problem properly the day before and smiled insolently at his teacher. Angelo smashed him with a heavy blow.

Angelo asked Nugent to do the next two mathematics problems, ready to cane his pupil if errors were made. Nugent had prepared both problems the night before, answered correctly and achieved his purpose. Everyone in the classroom including Angelo himself knew that the teacher was being unjust, and from then on antagonism existed between the two. Francis Nugent from this time on studied intensely; he never went to bed before twelve o'clock. Angelo continued to be one of his teachers even into the final grade in school, and they drove each other unmercifully. When Nugent was graduated from the West Abbey School, he took the examinations for Civil Service, and, although he was competing against boys from the rest of the British Isles, he won first place in three out of five subjects.

When the story's narrator asked Sir Francis Nugent if the diligent and slavish labor of his school years was worth it, Nugent answered "Yes" with some qualifications. He became a brilliant student but lost his youth in the process; he hated his father and mother from the day they had punished him and made him cry: "They did the one thing to me that I couldn't stand up against. They did what that little cur Angelo planned they'd do. They broke my spirit with pity. They made me cry with pity." [48] Nugent's hatred eventually turned to pity, and then his parents became objects that he loathed: "A boy can be sorry for people who are weak and pitiable, but he can't respect them. And you can't love people if you don't respect them. I pitied them and I despised them." [49] Sir Francis Nugent's success, he insists, was accomplished in spite of this pity which injured him for all time. A hard, calculating-machine attitude replaced common humanity, and he became a mechanical figure rather than a whole human being. Nugent condemns pity as "disintegrating" and "disgusting"; it forced him to hate his parents and prevented him from having a normal childhood.

After the death of Sir Francis's father, the mother came to live with him in London, and now her corpse is on the train returning to her birthplace. When Nugent sees his first sight of Cork after many years, his eyes looked "thirstily" at children playing in the streets; the word "thirstily" appropriately connotes Nugent's attitude toward the childhood he wished he had been able to have. Although he has regarded pity as despicable, pity is something that can never be completely discarded. He wished to bury his mother in London, but she had requested that she be returned to her native city for interment. He acceded to her wishes out of pity and in so doing does, as the narrator points out, "the kind thing." Nugent's only response to this comment is a barely audible repetition of the word "kind."

"Up the Bare Stairs" has the excellence of the imponderables of life, of the strange quirks which compose existence and are found in the development, success, or failure of individuals; how things may be done for the wrong reason and distort or twist personality and yet result in accomplishments of worth and value.[50] The deprivation which a person may undergo on one level may furnish the qualities which will lead him to success on another. Sacrifices that are made in some way injure the people who are making them—the sacrifices of Nugent's mother and father helped lead to his success but eradicated his love and respect for them. The sacrifices which he made deprived him of a normal childhood—something which he would always feel the lack of. The interrelation of so many different factors in one man's worldly success studied with psychological accuracy makes "Up the Bare Stairs" a moving case history of a rags-to-riches hero who pays dearly for his fame and fortune. Again, as in reading any of O'Faolain's superior stories, the ironies and paradoxes are so penetratingly presented and analyzed that the mystery and wonder of existence teases us out of thought and troubles the imagination.

Molly and Paddy Maguire, the husband and wife in "The Fur Coat" have been married for many years, and their life has not been easy. But after many exhausting and lean years Maguire has obtained a sound clerical position working for the Minister for Roads and Railways. Now for the first time in their lives they have some financial security, and Maguire promises his wife that she may buy a fur coat. Owning a fur coat has been Molly's one desire, and now a life-long goal and dream can be achieved. It develops, however, that Paddy Maguire has no idea of the price of a fur coat. When he tells Molly to go and buy the best, he learns that the most elegant coat is priced at over a thousand guineas. But his wife has no intention of buying such a costly garment; she is more than willing to settle for a reasonably priced coat. Her husband tells her to hurry down to the store and purchase such a coat.

But Molly is in no rush. She does not wish to buy something cheap-looking, but she also does not wish something that would be too impressive. She does not want her neighbors or friends to feel that she is becoming affected or getting "grand notions." Molly keeps turning over in her mind every aspect of the possible purchase. She considers the pro's and con's of not having the coat, of having the coat, of having a particular type of coat. All of this debating and indecision causes a quarrel with her husband in which she angrily claims he is too parsimonious to want her to have the coat. After good relations are restored, Paddy leaves his wife a check for one hundred and fifty pounds for the purchase of a fur coat. Molly, however, refuses to use the check to buy the coat. Above all else in the world, she wishes to own a coat, but she admits that she just does not have the "heart" to spend money for it. This "heart," she asserts, "was knocked out of me donkeys' years ago." When her husband positively insists that she take the check and buy the coat, she maintains she "just couldn't" although she really just does not know why she "couldn't."

"The Fur Coat" is another expertly told and deeply felt narrative. Both Paddy and Molly are very much accustomed to financial hardship which has come not only from their own lives but also from a peasant background in which money was never plentiful and starvation was all too often hovering about. As a consequence they both—although Paddy to some degree less than Molly—regard something like a fur coat as a showy extravagance. Although life is now financially satisfactory, the peasant background, saturated both in history and in stories and experiences of ancestors, causes worry that next year or the following year may be just the reverse of the present, and again penury and deprivation may set in.

While this tale is not calculated to appeal to the present-day affluent younger generation, readers who have known their grandparents or even parents of a peasant background from the old country—no matter what the old country—appreciate the truth and universality of this narrative. The reader feels the years of privation, the sudden promotion and affluence, the promise; then the caution, the doubt, the mental examination of the matter from all angles; the debate; and the final rejection of the longed-for hope because of the power of past events and an ingrained prudence and insecurity, and even the not quite understandable reason for the resulting reaction. Again the story is handled quietly, logically, building inevitably to its climax—although the reader is not quite certain of the climax—and then, when the climax does come, it is the only one that really would have made sense and squared with one's knowledge of the thrifty and often deprived peasant strain found in these characters. Two central impressions result from a reading of "The Fur Coat"—one says of the story "how true it is"; the other, "how Chekhovian!"

The other stories in *The Man Who Invented Sin* volume are not quite so masterful. They are handled with verbal skill and with careful artistry, but, for the most part, they tend to be less significant in permanent meaningfulness. Samples of such stories would be the stylistically elegant "The Trout" in which a young girl takes a trout from a well where it will be caught by a fisherman and puts it in a river where it will have freedom and a chance to escape death for a time); "Innocence" (where a boy's first confession stirs his father's memory of a boyhood confession when he professed to have committed adultery, although he did not know what the word meant); "Passion" (a delicate and tender handling of the transiency of beauty theme); and "Unholy Living and Half Dying" (in which the grip of religion in Ireland is shown to affect even the irreligious).

A steady development in proficiency and maturity has occurred in each of O'Faolain's short-story collections. The superior stories in his second and third compilations are characterized by subtlety, compassion, understanding, irony, and a perceptive awareness of the complexity of human nature. Themes and insights are suggested and implied rather than flatly stated, and the themes are significant. In these superior stories O'Faolain demonstrates authorial objectivity and detachment; he avoids description for its own sake; and he successfully infuses a poetic mood—subdued and delicate—over his narratives. He makes excellent use of suggestion and compression in handling style. Overall, then, it may be affirmed that stories such as "A Broken World," "The Man Who Invented Sin," "The Silence of the Valley," "Up the Bare Stairs"—to mention a few—exemplify considerable artistry and expert control of modern short-story techniques.

CHAPTER 4

The Bell

I *Origin and Policies*

WHILE O'Faolain was writing short stories and novels and living quietly in Ireland, he was also keenly observing the political, social, and cultural life of his native country. He became convinced that Ireland badly needed an intellectual journal which would be free from the restrictions of sectarian control. World War II had closed markets for many Irish writers,[1] and, in any case, the authors required an acceptable vehicle in their native country in which to publish mature fiction and commentary. Thus was *The Bell*, subtitled *A Survey of Irish Life*,[2] established. This journal became the most literarily significant publication printed in Ireland since "AE's" *Irish Statesman.*

The Bell was edited by O'Faolain and its first monthly issue appeared in October, 1940. In a preliminary statement O'Faolain announced that time would give the journal its own specific character.[3] It was clear from O'Faolain's remarks that the magazine wanted especially to encourage writers who would describe their own experiences and their individual impression of the country. "You," O'Faolain declared, "who read this know intimately some corner of life that nobody else can know. You and Life have co-operated to make a precious thing which is your secret." [4] The job of *The Bell* was "to encourage Life to speak" through the writer. All areas of Irish life became common subject matter for the magazine.[5] In practice the new periodical became—as Vivian Mercier once suggested—a combination of *Horizon, New Statesman and Nation, John O'London's Weekly,* and *World Review.* Mercier cites American equivalents as *Harper's, Partisan Review, The New Republic,* and *Saturday Review.*[6]

The Bell presented a rich and varied menu. Articles and contributions were submitted by well-known figures connected with Irish literary life. Such writers as Flann O'Brien (Myles na gCopa-

leen), Maurice Healy, L. A. G. Strong, Maurice Walsh, Lynn
Doyle, Michael McLaverty, and Margaret Barrington produced
material for this journal. Short stories and segments of other creative work appeared by Frank O'Connor, Maura Laverty, Bryan
MacMahon, Liam O'Flaherty, Peadar O'Donnell, and O'Faolain
himself—again to select just a few names. There were personal
reminiscences of literary and other important Irish personages—
Frank O'Connor's portrait of "AE" is a splendid illustration of this
type of material—and thoughtful critical commentaries—Elizabeth Bowen discussing James Joyce, for example.

Such books as Lennox Robinson's *Curtain Up,* Eric Cross's *The
Tailor and Ansty,* Maura Laverty's *Never No More,* and Jack B.
Yeats' *Ah Well!* were first presented to the reading public in *The
Bell.* Also notable was the publication of extracts from *The
Speckled Bird,* a hitherto unpublished novel by William Butler
Yeats. *The Bell* also offered poetry by all of the best modern Irish
poets: Patrick Kavanagh, Austin Clarke, Robert Farren, Robert
Greacen, Valentin Iremonger, and others. Furthermore, the magazine gave younger writers such as Brendan Behan and James
Plunkett an opportunity to make a forceful debut upon the literary scene. The magazine also devoted much space to fascinating
documentary articles on all phases of Irish life—prison conditions,
slum living, street ballads, to point out a few random subjects. In
presenting documentaries the journal was attempting to examine
and describe Ireland thoroughly and to have Ireland reveal "herself truthfully, and fearlessly." [7]

The Bell regarded itself as an arbiter of taste for modern Ireland. It believed that Ireland was at the beginning of a new period in its history, for Irish life had not stopped at 1916 as many
seemed to believe. The revolutionary or political era was completed, and now a new creative period was in embryo. Standards
and taste, therefore, had to be formulated and established. This
was a primary goal of *The Bell;* it conceived of itself as a modern
Irish version of the *Tatler* and *Spectator* papers. Thus, for example, the Abbey Theatre was reprimanded for lowering its standards in recent years by presenting inferior escapist material or
mere Naturalism. In one of his editorials O'Faolain appealed to
his readers: "Whenever you see something fine that any of our
people are doing anywhere tell us about it. Whenever you see
anybody creating something cheap and ugly, and a large number

of people being deluded by him, tell them and tell us about it. Only in that way can we build up real standards worthy of our dreams about a great, modern Ireland." [8] This statement serves as a concise commentary on the intentions and editorial policy that *The Bell* attempted to carry out.

As a result, its editorials became increasingly didactic. In a commentary on *The Bell* Vivian Mercier wrote about how closely O'Faolain himself guided and directed *The Bell* and noted that actually O'Faolain and *The Bell* were one and the same.[9] So *The Bell's* crusade was O'Faolain's, and the close identification of the two gives us a basic awareness of O'Faolain's own ideas and aims. And one of the main aspects of Irish life which was to draw the ire of *The Bell* was the practice of literary censorship.[10] Although O'Faolain's editorials became critical of the Irish Censorship Board, they were particularly agitated by unofficial censors who took their cue from the Literary Censorship Act.[11] This censorship was associated with a "rampant Catholicism" which found book-banning congenial. Worse than the Censorship Act itself is

the censorship-consciousness of a number of people for whom there is no other word but obscurantists—that is, they obscure the light, they sentimentalise everything into a pretty fable which is no less a lie for being pretty, and is far more insidious. The effect of this on the 'general intellectual atmosphere' is corrosive. What is still worse, these people defend themselves mainly in the name of . . . Gaelicism and . . . Catholicism, and thereby bring both into contempt.[12]

Censorship in Ireland prevented a free exchange and discussion of ideas. It helped to develop an indifferent and uninterested attitude on the part of the great mass of people. Except for the intellectuals, the great majority of people in Ireland seemed willing to accept this rigid thought control; and, consequently, Ireland could not advance intellectually as it should.

While censorship was to become a basic target of *The Bell*, Catholicism was attacked only as it related to such literary restrictions.[13] Modern Gaelicism, however, was disapproved of; the Gaelic Leaguer was accused of clinging too tightly to a past that was either dead or has been slowly dying. O'Faolain, himself at one time a Gaelic enthusiast, was one of many who "grew up with the Yeatsian discovery of the glory and inspiration of that 'ancient memory'"[14]; but now the grandeur and usefulness of this aura has passed, and "every single iota of colour and romance has been knocked out of the inspiration of Gaelic and the Gaelic tradition." [15] O'Faolain insisted that Gaelicism tended to result in isolation and provincialism and was of course impractical.

In this vein O'Faolain cited a comment by Dr. Lyons, the Bishop of Kilmore, who maintained that movies and radio programs presently brought in ideas which were antagonistic to "native culture." [16] O'Faolain also referred his readers to Daniel Corkery's theory that at present the only genuine artists in Ireland are painters. This is the case, argues Corkery, because Irish writers have not severed ties with England.[17] Another example of the extremism of present-day Gaelicism was the proposal to remove the Irish Minister for Defence from office because army members participate in such recreational sports as hockey and soccer "which are not 'national games.'" [18]

O'Faolain praised the initial concept of and the original potentiality of the Gaelic League, but he asserted that it had failed to live up to its expectations. The main reason for its failure was, he shrewdly observed, "that, in Ireland, political nationalism has for too many generations absolved us from the need for intelligent, constructive thought. The result has been that we have forgotten . . . that ultimately every problem is not a problem of nationality but of civilization." [19] He noted that, for modern communication, Gaelic was highly inferior to English, but he stressed its value in helping one to understand pre-1750 Ireland.[20]

O'Faolain strongly objected to the Gaelic League's slurs on other racial groups, to its concern about making Ireland "the master of Europe," to its attacks on Irish literature in English, to its censures of all Anglo-Irish writers, particularly Yeats and O'Casey.[21] The League, he noted, wished "to abolish utterly all books other than those written (or to be written) in Gaelic, and to abolish English utterly as the general, practical language of the island." [22] Gaelic Revivalism has gone to extremes; it is too closely bound to the past—a past that "has misled so many countries—especially the past sentimentalised and exploited and smugly accepted as the unalterable Law." [23] *The Bell* was concerned with what could be learned from the past to help the present and the future; *The Bell* was not concerned with the past merely for its own sake.

The Bell gradually came to find fault with current "stuffed-shirt middle-class mentality." [24] This middle-class group, which included professional men and civil servants, developed after the establishment of the Free State and is "full of pietism, profits and ignorant bumptiousness." [25] Composed of the people in the town and large cities, this group controls both houses of the Irish parliament;[26] and this situation handicaps the farmers, who cannot be assisted unless the urban leaders give approval.

According to O'Faolain, the middle-class interests wish to preserve the status quo and, consequently, they support or remain indifferent to questions such as literary censorship. This group is nationalistic and narrow, isolationist and reactionary. One of the unhappiest aspects of this condition is that present-day Ireland is a mockery of all that the freedom fighters from the earliest days of their struggle up to 1924 ventured in their aspirations for a finer country. Present-day Ireland (the 1930's and 1940's) is not the Ireland that men like O'Connell, Parnell, or Wolfe Tone hoped for and desired. O'Faolain's work and his editorials in *The Bell* have on occasion been censured for being too defeatist and too pessimistic; yet, when it is kept in mind that O'Faolain was constantly contrasting Eire of that day with the way the rebels of twenty, thirty, forty, and more years ago dreamed it would be, then the charge of pessimism and defeatism was unwarranted:

How differently we had once dreamed it all! We had not merely seen the English flag and the English army go, and the Royal Irish Constabulary, and the sepoys of Dublin Castle. This was but the clearance. We had not merely seen even those first steps of the new thing— land for the landless, homes for the poor, factories rising, rivers harnessed, a fair share of our own people in business, and end to emigration and unemployment. That was but the framework. We had looked forward to seeing all classes united, all religions equal, all races welded, all ideas welcome, that hammering and clanging of a young nation at work which Milton so finely describes in his famous "Speech for the Liberty of Unlicensed Printing." We visioned fresh and eager life sloughing its old skin.[27]

O'Faolain wanted Ireland to be a society created to a "desirable image of life." He was more interested in the everyday life of Julia Murphy than he was in the life of Julian the Apostle. "Just as when the Legion of Mary talks about the evil of smut what I want to talk about is the evil of slums." [28] This vision of a prosperous, open-minded, intelligent, progressive, and enlightened country has been thwarted by the predominance of middle-class smugness and by its willingness to compromise with authoritarianism and mediocrity.

In addition to deploring literary censorship, Gaelicism, and the attitudes of the middle class, O'Faolain attempted to shake Ireland out of its insular viewpoints. He observed that radio, movies, more frequent traveling between countries, and similar characteristics are letting in the outside world more and more, a world that Ireland wrongly wishes to shut out. He argued that for "fifteen hundred years the central fixation of the Celtic mind has been the desire for an ascetic or indifferentist withdrawal from modern life." [29] Such an attitude was equivalent to "Lazarus in his tomb." O'Faolain intended to stir Ireland out of its sleep, out of its preoccupation with itself and its own local affairs.

In order to advance and come alive, the country must move out of the eighteenth and nineteenth centuries; it must take its place with all the nations of the twentieth century and assume the responsibilities which such a step entails. "The truest Irish patriot of today," wrote O'Faolain in December, 1943, "is the man who can look at Ireland as a modern man, and as a Citizen of the World, who happens to be resident in this corner of it." [30] At the time these words were written, they were shocking to a large number of the Irish people.

Following up this theme, O'Faolain inaugurated in the next issue a series of editorials called "One World." Using a quotation from Socrates as one of the mottos for this series—"God has placed us upon this great city like a hornet upon a noble horse to sting it and keep it awake,"—O'Faolain endeavored to make Ireland more knowledgeable about international problems. Censorship in Ireland during World War II attempted to keep the country as isolated as possible. Irish newspapers, for example, were not allowed to send out foreign correspondents, and the press was prohibited from detailed commentary on the bare news items received. Thus the "One World" editorials were "our modest contribution against Isolationism and Little Irelandism." [31]

In editorial after editorial O'Faolain stressed that isolation from the world and its problems is no longer possible now or in the future. He spoke of a possible postwar European Federation and of Ireland's relationship to such an organization. He discussed the question of a future United Nations organization and the necessity of Ireland's taking its position in such a group. He noted that the world's moral, social, and economic problems are also Ireland's problems and that no country could solve its problems in isolation. He drew repeated parallels which allied aspects of the present Irish scene to characteristics found in countries such as Italy, Poland, Denmark, and Yugoslavia. He continually expanded the mind of his reader and demonstrated the requirements of "One World" with specific examples of its need.

O'Faolain also favored a forget-and-forgive policy against former British injustices and pleaded that the Irish should become free-minded enough to regard England naturally. In so doing, Ireland would unburden itself from the suspicions and prejudices of the past. He observed that Ireland has a neurosis on the question of Britain, and he hoped that this "age-long, near-neurotic, itching, worrying, sense of non-freedom which is the inheritance of centuries of oppression would at last come to a blessed end." [32]

All of the "One World" editorials were written in this vein of reasonable, well-rounded, and mature attitudes—in short, in the vein of common sense. Today, of course, many of these ideas are dated and often seem far too obvious. Ireland took its place in the United Nations in December, 1955, and has grown much less isolationist and provincial in the 1950's and 1960's. Nevertheless, at the time they were written, the "One World" editorials made a valuable historical and intellectual impact on the Irish scene. Some intelligent and influential Irish writer had of necessity at that period to enunciate what to the majority of the people in Ireland were startlingly advanced ideas.

On the negative side, it should be noted that the "One World" editorials suffered from a rambling digressiveness which often jarred the unity and progressive development of ideas within individual editorials. These defects, however, resulted primarily because of the restrictions of government censorship which limited the amount of material and prevented fully developed discussions. O'Faolain explained the matter when he said that, under the limitations of wartime censorship, the task of writing about world problems and Ireland's relationship to these problems "was just barely possible for the editor, though nobody realised better how inadequate, indeterminate, over-generalized and merely allusive these articles have, perforce, had to be." [33]

After the Allied defeat of Germany in 1945, O'Faolain wrote of the price Ireland paid for neutrality: "We have suffered by the prolonged suppression of our natural sympathies with tortured humanity, our admiration for endurance and courage; our moral judgment has been in abeyance; our intellectual interest in all the ideas and problems which the rest of the world is still straining to solve has been starved. . . . There is a great leeway to make up, many lessons to be learned, problems to be solved which, in those six years of silence, we did not even allow ourselves to state." [34] Happily, O'Faolain overstated the case here. Yet because of his writings for *The Bell*, many of these problems, within the limits of the censorship restrictions, were stated; and intellectual interest in world issues was maintained.

O'Faolain continued as editor of *The Bell* until April, 1946. For that issue and all others for the rest of its existence (to 1954), the journal was edited by Peadar O'Donnell. In the April, 1946, issue O'Faolain announced under the heading "Signing Off" that he wanted to devote more time to other literary areas, and he asserted that he had "grown a little wary of abusing our bourgeoisie, Little Irelanders, chauvinists, puritans, stuffed-shirts, pietists, Tartuffes, Anglophobes, Celtophiles, *et alii hujus generis*." [35]

II *Post-Editorship Contributions*

O'Faolain's connections with *The Bell* were not completely severed. For a while he served as its book-review editor, and he periodically contributed articles and short stories during the remaining years of the magazine's existence. That O'Faolain's interest in polemics was to continue can be seen from several articles published in *The Bell* after his tenure as editor. The most famous of these was his 1951 essay on "Auto-antiamericanism," a term he coined to describe those individuals—in Ireland especially—who were anti-American in their attitudes and activities.[36] The dispute started when Miss Louie Bennett, an Irish trade-union leader, protested in *The Irish Times* the loans made by the Economic Cooperation Administration to develop Irish industry. She argued that such financial aid was a conscious attempt to entangle Ireland in America's plans for future wars. When O'Faolain responded in *The Bell*, he noted that the sixteen million dollars Miss Bennett was particularly disturbed about was a gift to Ireland and not a loan, and that this gift had no strings attached. He maintained that Miss Bennett's feelings exemplified "Auto-antiamericanism," which he felt was present in some quarters in Eire. O'Faolain attributed "Auto-antiamericanism" to four factors: (1) British influences (reflecting Britain's decline as number one power and a basic sour-grapes attitude); (2) A climate of unbelief where motives are questioned and cynicism is rampant ("It is the phenomenon of our time that nobody any longer believes in anybody");[37] (3) A general suspicion that the United States was primarily concerned with selling its goods in foreign markets; and (4) a chauvinistic sense of patriotism.

In arguing against Miss Bennett's position, O'Faolain put considerable stress on how American financial support and "know-how" had been particularly valuable in changing the Calabria section of Italy from an indescribably poverty-stricken, backward area to a more proeperous, self-respecting community. O'Faolain himself had visited Calabria and witnessed the effect of American assistance. His fiery eloquence in this section was typical of his best polemical writing:

Well? If some sceptic went down there [Calabria] he would say, "Ha, ha! But what is the U.S.A. getting *out* of it?" I suppose he would. He would look for the catch rather than for the faith. I will tell you what the U.S.A. is putting *into* it. The whole of Marshall Aid to the end of 1950 has cost every crude, rude, grasping, vulgar, selfish, racketeering American fifteen shillings a week out of his back-pocket. All those billions are a free grant to Italy.

You have never seen the town of Matera in Lucania? A pity. It's worth seeing. The entire poor quarter consists of holes dug out of a mighty cliff face, honeycombed with them, with one wall of mud or stones closing the opening, and in this wall a door—the only ingress for light and air and the only egress for smoke; housing father, mother, children, grandchildren, the mule, the hens, and maybe a pig. No sanitation whatever. These truly wretched people had to wait until far-off Americans came to build houses and sewers for them. I could mention half a dozen such examples, the burning memory of which makes me just wonder whether the people who believe America has only selfish arms in Europe are not the meanest, most ungrateful abortions on earth.[38]

The most shattering section of his "Auto-antiamericanism" essay in *The Bell* was reserved for the conclusion of his article. The following passage demonstrates why O'Faolain's views were so unpopular with the great mass of the Irish people. Emotion and

eloquence carried him away on occasion, but at this time [1953]
he hit too close to the truth to be ignored:

I put it to readers of this article that before we start to pick holes in
America we should first examine our own conscience. What is *our* foreign policy? *Our* contribution? I put it to you that our policy is a mean
one. We are slipping into the attitude that our hands are too lily-white,
our souls too pure, to touch the muck of the world, that we just *hope*
nothing will happen; that we are remote from it all; ready to be pro-
tected again by American G.I.'s, Dutch flyers, British sailors, French,
Belgian or Italian blood, with nothing of our own but a joke army, a
joke navy and a joke air force—all manned, agreed, by gallant men;
together with geography, geology, and God's special regard for his
chosen people. In short, we are snoring gently behind the Green Curtain that we have been rigging up for the last thirty years—Thought-
proof, World-proof, Life-proof. The only people *we* are ready to fight
for are the angels. For we keep on saying we will fight, if needs be,
for Christ that is against Communism; but, then, we add, only on
terms! If they give us our Six Counties we will fight for Christ. Not
otherwise. 'Who will buy Christ?' we cry. 'Going for a song! Just for
half a dozen bits of mortal soil!' Or, if you like to put it another way—
Ireland is on the market.[39]

It is perhaps unnecessary to declare that much of what O'Faolain said is not pertinent today. Irish troops, for example, participated with a sense of humanitarianism and moral obligation for
world issues in policing activities in the Belgian Congo as well as
during the crisis in Cyprus. How much of this progression toward
accepting world responsibility was ultimately due to ideas publicized and reiterated by O'Faolain and others of his caliber will
never really be known, but what would have been unheard in the
Ireland of the 1930's and 1940's (except from the lips of an O'Faolain) was successfully put into practice on at least two occasions
not so many years later.

O'Faolain's "Auto-antiamericanism" essay stirred up heated re-
buttal, as its author had foreseen. Peadar O'Donnell limited replies to one issue of the journal and then gave O'Faolain an opportunity to comment on his critics.[40] The correspondents' replies
proved that Miss Louie Bennett's view was not an isolated opinion; in general, individuals who disagreed with O'Faolain felt that
the United States wanted Ireland to become one of its satellite
supporters, and eventually it intended to force Ireland to join the

United States in future wars. These writers marshalled their arguments with vigor. They represented various positions on the topic —isolationism, humanitarianism, nationalism, Communism, etc. Even Peadar O'Donnell disagreed with O'Faolain when he insisted that peace should be the foremost Irish aim, and, if a war broke out, then Ireland should continue neutral and uninvolved. In the pages of *The Bell* the question remained unresolved, but again O'Faolain had brought an important issue out into the light of reason, stirred up interest, and forced people to articulate their views and at least to consider a broader, all-embracing attitude removed from provincialism and petty nationalistic concerns.[41]

In discussing O'Faolain's "forceful, witty, and thoroughly informed" essays written for Ireland's most important journal of the last thirty-five years,[42] John V. Kelleher, one of the most learned observers of the modern Irish scene, best summed up O'Faolain's career as an editor and writer for *The Bell:* "[O'Faolain] did produce piecemeal in his articles and editorials the fullest analytic description of contemporary Ireland, and of its strengths, faults, and derivations, ever given. More than anything else these writings, close in manner and approach to the best eighteenth-century pamphleteering, justify his title as first Irish man of letters."[43]

CHAPTER 5

Blending Sensibility and Intelligence

I *I Remember! I Remember!*

THE volume *I Remember! I Remember!*, published in 1961, contains several of O'Faolain's best stories. A previous book of collected short stories, entitled *The Finest Stories of Sean O'Faolain* (1957), was composed of selections from the *Midsummer Night Madness, A Purse of Coppers,* and *The Man Who Invented Sin,* plus eight additional stories which are not especially effective. Some of these eight tales were intended to be satirical; but, as O'Faolain was to confess, "they mostly failed dismally to be satirical; largely I presume . . . because I still have much too soft a corner for the old land. . . . Some day I may manage to dislike my countrymen sufficiently to satirize them." [1] Stories in this category, such as "Persecution Mania," "An Enduring Friendship," and "Childybaun," are too obviously manipulated and are neither biting nor wry enough for successful satire. The *I Remember!* compilation, however, shows O'Faolain striking off in a new direction and continuing his proficiency in handling the short-story form.

The title story treats the relationship between Sarah Cotter and her sister Mary. Sarah received an injury to her spine when she was young and, as a result, she has been restricted to a small house in Ardagh, Ireland, for twenty-five years. Twice a year, for a week at a time, Mary, who is married to an American buyer, visits her sister. Mary is in a position to visit her sister more frequently, but she is disconcerted by Sarah's prodigious memory. Sarah's ability to remember everything that was ever told to her begins to make Mary uncomfortable. Sarah contradicts Mary's memories of the past: for example, Mary recalls a very exciting day before her marriage when she and Corney Canty went fox hunting near Ballycolle woods and cornered the fox in a nearby quarry.

As Mary recalls the happening, Corney at that time was a dashing figure aged about forty. Sarah, however, punctures this remembrance when Mary's husband is present. Mary had always related this story of the adventurous fox hunt with Canty as one of the most interesting days of her life. Sarah was a witness when Canty applied for an old-age pension, and she relates that, judging by the age he wrote down on the pension form, he must have been in his middle sixties when the fox hunt with Mary took place. Mary's husband laughs heartily, but Mary is distressed because her happy memory of that occasion has been shattered and her insistence that Corney exaggerated his age deliberately in order to obtain the pension is met with disdain. Mary's husband regards Sarah's revelation as a factual confirmation that his wife exaggerates her stories a great deal.

On another occasion Sarah suddenly mentions Nathan Cash. Mary, having forgotten that she had even mentioned Cash to her sister, at first feigns ignorance of the name; but Sarah relates most of the facts. Cash was a director of the Bell Telephone Company in Newark and eventually divorced his wife Jane Barter. He had been having an affair with another woman, but Mary had never told Sarah who the other woman was. Later, Cash had married a girl named Carrie Brindle (Mary had also forgotten that she had told Sarah this), and now Sarah wonders how things are working out with Cash and his new wife.

The reader can ascertain that Mary had had the affair with Nathan Cash when he was married to Jane Barter. Mary's frightful despondency and loneliness over the breakup of the romance is indicated. Sarah's memory reminds Mary of the sad and embarrassing elements in her past life; as a consequence, she vows never to see Sarah again. She does not want to be disillusioned by the remembrance of grim reality or by unromanticized detail. Mary breaks off the bond with Sarah, although Sarah has no other close relative to visit her in her sick room nor is she evil, malicious, or unkind, since she has no idea of the disturbance she is causing.

"I Remember! I Remember!" is immensely effective because it plays so expertly with the threads of memory in every person's life and demonstrates how the passing of time changes fact and reality. Remembrance of certain events and people dim and become obscure while other aspects of the same events and same people glow and grow in importance. To have these later concepts altered or disturbed by truth or reality can cause much distress. Things settled become unsettled, and one's outlook can be slightly or greatly disarranged and unbalanced, thus causing anguish and pain.

These lines are buried in the middle of the story: "Not that life ever is like a river that starts from many tributaries and flows at the end straight to the sea; it is more like the line of life on my palm that starts firmly and frays over the edge in a cataract of little streams of which it is impossible to say where each began." [2] These little streams of life and memory are so involved, so mysterious and yet so delicate, so tenuous. These streams change imperceptibly, and yet they change, and then each one in his own way must come to grips with the alterations of the streams of life and time for the sake of peace, for the sake of sanity, for the necessity of fitting into the little shallows on the banks of the stream.

Can one really ever accept reality? Must reality really be completely forgotten or in some manner distorted or softened so that life can go on? These are questions O'Faolain asks but does not answer. Mary Carton answers these questions only for herself. But time and memory must serve to answer these questions for each person on an individual basis. Unquestionably, some form of compromise must be involved since that is the way an individual must usually play the game of life or else be destroyed.

In "The Sugawn Chair," another story constructed on the movement of time and memory, the narrator recalls that, when he was young, his mother received a sack every year from the farm where she was born. This sack, containing apples and potatoes, produced mixed feelings of joy and sorrow. The boy's father was also born on a farm, and, although the mother and father had lived in a city for many years, they both longed for the rural areas.

One October when the sack arrived, the father went up to the attic and brought down the old sugawn rocking chair that had originally come from his home. Straw was purchased, and the father and two of his cronies attempted to make straw ropes for the seat. The two cronies were also originally from the country, and again—as occurred when mother and father exulted over the annual country sack—more rural words were spoken with a poetic, picturesque ring and connotation. While resting from their work, the three men grew nostalgic about farm life, and the father pronounced his frequently stated wish to return to the country and to buy a small farm. This dream, shared by the mother, was a constant hope and wish but one completely impossible because of financial problems. But the beauties of nature were recalled and even the boy, who visited his uncle on the farm during the holidays, could appreciate the lure of the turf, the misty air, and the flowers.

As the work on the chair progressed, frustration with the job of reseating grew. Each of the men could recall how the job was done when he was a boy in the country, but now either the straw was not right or he had lost the knack. In any case the men could not repair the chair, and it was returned to the attic with the seat still unrepaired. The broken sugawn chair remained in the attic long after the father died. When the narrator's mother died, no one wanted to buy the chair so it was left in the attic. As the narrator beheld this piece of furniture, he recalled the annual rejoicing over the October sack, how united and youthful his mother and father were on that occasion, and how their first romantic ardor was then recaptured for a brief time.

O'Faolain succeeds so well with this story because its truth can be immediately validated. The intensity and wonder of youthful love is contrasted with the later married years when work, responsibilities, and repetition have taken the wonder out of life except on special occasions when the glorious moments of the past are recalled. Much meaningful poignancy is conveyed in the constant desire the couple has to return and settle on a farm. But time knows—and the couple knows deep down within—the impossibility of doing so.

The failure to restore the chair stirs in the father the realization that he has lost much of his youthful farm knowledge. This failure to repair the chair becomes, on a larger plane, a symbol of the impossibility of returning to the past for any length of time. Past time, the life and youthful existence on the farm, in the fresh, green, spring days is broken too; it can never be repaired; it has passed forever. A loneliness, a remembrance of things past, forms a pensively sad mood over the narrative and gives it a distinctive bittersweet tone amidst the inevitable passing of life and youth and recurring dreams. Tone, mood, and theme blend to perfection in this brief story, and the artistic achievement is even more impressive since one realizes how this story could have easily become marred by sentiment and maudlin emotionalism.

At times, the story moves perilously close to the line dividing expert artistic control of mood and sheer sentimentality. The mother's sudden weeping over the sack of apples and potatoes might have become maudlin, but this scene is counterbalanced immediately by the watchers laughing wildly at her for being momentarily carried away. The reader laughs at the mother's foolishness, yet understands why it occurs; he then perceives that such a reaction on her part is normal and logical under the circumstances. Sentimentality could have occurred in the stress given to the mother and father when they live over their period of courtship again, but the reader is given only a fleeting glimpse of this, an inkling which can, nevertheless, be verified by one's own personal experiences or observation. Since the glimpse or insight is so delicately and lightly handled by the artist, it does not fall into defective emotionalism. The melody is soft and gentle; the strains are in the background; the nuances of mood and tone are so carefully arranged that the story yields a haunting quality most allied to a musical composition modulated to just the right proportion of pitch and harmony.

The title of the story "A Shadow, Silent as a Cloud" is richly evocative in itself. The shadow in question passes over the head of Jeremiah J. Collis, a well-to-do Dublin architect. This shadow is caused by a waitress named Lily Collis (née Braden) whom Jeremiah meets at a banquet. Lily and Jeremiah were children together in rural Rathfarnham, and, when she was twelve years of age, he had asked her to marry him. Many years after, she had married a cousin of Jeremiah's. Before meeting at the banquet, Lily and Jeremiah had not seen each other for thirty-seven years. They reminisce about the beauty and tranquillity of Rathfarnham (Jeremiah has also spoken of the beauty of this area in an address he gave at the banquet), and they recall old friends and relatives. Lily wonders if the fifty-three-year-old architect is married, but he maintains he was too busy becoming successful to have time for thinking of marriage. Lily notices, however, that he is apparently very much attached to young Stella Shannon, who is also attending the banquet.

During an interlude in the proceedings, Jeremiah asks Stella to marry him. She refuses because he is concerned only with his work, a monomania that she could not endure. If he would give up some of his architectural projects and center more of his attention on her, she would marry him. But his nature will not allow him to do this. Stella decides to marry Condon Larkin, a young, frequently intoxicated architect whom she feels needs her very much. By marrying Larkin, Stella will ruin her life. A certain wild inevitability in each individual's nature makes each what he is, and he cannot alter his pathway. Life puts each individual in a certain time, place, and niche, and it is difficult to break this pattern. Jeremiah comes to believe that

there is no such thing as saving your life or squandering your life because nobody knows what life is until he has lived out so much of it that it is too late then to do anything but go on the way you have gone on, or been driven on, from the beginning. We are free to be, to act, to live, to create, to imagine, call it whatever you like, only inside our own destiny, or else to spit in the face of destiny and be destroyed by it. If a man won't do that all he can do is to bake his bread and throw it on the waters, and hope to God that what he is doing—he gazed up and around him—is the will of the night, the stars, the god of this whole flaming bloody unintelligible universe.[3]

Jeremiah Collis is a famous and important man in the architectural field, but he will suffer the deprivation of not having a wife and children. He desires to have a family, but career goals are stronger. When he meets Lily, he recalls the old and more halcyon days; he admires Lily and the Collises for basic honesty and for a sense of truth and endurance. Jeremiah, on the other hand, does not have the genuineness and sincerity possessed by his relatives. He can give a spurious speech in which he talks about the beauty and past historical associations of places like Rathfarnham and Templeogue, but his feelings are hypocritical; and he deals in sentiment because of its effect on his audience. He wants the rural beauty of such places destroyed so that he can build modern housing projects.

Lily half-consciously reminds him of the old beauties of the past and of genuine, solid beliefs. She makes him see his own lack of sincerity and his smallness in contrast to more deeply felt and sincere standards and beliefs. While this shadow is moving momentarily over him, Jeremiah is a better balanced individual, more humane, more down-to-earth. But the shadow passes, and Jeremiah is back on his pre-ordained path, arguing and demonstrating the value of his massive, up-to-date housing development.

For a time memory causes his whole life to flash before him; he sees the young Jeremiah and middle-aged Jeremiah; and he sees his basic unwillingness and, really, helplessness to change his character. He realizes that creation is destruction and that in both his career and in his own personal life these same phenomena are happening, but a change cannot be effected. The past, present, and future not only move irrevocably in the external world; they do so also in the personal life of Jeremiah Collis—and O'Faolain implies—in the personal lives of every man and woman.

"A Shadow, Silent as a Cloud" is another realistic commentary on aspects of time and memory; of different values at different periods of life; of points of no return; of tragedy that cannot be forestalled; of brief moments when things are seen clearly but then rejected for one reason or another; of loneliness that is indirectly or directly chosen; of things that seemingly must inevitably be, although in many instances they should not be the way they are; of star-crossed and handwriting-on-the-wall manifestations which can only mystify man the more he studies them and seeks explanations.

In another story about memories, Daniel Cashen, an elderly County Roscommon industrialist, owns a woolen factory which produces excellent products. The narrator of "A Touch of Autumn in the Air" relates that he did not meet Cashen until the latter was an old man. On one occasion the narrator remarked that, although the day was sunny and pleasant, there was a touch of autumn in the air. This comment startled Cashen because it brought to his mind the problem of why some things are remembered while others are forgotten. This question Cashen had not previously considered, and the matter obviously troubled him.

Cashen then recalled an autumn holiday period spent in a rural area of Ireland when he was fourteen years old. The weather was the same as that of the day just mentioned, and this similarity stirred the reminiscence. Cashen recalled individual particulars of this period almost sixty years ago. Some things he remembered well, such as a flickering stream near a tiny stone bridge close to his uncle's farm. Other details were hazy—for example: Was the red barn in which he so often played constructed of wood or corrugated iron?

Before Cashen's conversation with the narrator, he had visited a shop where toys and sweets were sold. The aroma in this store carried him back to the boyhood vacation so many years ago. Cashen and his cousin, Kitty Bergin, had eaten Conversation Lozenges—little candies with generally romantic inscriptions colored on them. It was evident that a feeling of love and attachment began to dawn between the two teen-agers. When Cashen asked if he could buy some Conversation Lozenges, the storekeeper had never heard of this kind of candy. At the same time, Cashen saw a nun in this store and examined her with curiosity; he wondered why he should remember the Conversation Lozenges and Kitty Bergin and a statement she had made that she might become a nun. Cashen was bewildered by it all: Why these particular memories and so few of other occurrences? "The pain in his eyes was the pain of a man who has begun to lose one of the great pleasures of life in the discovery that we can never truly remember anything at all, that we are for a great part of our lives at the mercy of uncharted currents of the heart." [4]

Cashen was not a sensitive type; he was a hard-working, practical man who lived for his work and labored from dawn to twilight; but now he was attempting to analyze and explain things that were not in his experience. Deep down in his innermost being were the joys of that holiday on Uncle Bartle's farm when there was tranquillity, contentment, and the possibility of love. These memories had been sublimated to ambition and the quest for financial power, but such memories could never be obliterated. They represent the other Daniel Cashen, the Cashen he did not allow himself to be. He had rejected such joys, just as Jeremiah Collis had done in "A Shadow, Silent as a Cloud." Collis was still young enough and career-obsessed enough to put such memories out of his mind almost at once; Cashen, on the other hand, in his mid-seventies and near death (he dies a few days after his conversation with the narrator) is not able to shake off the silent shadow of memory. Memory's effects and peculiarities perplex him as the memories stir up a realization of joys he has missed. If there is no regret, there is wonder, a realization of the mystery and inexplicableness of it all.

Perhaps the central fact of his life was that he had felt small and inconsequential in that remote pastoral setting, and somewhere in his nature he had felt the need to rise above this role, to overcome poverty, to improve upon his ancestral roots. Ironically, on his death most of his money—no small amount—was bequeathed to his relatives, most of them poor and still living in the region of his Uncle Bartle's farm. What Daniel Cashen missed they perhaps have already; what Daniel Cashen had, they will now share. If there are eternal verities at work here, they are the joys of nature and of ordinary love which, in the long run, lure and tease even when financial success is attained.

Of the remaining stories in the *I Remember! I Remember!* collection the most worthy of comment is "No Country for Old Men," which takes its title from a line in Yeats' poem "Sailing to Byzantium." The story begins with a newspaper item announcing that Joseph Cassidy, age sixty-three, and Frederick Wilson, age fifty-seven, had been found guilty at a trial in Belfast of entering Northern Ireland and taking part in a raid on a police barracks during which a policeman was killed.

Both men, who insisted that they had not participated in the attack, maintained that they had entered Ulster in order to recover a stolen truck belonging to Celtic Corsets, Ltd. Cassidy is the owner of the corset company; Wilson, the concern's accountant. Since Cassidy was found carrying a revolver, he is sentenced to one year in prison; but Wilson receives a term of six months. The newspaper account also mentioned that Cassidy and Wilson had participated in the 1916 Easter Rising and had served in the same brigade during the later struggle against English rule in Ireland.

This information was the essence of what appeared in the news accounts, but Irish newspapers are notoriously reticent about such matters, and, obviously, questions remained to be answered. Joe Cassidy was not the type of person who would now risk his financial position, and Freddy Wilson was considered too sly an individual to fall into the hands of the police. It develops that Joe Cassidy's son Frank, a member of the Irish Republican Army, had stolen his father's truck in order to participate in an attack on an Ulster police barracks. When Cassidy learned of the theft, he pursued his son in a car. Freddy Wilson had accompanied Frank, but not to take part in the raid; he was fleeing from Southern Ireland after stealing a large sum of bonds from Joe Cassidy's firm.

When Cassidy picked up the trail and discovered Frank a short distance across the border, he also encountered Freddy Wilson. The raid had ended, and Frank was attempting to get the body of one of his comrades back to Eire. Joe and Freddy sent Frank to safety in Joe's car, and the two men took the truck and attempted to return to the South with the body of the dead youth. Lights of cars in the distance indicated that Ulster troops were patroling the roads. Cassidy was startled when Freddy Wilson produced a gun, an old-fashioned type called "Peter the Painter" which had been popular during "the Troubles." Once during a raid in the old days Freddy had saved Joe Cassidy's life with such a gun by killing a Black and Tan soldier. When Cassidy inquired if Wilson would use his gun if they encountered Ulster police, Wilson said he would. Cassidy responded that he knew Wilson would have done so in the days of the rebellion, but now he was not certain of Wilson's eagerness, because of his age, to meet trouble.

Freddy Wilson had lived outside of Ireland after "the Troubles." He had returned only a few years ago to work for Joe Cassidy at Cassidy's insistence, and on this night he had attempted to steal four thousand pounds of Celtic Corsets, Ltd., bearer bonds. Cassidy wanted Wilson back with him because they had been young and had felt immortal together in the Black and Tan period. "And you can never understand why you stopped feeling like that." [5] Time has destroyed this feeling, and the individual asks why. But in those days time was not important to either Cassidy or Wilson; at present, time weighs heavily on both men. They no longer regard it in an instinctive, animal-life manner, and the notion of immortality which youth feels is past. Nothing surprises a man more than the realization of old age, and this realization is particularly disturbing when it is contrasted with an exciting and meaningful youth.

Freddy recalls that Joe Cassidy had fought for the Free Staters in the Civil War. If Freddy had stayed in Eire during the Civil War, he would have been an Irregular. If Cassidy and Wilson had met under these circumstances, the old friends who had fought side by side against the British would have attempted to kill each other. So does time change; so do men change; and so are time and men bound together.

Freddy Wilson had kept his old gun because he believed that he would kill Joe Cassidy someday. Cassidy was a leader of the Free State forces, and Freddy's best friend was killed by Free Staters during the Irish Civil War. Since Cassidy has also been one of the rising middle class who had prospered from the Free State, he represents materialistic, Philistine Ireland (the Ireland that O'Faolain condemned in his *Bell* editorials); and Freddy hated Cassidy for selling out the splendid and high hopes of the original struggle.

Contrast is also indicated by the presence of the dead Irish Republican Army youth who represents a continuance of the spirit of the old days—now for the most part dying or lying dead in the darkness—while the corpulent Cassidy has been one of thousands who have corrupted the former idealism and grandeur of the old cause. Coming to accept the situation, Freddy, in a cynical mood of purposelessness, decides not to kill Joe Cassidy. He recommends that they bury the dead lad since they are now obviously in the safe territory of the Republic. In making this suggestion, Freddy is burying everything in which he and Cassidy had ever believed during the grand old days. The Ireland of the future, as those who fought against the Black and Tans envisioned it, is dead. The present bourgeois and authoritarian Ireland (symbolized by Cassidy) cannot be dislodged. Freddy begrudgingly accepts the reality and evil of the situation.

A little later, after another period of rest, Freddy suggests that he and Cassidy return to the North and make their own two-man raid. It will be a last gesture of courage, of recapturing the immortality of their youth. Moreover, such an act would be a purification and an atonement (particularly for Cassidy), a final burst of idealism before death. Cassidy, however, refuses; he is beyond idealism. Now he is interested in safety, in a return to his business, in a retreat to the mediocre round of old age. He will never do another idealistic thing from now until the day of his death. Death dominates the story: the death of the Irish Republican Army lad whom the two men have brought with them and buried, and the figurative death of both Wilson and Cassidy—the dreams and ideals of their youth are dead and the odor of their spiritual deaths suggests their eventual physical deaths.

"No Country for Old Men" is doubly affecting because it combines action with contemplation. It re-echoes some of the effectual chase-and-pursuit intrigue which was so fascinating in *Midsummer Night Madness*. A sense of movement, suspense, and physical peril enlivens this narrative and enhances the usual depth of thought and quiet analysis which is so characteristic of O'Faolain's later short stories.

All of the stories in the *I Remember! I Remember!* collection are mood pieces. They are tonal compositions distilling an atmosphere in which spring and autumn are contrasted in the light of the slow but inexorable and irrevocable movement of time and memory. These narratives are written, fittingly, from the viewpoint of middle age or old age, and they reflect the fact that Ireland has become more and more urbanized and more a part of the outside world.

Urban Ireland with its prosperity and housing developments is far removed from the rural, peasant Ireland that so many of the individuals in these stories knew in their youth. Consequently, many of these figures reflect on their youth; and they also contrast the past and the present. Life's hopes, disillusionments, frustrations, the passing of old friends, pervasive memories, problems of love, the compromises of time—these and similar matters pass in review in these stories. Disenchantment is probed through "the long humiliation of life." [6] The romance of the past is punctured or scarred by present reality and future dissolution.

The autumnal fall of the leaves hangs over most of these tales and awakens the recurrent question of *why*. Spoken and unspoken griefs, laments, and realizations of imperfection, disappointment, and lack of satisfaction are basic in the delicate and sensitive texture of these narratives. The stories continuously stir meditation. Memories are awakened, most of which are pleasant; but these memories have different effects when brought into present situations. The crippled sister in "I Remember! I Remember!" exists and is nourished by her ability to recall facts so thoroughly. Yet these same memories destroy her sister's peace of mind and alter the romantic notions of the past which she treasures.

For the mother and father in "The Sugawn Chair" their happiness—youth and the thrill of first love, the ecstasy of the early married years—is all in the past, one which serves as a refuge from the unglamorous reality of the present. But Jerry Collis can linger over the past, and then put it out of his mind. Collis in his drive for material success has reflected on the old days, but he has never taken them too seriously. His meeting with Lily, however, reawakens a faint aura of meaning which he possesses deep in his subconscious. But being the kind of man he is, this aura is a brief shadow which he forces away and will not allow to pass before him in the future (he will avoid Lily's husband who is the headwaiter at a restaurant Jerry has frequented regularly). He will push out of mind and sight any reminders of the past which might deter him from his ruthless present.

Other stories remind us of other aspects of past and present: the contrast between idealistic and heroic youth and the drabness of advancing old age ("No Country for Old Men"); the past does not necessarily repeat itself even given almost the same set of circumstances ("Miracles Don't Happen Twice"); lingering over and living in the past and a refusal to face present reality causes disaster and unhappiness ("The Younger Generation"); past opportunities, if taken advantage of, would have resulted in the avoidance of present frustration; and yet some individuals would rather live in their dream worlds than try to make their dreams come true ("One Night in Turin"); for some people, facing the lonely truth of the present is preferable to living on the lies and exaggerations of the past ("Two of a Kind").

Joys and consolations are to be found by hanging on to the past; but frustration and bitterness may also be savored by clinging to the past. Each human being reacts differently, therefore, to that which has vanished. Memory, an essential ingredient in every individual, is always stirring about within us. But, whatever it brings to us at different times and in different places and in various moods, the overall reaction in these stories is essentially that of loss or regret. In this volume O'Faolain plays almost every variation possible on the theme of memory, and with his probing comes foremost a sense of sad compassion, of tragic tenderness. If a character's romanticizing of the facts distorts reality, this result is presented with a mellow realization that this is the way life is; this is the way people are.

Is some character to be censured for this situation? Not in O'Faolain's handling! He understands and forgives, but the objective note of irony is always maintained. This chord has grown in O'Faolain from his earliest days. In the *Midsummer Night Madness* it tended to be heavy-handed, overly stressed, at times harsh, at times lost or jarred erratically by the lush style and the poetic romanticism. As O'Faolain has developed in artistry over the years, his intelligence has caught up to his earlier sensibility. The objectivity, compassion, and irony have grown in maturity, thoughtfulness, and subtlety. Sensibility has blended with intelligence. (The blending of the incongruous with the heroic in "No Country for Old Men," for instance, is masterfully balanced.) Nowhere is there greater opportunity for irony than in the dreams of the past and the relative mediocrity and distress of the present. O'Faolain has successfully seized on this subject in the *I Remember! I Remember!* stories; and he has also managed to hold firmly to poetry, contemplation, and compassion.

II *The Heat of the Sun*

O'Faolain's most recent collection of stories, *The Heat of the Sun* was published in 1966. This book is much less satisfying than the *I Remember! I Remember!* collection, because too many of the narratives are tales rather than short stories. In a foreword to his latest compilation, O'Faolain asserts that a tale is much more roomy than a short story, that it incorporates more scenes and plot, and that it is a more leisurely form of writing. Such qualities are not, however, characteristic of O'Faolain's finest work. Before his latest book O'Faolain had written, from time to time, a few tales, but they were not particularly successful productions. In O'Faolain's handling, the longer length of the tale lends itself to greater discursiveness, to a slackening of tight and deft control, to more obvious manipulation of the plot and, barring an exception here and there (certainly "In the Bosom of the Country" is one) to more shallow characterization. Too much material is covered in too short a space; as a consequence the reader is often jarred by a deficiency in story probability and verisimilitude. The bones of the narrative protrude rather sharply and yield an impression of thinness and even, at times, of flimsiness. Tales such as "£1000 for Rosebud," "One Man, One Boat, One Girl," and "A Sweet Colleen" tend to ramble too expansively and to distract the reader. They also lack the vast wealth of insight and the chiseled craftmanship one has come to expect from O'Faolain.

On the other hand, these comments do not pertain to the short stories. The better short stories in his newest volume—"Dividends," "The Human Thing," "Billy Billee," and the title piece—are typical of O'Faolain at his best. Irony, the quiet probing into character and life's meaning, the beauty, compression, and economy of style, and the layers of insight which cause repeated reflection—these qualities are again displayed with grace and facility.

Thematically, too, *The Heat of the Sun* is most rewarding. As he had played on the theme of time and memory in the *I Remember! I Remember!* collection, O'Faolain now studies the many aspects of love, and even the unsuccessful tales support the volume's overall motif with considerable variety. Love is seen in its first fiery bloom and in its later dying embers. It is also looked upon in retrospect and viewed in its phases of foolishness, blindness, selfishness, impulsiveness, misunderstanding, pity, tenderness, sacrifice, innocence, comfort, and companionship. It is also observed as reality and illusion and examined as a constant attempt by humans to assuage loneliness and give meaning to existence even though such attempts too often fail or survive for only relatively brief periods. Completely satisfying love is an ideal that man can attain for only a short time, and this very fact makes love both more desirable and more frustrating. In *The Heat of the Sun* collection, love, seen in its infinite variety and in its extremes of misery and splendor as well as points-in-between, is always haunted by transiency, which makes us persistently conscious of time's ascendency and aware that we are simultaneously blessed and cursed in the bittersweet, joyful melancholy of existence.

CHAPTER 6

O'Faolain's Achievement

D URING the period from the late 1930's to the mid-1950's, Ireland required a significant creative writer who would crusade to eliminate the country's cultural shortcomings. James Joyce and Sean O'Casey testified to the talent of Irish writers, but both were exiles and, as such, they were removed from the home scene. Both Joyce and O'Casey lost a certain immediateness in their writings because they had to draw on memories of the distant past—as was particularly true of Joyce—or else write variations on one theme—as was particularly true of O'Casey. Admiration for the work of O'Casey especially must be tempered by a regret that he had not remained in Ireland, battled on the scene, and stayed close to the everyday material he needed.[1]

While the position of exile has its particular frustrations, it is in many ways easier to be an exile than to continue to live in a ghetto and to fight and struggle against the ghetto's prejudices and pressures and to rise above its limitations. Courageous is the portrait of the modern writer in Ireland who, "attacked on every side by political prejudice, national enthusiasm, pietistic evangelism . . . [fought] tooth and nail for his vision of life." [2] What was needed during this crucial period was a champion who would enter the lists and have the incredible mental stamina and persevering endurance—for it took these qualities to face intense pressures from Church, State, and the vast majority of the people living in Eire—to give witness to the truth and to say, in Leslie Fiedler's terms, the "Hard No." In making a wholehearted commitment to truth, an Irish writer would appear to be a traitor to the people whom he loved. This function so greatly needed in the Ireland of the 1930's, 1940's, and 1950's was supplied by Sean O'Faolain.

Especially as editor of *The Bell*, O'Faolain became the Irish Matthew Arnold of his time by doing battle with the rabblement

and the Philistines; by extolling intelligence, enlightenment, and
common sense; by becoming a spokesman for civilization.[3] He
constantly endeavored to improve Irish society and to create a
favorable climate for ideas and for Irish writers. He believed that
time would improve conditions and observed that "men of genius
accelerate the processes of time for their country." [4]

O'Faolain himself was a voice of acceleration. His efforts
against oppressive censorship, for example, have helped to abate
this problem considerably.[5] Exceedingly well equipped for this
function—a man of wide knowledge and very research-minded—
O'Faolain was able to trace historically the various social, political, and cultural concepts which compose the Irish scene. O'Faolain supported his ideas with scholarly and factual materials, but
this intellectual background was reinforced by first-hand participation in the Volunteers, in the Irish Republican Army, on the
Republican or left side in the Irish Civil War. O'Faolain at first
enthusiastically supported DeValera but then became a severe
critic of many of his policies when the dreams that the rebels had
fought for had been compromised and stained by his governmental rule.[6] O'Faolain participated in the Gaelic language revival
movement, but he became disenchanted with the excesses of the
Gaelic Leaguers. Nevertheless, he had the breadth of view and
depth to admit in 1943 "that an Irishman without a knowledge of
Gaelic is . . . intellectually and spiritually disinherited." [7]

In his creative work O'Faolain fought a second battle. He,
Frank O'Connor, and others commenced their writing careers
with the desire to avoid the subjective and Romantic literature of
such writers as Synge and Yeats and to model their own writing
on the Realism of the Russian novelists. A writer such as Synge
produced excellent writing for his particular period, but now a
new age of Irish history had begun; and, with the passing of "Romantic Ireland," a period of disillusionment set in, a period when
materialism and narrow nationalism were prevalent. In such a period, the temptations for an Irish writer would be sentimentalism
and an adherence to the notions of the Celtic mist. Instead of
truth, the public wanted platitudes and escapism.[8] Writers like
O'Faolain and O'Connor, however, adopted a penetrating, realistic approach to basically unsympathetic material. What O'Faolain
said of the-beginning-of-the-century Yeats could be said of O'Faolain himself: he had the "stature of mind, the spiritual physique,

to refuse to escape from the unsympathetic material of the life about him. He has transmuted it, as every artist must: but he has never been disloyal to it." [9]

H. E. Bates, in his study of the modern short story, notes the influence of Turgenev's fiction on O'Faolain. Turgenev's deep feeling for the beauty of nature, his compassion, and his poetry are qualities which, Bates maintains, have been carried over into the work of O'Faolain. [10] O'Faolain himself, as has been indicated earlier, has admitted the influence of Turgenev and Chekhov. He especially acknowledged their ability to penetrate deeply into the essence of the tragic or humorous situation they were describing. He praised their realism, their lyricism, their ability to convey mood effectively; and he admired their deep knowledge of human nature. [11] O'Faolain's growth in these qualities has been observed in the preceding chapters.

Chekhov, in particular, is O'Faolain's *maître*. Chekhov appealed to O'Faolain primarily because he was a Realist who "held on to poetry, to mood, to poetic feeling . . . being true to common life." [12] O'Faolain also deeply admired Chekhov's compassion and understanding: "To Chekhov there is in every man, even if he be a fool or a scoundrel, a sacred mystery to be plumbed." [13] This mystery is part of the greater mystery of life which fascinates O'Faolain just as much as it intrigued Chekhov: "life posed questions . . . life had no answer for them." Paramount always was the "inscrutable mystery of human suffering." [14] Chekhov was one of those writers "who seem to compass all life and balance all life, and yet leave us questioners of life at the end. They have detachment without loss of emotion; passion without loss of justice; judgment without loss of sympathy." [15]

Because of the circumstances of the time and because of the Celtic temperament, anger would seem to be a natural reaction for a short-story writer in modern Ireland. Yet, although he frequently vented his anger in his nonfiction work, particularly in his editorials in *The Bell*, O'Faolain has transcended this possible source of weakness. In one of his essays he asserts that, for the creative writer, "anger is not a fruitful emotion." [16] The Irish writer, O'Faolain avers, should "struggle desperately against anger and didacticism . . . fight . . . for the lyricism and sweetness that anger and contempt would destroy; for humour, and good humour; and above all, for intelligence and detachment." [17]

And, in his best work, O'Faolain has achieved this goal. His objectivity in his most successful writing is impressive, and he adheres to the technique of the greatest writers who hold "the balance of life so evenly between their characters, good and bad, that it is next to impossible to define their own attitude to their people." [18]

At times O'Faolain has failed in his purposes. In most of the stories of the *Midsummer Night Madness* volume and in some of the stories in *A Purse of Coppers* and *The Man Who Invented Sin* collections, O'Faolain has violated his own principles. On occasion, he has underscored the obvious, been too didactic, and has wasted words in presenting the story and in conveying information. Narratives like "A Born Genius" and "One Night in Turin" are flawed, therefore, because they do not possess the compression and unity which is required of artistic short stories.

O'Faolain's fiction has been accused of other weaknesses. Frank O'Connor claims that O'Faolain's writing should be built on humor and satire; he praises, for example, O'Faolain's play *She Had to Do Something* for these qualities.[19] In point of fact, this play is a very superficial, flimsy comedy that does absolutely nothing to enhance O'Faolain's literary reputation. O'Connor is trying to form O'Faolain in his own image and likeness, and such an attempt is short-sighted and would be crippling to any writer whose talent and aims are of a different nature. O'Faolain's work contains humor, but it is not a pronounced quality in his books, nor is his humor boisterous. His humor is sly, subtle, a muted note in his stories. One never laughs out loud when reading O'Faolain, and this reaction he intends.

Perhaps the most damaging charge that can be leveled against many of O'Faolain's short stories is that they lack passion or fire. From the dedication to Edward Garnett in *A Purse of Coppers* we learn that Garnett wished O'Faolain to be more passionate.[20] O'Faolain, however, equating such passion with Romanticism, rejected this approach. O'Faolain also felt that such passion would lead to anger which would, in turn, reduce objectivity and lyricism. Instead of emphasizing sensibility over the intellect—a pronounced weakness in Irish writers[21]—O'Faolain aimed to blend sensibility and intelligence, and he believed that a more passionate approach would force the sensibility to predominate over the intelligence. In the *I Remember! I Remember!* collection, he achieves the perfect unifying of the senses and the intellect.

In "Lady Lucifer," one of the short stories in *The Man Who Invented Sin* volume, O'Faolain talks about an author whose stories are "about little spurts of passion." Such stories might be labeled "Faint Gestures." [22] Perhaps many of O'Faolain's own stories might be faulted as being faint gestures: as too calm, as too understanding, and as revealing too much resignation. [23] At times O'Faolain can be censured for looking "at life coldly, observing and recording without any apparent emotion." [24] Since O'Faolain is frequently not interested in plot—in the accepted sense of the word—his short stories often lack a narrative drive or pull which a bit more passion or fire would compensate for. But he insists on the cold, realistic approach.

Recommending words suggested by Yeats for his epitaph— "Cast a cold eye/ on life, on death"—O'Faolain declares that the "hard and realist literature of our time is performing its own role. It keeps us looking both life and death coldly in the face until, some day, the Jacob's ladder of our vision will rise again out of this Irish clay and lift us to where we were in the days when we were not afraid to shudder at our dreams." [25]

In considering how successful O'Faolain has been in achieving the short-story goals he has set for himself, one must respond, "Exceedingly well, in his best writing!" As James T. Farrell has remarked, O'Faolain is "saturated with a sense of Ireland, but he is not parochial. . . . Besides the skill, the insight, the fine style which he brings to his work, you recognize on reading and rereading him that his perspective is balanced. He has an eye for the comic as well as the sad, a good ear for Anglo-Irish speech, and the heart to feel with his characters." [26] Following Chekhov's standards, O'Faolain gives us Realism combined with lyricism; a pervasive sense of mood; compassion; a deep awareness of the inherent mystery of existence, and detachment, combining sensibility and intelligence.

In handling style O'Faolain has also progressed from the exuberant, lush Romanticism found in his first collection of short stories to a controlled prose—still rich and lyrical—but toned down so that it is in keeping with realistic subject matter. Horace Gregory has made the most perceptive observation about O'Faolain's post-Romantic style: "Nor has O'Faolain dropped into another common pitfall of lesser Irish writers—that of writing 'poetic prose'—he can be and is eloquent enough, yet the nearly 'styleless' style in the prose of his later writings is prose in the sense just as Yeats' later verse 'withered into truth.' " [27]

One more issue remains. O'Faolain himself is worried over whether he is a Romantic or a Realist. Ostensibly, he is a Realist, but his subject matter must of necessity have some Romantic overtones. Talking of this problem in relation to writers in general, O'Faolain comments: "For any kind of realist to write about people with romantic souls is a most tricky and difficult business, even when he is a Stendhal gifted with a lovely irony, a Chekhov holding on firmly to the stern morality of the doctor, a Turgenev informed by an intelligent humanism, or an E. M. Forster blessed with a talent for quiet raillery. If one has not some such gift, the subject is an almost certain pitfall." [28]

O'Faolain acknowledges that one could write angrily about such material—but, as we have seen, he has rejected this course, or one could turn to satire—as Frank O'Connor suggested. But O'Faolain informs us that he cannot be a satirist.[29] Nevertheless, no writer, O'Faolain maintains, should remain the same; any serious author should keep evolving, changing in some manner, and seek new forms. The genuine artist should possess a willingness to experiment. This O'Faolain has continued to do. His study of various ramifications of time and memory in *I Remember! I Remember!* and the probing of love in *The Heat of the Sun* are recent manifestations of his own continuing evolution to new themes and subject matter.

O'Faolain's perplexity over Realism and Romanticism in his own case appears, therefore, to be idle speculation. O'Faolain is essentially a Realist—in his objectivity, in his conscious intellectual handling of material, in his use of irony, in his grasp of truth, and in his portrayal of life as it is. Yet, at the same time, his work contains lyrical and atmospheric qualities that are usually labelled "Romantic." Like Chekhov, O'Faolain is a realist who can blend truth with mood and poetry so that his portrayal of existence is enhanced by nuances and subtleties which give a deeper meaning to the writing and a closer look into contradictions, deceptions, and mysteries.[30] O'Faolain is more poetic and contemplative than Chekhov but less detached and less ironic.

Like Chekhov, O'Faolain is essentially an optimist. Despite man's follies and foolishness, O'Faolain still believes in humanity; he affirms man, although he is aware that man and man's problems are continually perplexing, that sadness and tragedy are common, and that existence is an enigma, which, nevertheless, must be probed and studied. The artist seeks answers even if there are no answers; and, above all, the writer uses all his intelligence and sensibility to ponder "the inscrutable mystery of human suffering." O'Faolain's best short stories must earn him the title of the Irish Chekhov. This statement redounds to the credit of both of these artists.

Notes and References

Preface

1. *Irish Short Stories*, ed. Valentin Iremonger (London, 1960), p. 13.

Chapter One

1. The number of Corkmen who joined the Civil Service after the signing of the treaty with England was so large that this situation became one of the most famous jokes ever created by *Dublin Opinion*. See Vivian Mercier, *"Dublin Opinion's* Six Jokes," *The Bell*, IX (December, 1944), 209–18.

2. *Vive Moi!* (Boston, 1964), p. 43.

3. *Ibid.*, p. 114.

4. *Ibid.*, p. 141. This alteration of name was done informally rather than legally at this particular time, according to a personal communication from O'Faolain to the present writer dated March 27, 1965. John V. Kelleher notes that O'Faolain is listed in the National University of Ireland Calendar as a graduate of University College, Cork, in 1922, under his given name, John F. Whalen.

5. *Vive Moi!*, p. 175.

6. *Ibid.*, p. 248. This narrative was one of the early important developing points in O'Faolain's short story career.

7. "About Myself," *Now and Then*, No. 41 (Spring, 1932), p. 35. This article is also printed as "Sean O'Faolain," *Wilson Library Bulletin*, VIII (March, 1934), 380.

8. *Vive Moi!*, p. 340.

9. John Chamberlain, "Sean O'Faolain's Fine Tales of the Irish Rebellion," *The New York Times*, March 27, 1932, Sect. 4, p. 7.

10. W. Y. Tindall, *Forces in Modern British Literature 1885–1956* (New York, 1956), p. 81.

11. *Constance Markievicz* (London, 1934), p. 15.

12. *Vive Moi!*, pp. 203–4. See also pages 296, 302, 314 for other comments about this story. Much of the material used in O'Faolain's first short-story collection has a factual basis; for example, the incident in the title story in which the policeman grabs a hot poker during an

eviction—*Midsummer Night Madness and Other Stories* (New York, 1932), p. 27—is based on an episode in which O'Faolain's own father was involved, *Vive*, p. 38.

13. "About Myself," p. 35.

14. *Vive Moi!*, p. 296.

15. *Midsummer Night Madness and Other Stories*, p. 167.

16. *Ibid.*, p. 177.

17. "About Myself," p. 35.

18. John V. Kelleher, "Loneliness is the Key," *The New York Times*, May 12, 1957, Sect. 7, p. 5.

19. *Vive Moi!*, pp. 247–48.

20. It should be noted, however, that O'Faolain's initial efforts were much more lavishly Romantic than the final versions of these stories. For example, the first published version of "The Bomb-Shop," *Dial*, LXXXII (March, 1927), 197–209, is considerably inferior to the final rendition. *The Dial* story is extremely subjective ("I" is used repeatedly), self-conscious, stiff and pretentious, and filled with frequent diary entries and a clumsy attempt to intersperse dialogue with description.

21. *Midsummer Night Madness and Other Stories*, p. 4.

22. *Ibid.*, p. 57.

23. *The Finest Stories of Sean O'Faolain* (Boston, 1957), pp. vii-viii.

24. *Midsummer Night Madness and Other Stories*, p. 3.

25. *The Finest Stories*, p. vii.

26. "About Myself," p. 36.

27. *Midsummer Night Madness and Other Stories*, pp. vii-xii.

28. Robert Cantwell, "Poet of the Irish Revolution," *New Republic*, LXXVII (January 24, 1934), 313–14.

29. *Vive Moi!*, pp. 224–25.

30. Sean O'Faolain, *The Short Story* (New York, 1951), p. 78.

31. *Vive Moi!*, pp. 28, 114–15.

32. See the preface to *She Had to Do Something* (London, 1938), pp. 7–24. Peter Kavanagh notes that this play was produced through the influence of Frank O'Connor, *The Story of the Abbey Theatre* (New York, 1950), pp. 171–72. In his introduction to O'Faolain's first short-story collection, Edward Garnett remarks that O'Faolain authored a play about Parnell. This drama was never produced or published, and O'Faolain says in his personal communication to the present writer dated March 27, 1965, that the manuscript has been lost.

33. Lewis Nichols, "Talk with Mr. O'Faolain," *The New York Times*, May 12, 1957, Sect. 7, p. 27.

Chapter Two

1. Grattan Freyer, "The Irish Contribution," *The Modern Age,* ed. Boris Ford (Baltimore, 1961), pp. 196–97, 206–07.

2. Frank O'Connor, "The Future of Irish Literature," *Horizon,* V (January, 1942), 59–63.

3. Sean O'Faolain, "Fifty Years of Irish Writing," *Studies,* LI (Spring, 1962), 102–03.

4. After *Come Back to Erin* O'Faolain wrote three other novels. All that remains of the first of these is the short story "Love's Young Dream," which is published in the *I Remember! I Remember!* volume. Another novel called *Alien with a Passport* was accepted for publication by Cape, but O'Faolain was dissatisfied with the book and withdrew it before publication. A third novel was reduced to the story "No Country for Old Men" found in *I Remember! I Remember!* (personal communication from O'Faolain to the present writer dated March 27, 1965). The novel O'Faolain mentions he was working on in 1957 was eventually released as "No Country for Old Men," *The Finest Stories,* p. viii.

5. *A Nest of Simple Folk* (New York, 1934), p. 124.

6. *Ibid.,* p. 148.

7. *Wilson Library Bulletin,* 380.

8. *A Nest of Simple Folk,* p. 393.

9. *Ibid.*

10. *Vive Moi!,* pp. 110–11.

11. *Ibid.,* p. 114.

12. *A Nest of Simple Folk,* p. 28.

13. One of the ironic oddities of the Irish famine is that food was being sent from Ireland to England at periods of great starvation, *cf.* Cecil Woodham-Smith, *The Great Hunger* (New York, 1962). O'Faolain reviews this book, "The Irish Famines," *Nation,* CXCVI (March 30, 1963), 269–71.

14. *DeValera* (Harmondsworth, England, 1939), p. 15.

15. *Ibid.,* p. 40. See also *Constance Markievicz,* pp. 175–76 and *passim.*

16. *Ibid.,* p. 27.

17. J. Donald Adams, "A Fine Novel Out of Ireland," *The New York Times,* January 7, 1934, Sect. 5, p. 1.

18. *Ibid.*

19. *Bird Alone* (New York, 1936), p. 106.

20. Donat O'Donnell, *Maria Cross* (New York, 1952), pp. 95–115. Despite some excellent insights, O'Donnell's literary criticism tends to seize on one *idée fixe* and to neglect other aspects of a writer's work. In the revised edition of *Maria Cross* (Fresno, California, 1963), p.

vii, O'Donnell has not taken the time to update his material on O'Faolain and take into account such a volume as *I Remember! I Remember!*

21. Benedict Kiely, *Modern Irish Fiction* (Dublin, 1950), pp. 85–87.

22. *Bird Alone,* p. 187.

23. For a short time Corney felt that their relationship was sinful, but this mood quickly passed, *Bird Alone,* p. 268.

24. A selection from the Tinsley burial arrangements called "My Grander" is excerpted in *An Anthology of Irish Literature,* ed. David H. Greene (New York, 1954), pp. 543–46.

25. *Vive Moi!,* p. 329.

26. *Ibid.,* p. 330. Writing in *The Bell* in 1953, O'Faolain declared:

Some seventeen years ago (1935–36) I wrote a novel (*Bird Alone*) about a man who seduced a girl, who died in childbirth, and whom the seducer should, in his Faith, believe damned. The probable effect on his life interested me. It was only necessary that the girl should sin once . . . . to underline the horror of the idea of eternal damnation for a single sin. It was with the greatest difficulty that I made it seem plausible that she should allow herself to be seduced at all, so powerful are the religious beliefs and social conventions of modern Ireland. (I may add that the novel was banned as indecent.) . . . one cannot . . . get very far or achieve much variety of action with so strict a morality. We are, in effect, very much in the same position as Hawthorne who managed to squeeze one great novel out of equally unmalleable material, in a society where, also, sin was furtive, revolt slight and brief, and convention rigid. As I have said, Communist writers are in an identical straight jacket. The personalities of their *dramatis personae* are not free.

("Ireland After Yeats," 45).

27. The Reynolds book was called *Faust: A Romance of the Secret Tribunals* and was published in London in 1847. Reynolds' telling of the Faust story is one of the most untypical versions of the legend O'Faolain follows the more standard Goethe version.

28. *Bird Alone,* p. 280.

29. *Maria Cross,* p. 111.

30. *Ibid.,* p. 114. What O'Faolain says of Daedalus could be said of Corney: "He is a Promethean rebel defying nature and God by the extent and intent of his rejection. He reinvokes Camus's statement about the individualist—that he must reject reality in order to affirm his own existence," *The Vanishing Hero* (Boston, 1957), p. 200.

31. Frank O'Connor, *An Only Child* (New York, 1961), pp. 97–98.

32. Sean O'Faolain, *Come Back to Erin* (New York, 1940), p. 70.

33. O'Faolain gave his own views on Saor Eire (Free Ireland) in "The New Irish Revolutionaries," *Commonweal,* XV (November 11,

1931, 39–41. See also letter from O'Faolain, *Commonweal*, XV (January 6, 1932), 273.

34. From the poem "September 1913."

35. *Come Back to Erin*, p. 108.

36. *Ibid.*, p. 275.

37. The real-life prototype of Bee Hannafey is the woman O'Faolain calls by the pseudonym of Anna Marie Kauffmann, *Vive Moi!*, pp. 268–70, 290–92, 294, 301.

38. Sean O'Faolain, *A Summer in Italy* (New York, 1950), p. 32.

39. *Come Back to Erin*, p. 366.

40. *Ibid.*, p. 172.

41. *Maria Cross*, pp. 109–10.

42. *Bird Alone*, p. 210.

43. Personal communication from O'Faolain to the present writer dated March 27, 1965.

44. John V. Kelleher, "Sean O'Faolain," *The Atlantic*, CXCIX (May, 1957), 69. As Professor Kelleher observes in an earlier article, Frankie Hannafey finds, upon his return to Ireland, the frustration and indifference from which he had attempted to escape. When he comes back to Erin, Frankie realizes that he has found his humanity but lost his purpose, *cf.* John V. Kelleher, "Irish Literature Today," *Atlantic Monthly*, CLXXV (March, 1945), 75–76.

45. *Vive Moi!*, p. 26.

46. *Ibid.*, p. 27.

Chapter Three

1. "Pigeon-Holing the Modern Novel," *London Mercury*, XXXIII (December, 1935), 159–64. O'Faolain lists his objections to Naturalism, "The Proletarian Novel," *London Mercury*, XXXV (April, 1937), 584.

2. "The Proletarian Novel," pp. 583–89.

3. "Plea for a New Type of Novel," *Virginia Quarterly Review*, X (April, 1934), 199.

4. O'Faolain's review of Siegfried Sassoon's study of *Meredith*, *Britain Today*, No. 151 (November, 1948), p. 44.

5. Nichols, p. 27.

6. Richard Diers, "On Writing: An Interview with Sean O'Faolain," *Mademoiselle*, LVI (March, 1963), 151, 209–15.

7. The influence of the Irish Realist Daniel Corkery must also be mentioned. Frank O'Connor notes that he and O'Faolain have developed their fiction from the Russians and that Corkery introduced the Russian element into the modern Irish short story, *The Writer Observed*, ed. Harvey Breit (Cleveland, 1956), p. 260. At a lecture (entitled "Essential Pleasures of Fiction") given at Manhattan College in

New York City on April 28, 1966, O'Faolain, during the question-and-answer period, noted the influence on his work of Daniel Corkery and Turgenev. He asserted that Corkery stressed the value of constant rewriting and revision and forced him to concentrate on what he wanted to say rather than on just how to say it.

8. O'Faolain has written a particularly perceptive essay on Chekhov, *The Short Story*, pp. 76–105.

9. Sean O'Faolain, "Ah, Wisha! The Irish Novel," *Virginia Quarterly Review*, XVIII (Spring, 1941), 268.

10. *The Short Story*, p. 52.

11. O'Faolain has written several articles under the title "The Craft of the Short Story." These articles were originally presented as talks over Radio Eireann. They were rewritten for *The Bell* and appeared in the following issue: VII (January, 1944), 337–44; (February, 1944), 403–10; (March, 1944), 529–36; VIII (April, 1944), 46–54; (July, 1944), 306–14. In addition to his book *The Short Story*, O'Faolain is the editor of *Short Stories: A Study in Pleasure* (Boston, 1961) which considers why and how good stories give various kinds of pleasure and enjoyment.

12. Nichols, p. 26.

13. "The Craft of the Short Story," *The Bell*, VIII (April, 1944), 47–48.

14. Nichols, p. 27.

15. "The Craft of the Short Story," *The Bell*, VII (January, 1944), 340.

16. *Ibid.*, 341.

17. *Ibid.*, 344.

18. *Ibid.* (February, 1944), 405.

19. *Ibid.*, 406.

20. *Ibid.*

21. *Ibid.*, 405.

22. *Ibid.*, 409.

23. "The Secret of the Short Story," *UN World*, III (March, 1949), 38.

24. "The Craft of the Short Story," *The Bell*, VII (February, 1944), 405.

25. "Are You Writing a Short Story?" *The Listener*, LIX (February 13, 1958), 282–83.

26. "The Craft of the Short Story," *The Bell*, VIII (July, 1944), 313.

27. *Ibid.*, 313–14.

28. *The Short Story*, p. 81.

29. "New Writers," *The Bell*, I (February, 1941), 61.

30. Diers, p. 209.

31. *The Short Story*, p. ix.

32. *Ibid.*, p. 170. O'Faolain equates genius with the literary personality of an author. By personality O'Faolain means the power of the author's own character which is developed by his experiences and his subjective, effectively individual interpretation of life.

33. *The Finest Stories*, p. 94.

34. *Ibid.*, p. x.

35. Many Irish seminarians at the famous Maynooth College were trained there by French Jansenist priests who had come to Ireland.

36. *The Finest Stories*, p. 97.

37. *Ibid.*, p. 99.

38. This theme has affinities with the conclusion used in "The Patriot."

39. *Ibid.*, pp. ix–x.

40. "Up the Bare Stairs" and "The Fur Coat" are omitted in the European edition.

41. *The Finest Stories*, p. 204.

42. *Cf. Vive Moi!*, pp. 136–37, 140–41.

43. *Ibid.*, pp. 142–43.

44. *The Finest Stories*, p. 300.

45. Robert H. Hopkins, "The Pastoral Mode of Sean O'Faolain's 'The Silence of the Valley,'" *Studies in Short Fiction*, I (Winter, 1964), 93.

46. *Ibid.*, 94–95.

47. From Yeats' "The Pity of Love."

48. *The Finest Stories*, p. 250.

49. *Ibid.*, p. 251.

50. O'Faolain discusses the origins of this story in *Vive Moi!*, pp. 119–20.

Chapter Four

1. *The Bell* paid its writers well during the period when markets in Britain and the United States were severely limited. "Dare We Suppress That Irish Voice?" *The Bell*, III (December, 1941), 173.

2. This subtitle was dropped after the January, 1941, issue, but it perfectly epitomizes *The Bell's* content. Curiously, the subtitle is used in the May, 1943, issue.

3. "This Is Your Magazine," *The Bell*, I (October, 1940), 5–9.

4. *Ibid.*, 6.

5. Peadar O'Donnell, "Signing On," *The Bell*, XII (April, 1946), 5–7.

6. Vivian Mercier, "The Fourth Estate: Verdict on The Bell," *The Bell*, X (May, 1945), 159.

7. "Answer to a Criticism," *The Bell*, I (December, 1940), 6.

8. "Standards and Taste," *The Bell*, II (June, 1941), 10–11.

9. Mercier, 157.

10. At first O'Faolain remarked that censorship was "easy to forgive," "1916–1941: Tradition and Creation," *The Bell*, II (April, 1941), 8. Frank O'Connor opposed this view, "Public Opinion—The Stone Dolls," *The Bell*, II (June, 1941), 65–67, and starting in this issue O'Faolain began to express a distaste for censorship, "Standards and Taste," 7–8. See also "Our Nasty Novelists," *The Bell*, II (August, 1941), 9. Some attempts were made in *The Bell* to defend censorship, notably in an article by Monk Gibbon, "In Defence of Censorship," *The Bell*, IX (January, 1945), 313–22. This essay drew several replies critical of Gibbon's position. Among the respondents in this controversy were George Bernard Shaw and Sean O'Casey, "Censorship," *The Bell*, IX (February, 1945), 395–409.

11. Officially called the Censorship of Publications Act and introduced in 1929.

12. "Fifty Years of Irish Literature," *The Bell*, III (February, 1942), 333.

13. Actually O'Faolain is relatively mild in discussing clerical control; cf. David Krause, *Sean O'Casey: The Man and His Work* (New York, 1962), pp. 353–57. O'Faolain's own religious views are perhaps closest to those expressed by the Irish dramatist Paul Vincent Carroll: "In religion, I cling from conviction to Catholicism, but God save me from its administrators!" *Twentieth Century Authors*, ed. Stanley Kunitz (New York, 1942), I, 254. O'Faolain describes his return to the sacraments of the Catholic Church in *A Summer in Italy*, pp. 167–77. *Cf.* also *An Autumn in Italy* (New York, 1953), pp. 27, 37.

Stephen Ryan feels that Irish writers tend to be less than fair to the clergy, "Ireland and Its Writers," *The Catholic World*, CXCII (December, 1960), 149–55. Ryan notes that Irish writers who are anti-clerical tend not to be anti-Catholic. Walter O'Hearn is unsympathetic to O'Faolain's criticism of the clergy, "The Irish Character," *Commonweal*, LI (October 28, 1949), 64–67. On the other hand, the views of Austin Clarke show the effect of narrow clerical domination, Richard J. Loftis, "Austin Clarke: Ireland of the Black Church," *Nationalism in Modern Anglo-Irish Poetry* (Madison and Milwaukee, Wisconsin, 1964), pp. 258–77. O'Faolain was bitterly attacked for his "Love Among the Irish," *Life*, XXXIV (March 16, 1953), 140–42, 44, 46, 49–50, 52, 54. See, for example, Rev. John Schultz's denunciation, "Police Told Two Foes Sabotage Church," *The New York Times*, April 20, 1953, p. 31. See also Peadar O'Donnell, "The *Irish Press* and O'Faolain," *The Bell*, XVIII (Summer, 1953), 5–7.

14. "Fifty Years of Irish Literature," 332.

15. *Ibid.*

16. "Ulster," *The Bell*, II (July, 1941), 9.

17. *Ibid.*

18. "The Stuffed-Shirts," *The Bell*, VI (June, 1943), 181.

19. "The Gaelic League," *The Bell*, IV (May, 1942), 77.

20. *Ibid.*, 80–81; "Gaelic—The Truth," *The Bell*, V (February, 1943), 335–40.

21. "The Gaelic League," *The Bell*, IV (May, 1942), 83; "That Typical Irishman," *The Bell*, V (November, 1942), 78–79.

22. *Ibid.*, (May, 1942), 84.

23. "1916–1941: Tradition and Creation," 6.

24. "The Stuffed-Shirts," 182; *cf.* "Beginnings and Blind Alleys," *The Bell*, III (October, 1941), 3–5.

25. "Attitudes," *The Bell*, II (September, 1941), 9.

26. "The Stuffed-Shirts," 188.

27. *Ibid.*, 191–92.

28. "Toryism in Trinity," *The Bell*, VIII (June, 1944), 195.

29. "Past Tense," *The Bell*, VII (December, 1943), 190.

30. *Ibid.*, 191.

31. "All Things Considered," *The Bell*, XI (November, 1945), 649. *The Bell* eventually conducted a survey among its readers to select the twelve best literary works which would help a visitor in Ireland understand what he saw. Correspondent Stewart Hill recommended, as one of his choices, his own selection of O'Faolain's *Bell* editorials during the years 1944–45, to be entitled "Without Fear or Favour," *The Bell*, XII (May, 1946), 177.

32. "One World," *The Bell*, IX (October, 1944), 3. O'Faolain's series of "One World" editorials are enlightening in helping outsiders understand Irish World War II neutrality and tracing it to the centuries-old antagonism toward Great Britain, Cyril Connolly offers some perceptive remarks on the England-Ireland question and Irish neutrality, "Comment," *Horizon*, V (January, 1942), 3–11.

33. "All Things Considered," 649.

34. "The Price of Peace," *The Bell*, X (July, 1945), 288.

35. "Signing Off," *The Bell*, XII (April, 1946), 1.

36. "Auto-antiamericanism," *The Bell*, XVI (March, 1951), 7–18.

37. *Ibid.*, 10.

38. *Ibid.*, 12–13. O'Faolain considers in detail the land reform movement in Italy in *An Autumn in Italy*, pp. 172–200, 203–7; at the same time, O'Faolain offers some interesting comments about Communism. In *Authors Take Sides on the Spanish War* (London, 1937), O'Faolain, who castigates both Communism and Fascism, declares that an artist should be an individualist.

39. *Ibid.*, 18.

40. "Auto-antiamericanism: Four Comments," *The Bell*, XVII (May, 1951), 8–28. O'Faolain's answer appeared in the June issue of *The Bell*, 57–59.

41. Even Donat O'Donnell acknowledges O'Faolain's overall efforts to stimulate and improve intellectual matters in Irish life, *Maria Cross*, pp. 113–14.

42. *The Bell* was not without faults. Some of its articles and stories were of an inferior quality; some of its materials would be of interest only to those who were intimately concerned with Irish life, and its book reviews and theater reviewing were erratic and usually below the standards upheld by other parts of the journal. Vivian Mercier and Donat O'Donnell have commented on *The Bell's* characteristics, *cf. The Bell*, X (May, 1945), 156–67. See also "Verdict on *The Bell*, No. 2," *The Bell*, X (August, 1945), 431–37.

43. Kelleher, "Sean O'Faolain," 68.

Chapter Five

1. *The Finest Stories*, p. xi.
2. *I Remember! I Remember!* (Boston, 1961), p. 11.
3. *Ibid.*, p. 52.
4. *Ibid.*, p. 65.
5. *Ibid.*, p. 231.
6. *Ibid.*, p. 229.

Chapter Six

1. "The Case of Sean O'Casey," *Commonweal*, XXII (October 11, 1935), 577–78.

2. "The Emancipation of Irish Writers," *Yale Review*, NSXXIII (March, 1934), 497.

3. O'Faolain and *The Bell* are concerned not with the language "of politics or insular nationalism, but of civilisation," *The Bell*, IV (May, 1942), 81.

4. "Ireland After Yeats," 47.

5. "Fifty Years of Irish Writing," 96. O'Faolain may be overly confident about the "improved" climate in this area. The recent banning of books by Edna O'Brien, one of the most talented of the younger Irish writers, is not conducive to optimism.

6. O'Faolain's early book on DeValera was very laudatory, *The Life Story of Eamon DeValera* (Dublin and Cork, 1933). O'Faolain later called this book "arrant tripe." He wrote a more balanced account in *DeValera* (Harmondsworth, England, 1939). On several occasions while writing for *The Bell*, O'Faolain was highly critical of DeValera; see especially "Eamon DeValera," *The Bell*, X (April, 1945), 1–18,

and "Principles and Propaganda: M. J. MacManus Writes in Defence of Eamon DeValera," *The Bell*, X (June, 1945), 189–205.

7. "Gaelic—The Truth," 340.

8. "Literary Provincialism," *Commonweal*, XVII (December 21, 1932), 214–15.

9. See "The Gamut of Irish Fiction," 19.

10. Bates, pp. 34–35.

11. "The Secret of the Short Story," 38.

12. *The Short Story*, p. 104.

13. *Ibid.*, p. 90.

14. *Ibid.*, p. 84.

15. "The Emancipation of Irish Writers," 497.

16. *The Irish: A Character Study* (New York, 1949), p. 176.

17. *Ibid.* For some pertinent comments on his writing, see *Vive Moi!*, pp. 224–27, 246–47, 365–68.

18. "The Emancipation of Irish Writers," 497.

19. O'Connor, "The Future of Irish Literature," 60.

20. See also *Vive Moi!*, pp. 321–32.

21. "Revamping Ireland," *Commonweal*, XXII (August 30, 1935), 417–18.

22. *The Man Who Invented Sin and Other Stories* (New York, 1948), p. 124.

23. William Saroyan makes the same point, "The Unholy Word," *The Bell*, XV (October, 1947), 35–36.

24. *Come Back to Erin*, p. 153.

25. "Romance and Realism," *The Bell*, X (August, 1945), 382.

26. James T. Farrell, "A Harvest of O'Faolain," *New Republic*, CXXXVI (June 17, 1957), 19–20.

27. Horace Gregory, "Imaginative Tales," *Saturday Review*, XL (May 25, 1957), 15.

28. *The Finest Stories*, p. xi.

29. *Ibid.* O'Faolain possesses an extraordinarily deep love for the Irish people. See, for example, "Love Among the Irish," 157. Yeats' line "The love I lived, the dream I knew" would be an apt summation of O'Faolain's overall attitude toward Erin.

30. *The Short Story*, pp. 102–4.

Selected Bibliography

PRIMARY SOURCES

1. Books

(Both the British and American first editions are recorded whenever a particular book was published in both countries.)

Midsummer Night Madness and Other Stories. London: Jonathan Cape, 1932; New York: Viking, 1932.

The Life Story of Eamon DeValera. Dublin and Cork: Talbot Press, 1933.

A Nest of Simple Folk. London: Jonathan Cape, 1933; New York: Viking, 1934.

Constance Markievicz; or The Average Revolutionary. London: Jonathan Cape, 1934.

There's a Birdie in the Cage. London: Grayson and Grayson, 1935. This novelette was later included in *A Purse of Coppers.*

Bird Alone. London: Jonathan Cape, 1936; New York: Viking, 1936.

The Born Genius. Detroit: Schuman, 1936. This story, almost a novelette, was later published in *A Purse of Coppers,* and also in *The Finest Stories* (1957) and *Stories of* . . . (1958) volumes.

A Purse of Coppers. London: Jonathan Cape, 1937; New York: Viking, 1938.

King of the Beggars: A Life of Daniel O'Connell. London: Thomas Nelson and Sons, 1938; New York: Viking, 1938. An abridged version of this book was published in Dublin: Parkside Press, 1945.

She Had to Do Something. London: Jonathan Cape, 1938.

DeValera. Harmondsworth, England: Penguin, 1939. A rewritten, thoroughly revised, and enlarged version of the 1933 biography.

An Irish Journey. London: Longmans Green, 1940.

Come Back to Erin. London: Jonathan Cape, 1940; New York: Viking, 1940.

The Great O'Neill: A Biography of Hugh O'Neill, Earl of Tyrone,

1550–1616. London: Longmans Green, 1942; New York: Duell, Sloan and Pearce, 1942.

The Story of Ireland. London: Collins, 1943.

Teresa and Other Stories. London: Jonathan Cape, 1947. *The Man Who Invented Sin and Other Stories*. New York: Devin-Adair, 1948. This Devin-Adair edition is the same as the *Teresa and Other Stories* volume except that two additional stories—"Up the Bare Stairs" and "The Fur Coat"—are added to the American collection.

The Irish: A Character Study. West Drayton, England: Penguin, 1947; New York: Devin-Adair, 1949.

The Short Story. London: Collins, 1948; New York: Devin-Adair, 1951.

A Summer in Italy. London: Eyre and Spottiswoode, 1949; New York: Devin-Adair, 1950.

Newman's Way. London: Longmans Green, 1952; *Newman's Way: The Odyssey of John Henry Newman*. New York: Devin-Adair, 1952.

South to Sicily. London: Collins, 1953. Published in the United States under the title *An Autumn in Italy*. New York: Devin-Adair, 1953.

The Vanishing Hero. London: Eyre and Spottiswoode, 1956; Boston: Little, Brown, 1957.

The Finest Stories of Sean O'Faolain. Boston: Little, Brown, 1957; *The Stories of Sean O'Faolain*. London: Robert Hart-Davis, 1958.

Vive Moi! Boston: Little, Brown, 1964; London: Rupert Hart-Davis, 1965.

The Heat of the Sun. Boston: Little, Brown, 1966; London: Rupert Hart-Davis, 1966.

2. Edited Works

Lyrics and Satires from Tom Moore. Dublin: Cuala Press, 1929.

Autobiography of Wolfe Tone (an abridged edition. London: Thomas Nelson and Sons, 1937.

The Silver Branch. London: Jonathan Cape, 1938; New York: Viking, 1938.

Adventures of Handy Andy [by Samuel Lover]. Dublin: Parkside Press, 1945.

Short Stories: A Study in Pleasure. London: Rupert Hart-Davis, 1958; Boston, Little, Brown, 1961.

3. Articles by O'Faolain

"Ah, Wisha! The Irish Novel," *Virginia Quarterly Review*, XVII (Spring, 1941), 265–74. O'Faolain maintains that modern Irish realistic novelists are most influenced by Russian authors, especially by Chekhov. The Irish novelist must go beyond Naturalism;

life is much deeper and more complex than Naturalism realizes. Irish writers have an ambivalent attitude toward the people of their country; the writers admire many qualities of the people, but they also see the shortcomings, and the authors must make judgments on such weaknesses.

"Are You Writing a Short Story?" *The Listener,* LIX (February 13, 1958), 282–83. O'Faolain declares that each story must have its essential core of illumination. The writer aims not just to present a story, but he seeks to convey the implications and shadings derived from the narrative.

"Being an Irish Writer," *Commonweal,* LVIII (July 10, 1953), 339–41. O'Faolain discusses the problem of writing realistically and frankly about a particular locale. If the writer speaks out truthfully, he arouses the community's anger and bitterness; if he does not reveal the community truthfully, he will do damage to his art and vision. Present-day Irish life is not very inspiring, but it does furnish writing material for the artist who wishes to transcend the strong pull of family and nationalistic emotions and loyalties which would dilute or abolish realism and accuracy. Laments the failure of modern Irish writers to use much comedy. Bitterness has too often overwhelmed the sense of comedy.

"The Case of Sean O'Casey," *Commonweal,* XXII (October 11, 1935), 577–78. O'Faolain understands why O'Casey became an exile, but he feels that the playwright should have remained in Ireland near to everyday life, and then he would have been influenced by the closeness of the people and events around him. Instead of being remote in his later work, he would be in the mainstream of Irish life.

"Dickens and Thackeray," *English Novelists: A Survey of the Novel by Twenty Contemporary Novelists.* Ed. Derek Verschoyle. New York: Harcourt, 1936; pp. 141–51. A discussion with particular emphasis on the deficiencies and strengths of Dickens as a writer, demonstrating how Dickens was a product of his times and noting that contemporary literature which stresses such qualities as subjectivity, the element of revolt and rebellion, and analysis, would find Dickens not to its taste. Of the two writers considered, the modern author can learn more from Thackeray than from Dickens.

"Don Quixote O'Flaherty," *London Mercury,* XXXVII (December, 1937), 170–75. Like Joyce, O'Flaherty searched for ideal beauty and perfection. Modern Irish writers are really searching for the Holy Grail, but Irish life, its restrictions and its people intrude between the writer and his grail search, and, as a result, only partial glimpses of the grail can be obtained.

"The Emancipation of Irish Writers," *Yale Review,* NSXXIII (March,

1934), 485–503. The modern Irish writer can preserve his vision of life at all costs even though he is assailed by nationalistic, religious, and provincial prejudices. He must always seek detachment in the presentation of his material and should aim for universality. Contemporary Irish writing should search for a new path of expression transcending mere Naturalism or hackneyed romanticism. Let the Irish writer move among ordinary people and bring forth beauty.

"The Gamut of Irish Fiction," *Saturday Review of Literature*, XIV (August 1, 1936), 19–20. On occasion British critics state that Irish fiction should give a more glamorous and romantic picture of Irish life. Sometimes Irish writers feel the same way, but when they realistically appraise the life around them, they understand that their previous thoughts were pipedreams. Irish literature must be made out of the lives of the ordinary people, out of town and farm life, etc. Such ingredients are not glamorous; to some degree such material is not conducive to artistic stimulus. Nevertheless the Irish writer must struggle against such a notion, against the unsympathetic materials he may find in the life about him. The genuine artist must never be false to the life he beholds.

"Getting at Which Public?" *Virginia Quarterly Review*, XXIV (Winter, 1948), 90–95. In Britain and in France there are select audiences of readers and critics which demand high artistic standards in the literature they purchase and recommend. These groups establish serious critical reputations, and a writer needs serious literary judgment more than popular success. In America it is difficult to determine which critical groups establish authorial reputations. Popular audiences want escapism or obvious Naturalism. In American fiction a reader finds much sentiment in Naturalism. The Irish writer's elite audience is primarily in England, and this demanding audience helps one to direct his literary productions to the highest standards. This situation is desirable and productive of better writing.

"Ireland After Yeats," *The Bell*, XVIII (Summer, 1953), 37–48. A brilliant exposition of the state of Irish writing in recent years. Pinpoints all of the aspects of modern Irish life which cripple and scar most serious writers. Condemns censorship, witch-hunting, complacency, materialism, and extreme authoritarianism. Urges the young Irish writers to be individualists and iconoclasts.

"The Irish and the Latins," *Commonweal*, LVII (March 13, 1953), 571–73. Italy possesses a strong appeal for an Irishman. The Italian attitude toward sex is so much more happy than the Irish attitude. Yet the corruption, indifference to poverty, etc., present in Southern Italy and Sicily are distressing as are some other features of Italian life; consequently, Italy becomes both a delight and a warning for the Irish.

"Irish Letters: To-Day and To-Morrow," *The Fortnightly*, CXLIV (September, 1935), 369–71. Irish writers who lived through the Troubles and the Civil War are uprooted, and this makes a focus for writing difficult. O'Faolain believes that realism is going to decline and that there will be a return to poetry, fantasy, and romance. Only in his own individual self can the modern Irish writer find certitude.

"Literary Provincialism," *Commonweal*, XVII (December 21, 1932), 214–15. O'Faolain discusses the difficulties of being a serious writer in the hostile and provincial environment of Ireland. Since the serious Irish writer is ignored or scorned by most of his own people, he tends to write of the past or to write falsely and sentimentally of Irish life, or else this situation drives the writer to exile. Spiritual exile of the writer causes him to produce inaccurate writing.

"Look Homeward, Angel," *The Impact of America on European Culture*. Boston: Beacon Press, 1951; pp. 37–47. Does not believe that the emigrant American really desires to Americanize Europe. The emigrant looks upon the old country in an unintellectual and sentimental fashion, emphasizing feeling rather than thought. Finds a bond of traditionalism and conservatism between America and the old countries of Europe.

"Love Among the Irish," *Life*, XXXIV (March 16, 1953), 140–42, 144, 146, 149–50, 152, 154. Discusses the sharp decline in Ireland's population and castigates customs which produce late marriages or bachelorhood and spinster existences. Condemns puritanism, unjust clerical oppression, and censorship since these conditions foster unhealthy notions about sex and marriage.

"The Modern Novel: A Catholic Point of View," *Virginia Quarterly Review*, XI (July, 1935), 339–51. O'Faolain argues that a Catholic novelist understands the cosmic significance of man's life and this understanding gives such a novelist a deeper insight into life. But Catholic novelists tend to slant their vision and to avoid a realistic presentation of evil. Ideal novels should present a deep and many-sided awareness of life, considering both life and eternity in their complexity. Worthy novelists should not shy away from a credible depiction of evil.

"Pigeon-Holing the Modern Novel," *London Mercury*, XXXIII (December, 1935), 159–64. O'Faolain censures fiction written by escapists, romantics, and Naturalists because they do not see life as it actually is. O'Faolain supports the kind of traditional novel which judges past, present, and future clearly and honestly.

"Plea for a New Type of Novel," *Virginia Quarterly Review*, X (April, 1934), 189–99. Attacks Naturalism in fiction because it stifles variety and confines the novel to a mere social document. More important effects should be sought than the mere presentation of reality. Hopes for a type of novel which would allow its characters to reach a timelessness. Such a novel would stress the poetry and mystery of life and carry far beyond the limited boundaries of ordinary photography.

"The Proletarian Novel," *London Mercury*, XXXV (April, 1937), 583–589. Communist writers, O'Faolain points out, have wisely stressed important environmental and community aspects of life, but a genuine artist must go beyond ordinary socialistic concerns and seek the elements of exaltation, variety, and mystery found in life.

"Revamping Ireland," *Commonweal*, XXII (August 30, 1935), 417–18. Contains some comments on Irish economic difficulties and the shrewd observation that a basic racial fault of the Irish people and their writers is to overdevelop sensibility and underdevelop the intellect.

"The Secret of the Short Story," *UN World*, III (March, 1949), 37–38. Praises the short stories of the nineteenth-century Russian writers; they demonstrated fine intelligence, realism, mood, and style. They fulfilled the essential function of the writer, that is, to ask questions. Asserts that French authors have excelled in short-story writing because they possessed the two most important qualities necessary for this art: emotional perception and reaction, and the ability to reach the essential core or truth of a situation.

"Written Speech," *Commonweal*, XXVII (November 5, 1937), 35–36. Notes the great variety of influences helping to give Irish prose its special flavor and picturesqueness. This unique flavor rests not only in word choice and sentence structure but also in the rhythm of good Irish speech.

SECONDARY SOURCES

Bates, H. E. *The Modern Short Story*. Boston: The Writer, Inc., 1941. Claims that O'Faolain by nature was a poet but was prevented from becoming an ordinary lyricist by the difficult conditions prevailing in Ireland. Stresses O'Faolain's ability to convey Irish atmosphere and to present feminine beauty effectively.

Bowen, Elizabeth. "Weeping Earl." *Collected Impressions*. London: Longmans Green, 1950. Discerning review of O'Faolain's biography *The Great O'Neill*. Praises the book for its art, poetic perception, and objectivity; records that the genius of a creative writer is evident in this biography.

Braybrooke, Neville. "Sean O'Faolain: A Study," *The Dublin Maga-*

zine, XXXI (April–June, 1955), 22–27; also published in *Renascence,* VIII (Winter, 1955), 59–63. Notes that the characters who struggle against State, Church, and sexual restrictions are applauded by O'Faolain. But the characters find it impossible to shed completely the lure and conditioning of religion. O'Faolain explores the problem of nationalism and its relation to Catholicism, the questions of progress and status quo, orthodoxy, and emancipation. Eden, the Fall, and Gethsemane become symbolic concerns of O'Faolain's art.

Cantwell, Robert. "Poet of the Irish Revolution," *New Republic,* LXXVII (January 24, 1934), 313–14. Discussion of O'Faolain's first two books of fiction. Censures those critics who praise O'Faolain for incidental qualities, e.g., his ability to create atmosphere. These critics miss the major point about O'Faolain's writing; namely, that he is obsessed with the Irish Revolution.

Cowley, Malcolm. "Yeats and O'Faolain," *New Republic,* XCVIII (February 15, 1939), 49–50. Cowley objects to O'Faolain's literary criticism because he feels that O'Faolain is too preoccupied with his own style when he is supposed to be analyzing the work of another writer. Cowley admires O'Faolain's novels and short stories but finds his criticism too abstract.

Diers, Richard. "On Writing: An Interview with Sean O'Faolain," *Mademoiselle,* LVI (March, 1963), 151, 209–15. O'Faolain answers questions about his writing career. His stories generally originate in character. He often destroys stories he has written, writes and rewrites constantly so that the process of composition is a painstaking pleasure.

Doyle, Paul A. "Sean O'Faolain and *The Bell,*" *Erin-Ireland,* I (Fall, 1966), 58–62. A study of O'Faolain's association with *The Bell* and the influence of his views on intellectual life in Ireland.

————. "Vive Moi!" *Best Sellers,* XXIV (October 1, 1964), 246–47. A review-article about O'Faolain's autobiography which points out the relationship between some of O'Faolain's stories and the personal experiences and reactions in his own life.

Farrell, James T. "A Harvest of O'Faolain," *New Republic,* CXXXVI (June 17, 1957), 19–20. Highly favorable commentary on *The Finest Stories* collection. Praises O'Faolain's style, his character portrayals and insights, and his balance in presenting both tragic and comic elements. Although O'Faolain's Irishness is pervasive, he is not parochial.

Finn, James. "High Standards and High Achievements," *Commonweal,* LXVI (July 26, 1957), 428–29. An analysis of the fiction collected in *The Finest Stories of Sean O'Faolain.* Praises O'Faolain for successfully communicating the special emphasis given to such

subjects as drinking and religion in Ireland. O'Faolain's materials
are raised from ordinariness and transient pleasure by his artistic
ability and the demanding standards he brings to his craft.

Gregory, Horace. "Imaginative Tales," *Saturday Review*, XL (May 25,
1957), 15–16. A review-article considering *The Finest Stories*
which contains, according to Gregory, "some of the best short
stories of the twentieth century." O'Faolain deals with universal
themes and revelations. O'Faolain is complimented for his quiet-
ness and for his avoidance of false emotion.

Halton, Thomas. "In the Irish Blood," *Catholic World*, CLXXXVII
(July, 1958), 252–56. An unsympathetic portrait of O'Faolain
and O'Connor by a priest critic who lives in Eire. Despite a
subdued attempt to express some appreciation, Halton is irked
by O'Faolain's anti-clericalism and his criticism of Irish foibles
and character deficiencies.

Hopkins, Robert H. "The Pastoral Mode of Sean O'Faolain's 'The
Silence of the Valley,'" *Studies in Short Fiction*, I (Winter,
1964), 93–98. This story is seen to reflect the conflicts between
primitivism and progress. The old Gaelic folk-world is being
destroyed by modernity, which brings a loss of innocence, contentment, and pastoral balance.

Kelleher, John V. "Loneliness Is the Key," *The New York Times Book
Review*, May 12, 1957, Sect. 7, pp. 5, 23. A long review-article
of *The Finest Stories*. Stressing O'Faolain's sympathetic and
understanding approach to his characters and subject matter,
Kelleher maintains that the theme of loneliness pervades the
stories and presents some shrewd comments on O'Faolain's style
which he finds to be a blending of realism and romantic sensibility.

————. "Sean O'Faolain," *The Atlantic*, CXCIX (May, 1957), 67–69.
Finds that O'Faolain is Ireland's most versatile and distinguished
present-day writer and the most romantic in viewpoint of any
twentieth century Irish author. This romanticism is balanced by
a keen, realistic intelligence, and the reconciliation between these
two opposites, while very difficult, brings to his best stories artistic
maturity and significance.

Kiely, Benedict. *Modern Irish Fiction—A Critique*. Dublin: Golden
Eagle Books, 1950; pp. 18–20, 85–87, 113–21, 142–43. Empha-
sizes the theme of exile found in O'Faolain's work; notes O'Faolain's interest in contemplative and nostalgic moments. Insists that
many Irish have not appreciated the greatness of O'Faolain's
fiction because they associate him with the fight against censorship
and other reforms which they oppose.

Lynch, Patrick. "O'Faolain's Way," *The Bell*, XVIII (March, 1953),
628–31. A review-article about *Newman's Way* which enthusias-

tically praises this biography because it so clearly and thoroughly explains the development of Newman's intellectual concepts. This work is superior to O'Faolain's other biographies because in his other studies he imposed subjective and partly mystical theories on his topics. In making this assertion Lynch uncritically accepts one of Donat O'Donnell's hypotheses.

Nichols, Lewis. "Talk with Mr. O'Faolain," *The New York Times Book Review*, May 12, 1957, Sect. 7, pp. 26–27. An interview in which O'Faolain talks of the great amount of revision and aging necessary for producing really effective short stories. Praises the work of Chekhov and explains that his own stories fit into the Russian tradition.

O'Connor, Frank. "The Future of Irish Literature," *Horizon*, V (January, 1942), 55–63. O'Connor feels that O'Faolain's novels are severely hampered by the provincial and deadening nature of his subject matter. O'Faolain is too oppressed by Irish problems and disturbed and anguished by conditions to write expansive art. Suggests that O'Faolain needs to use comedy and satire to make his novels more vital and robust.

O'Donnell, Donat. "The Parnellism of Sean O'Faolain." *Maria Cross*. New York: Oxford University Press, 1952; pp. 95–115. O'Donnell uses the word parnellism to mean freedom and rebellion from harsh State, Church, and sexual prohibitions. O'Faolain stresses the conflict between Catholicism and a clear-cut and liberal Irish spirit; he is torn between his love of the country and its people and his hatred of the frightful puritanism, paternalism, and censorship characteristic of Eire.

O'Hearn, Walter. "The Irish Character," *Commonweal*, LI (October 28, 1949), 64–67. A generally sympathetic discussion of O'Faolain's book *The Irish: A Character Study;* however, O'Hearn deplores O'Faolain's desire to reduce the power of the clergy in Irish life and have their influence replaced by that of the Irish intellectuals.

Pritchett, V. S. "O'Faolain's Troubles," *New Statesman*, LXX (August 13, 1965), 219–20. A feature review of *Vive Moi!* acknowledging O'Faolain as "one of the outstanding short-story writers and men of letters of his generation." Notes the realist under the veneer of romanticism, "the artist strict about form," and the fact that O'Faolain as a journalist and critic has "tried to educate the public moral sense of Irish readers."

Rago, Henry. "How to be a Foreigner," *Commonweal*, LIX (October 9, 1953), 15–17. Worthwhile travel books should possess compassion, integrity, and thorough observation. The traveler should retain his foreign qualities, yet at the same time identify himself closely with the country visited. O'Faolain's two travel books about Italy fulfill these requirements; they are unsurpassed among contemporary accounts of Italy.

Saroyan, William. "The Unholy Word," *The Bell*, XV (October, 1947), 33–37. A review-article of *Teresa and Other Stories* in which Saroyan records his delight with these tales but wonders if they are not too calm and too understanding.

"Talk with the Author," *Newsweek*, LIX (January 8, 1962), 67. O'Faolain discusses Americans and American writing. Believes that Americans are too conservative, optimistic, and deluded by the notion that they are free. Praises Cheever, Cozzens, Updike, and O'Hara for attempting to relate the individual to the society of which he is a part. In general, American authors, like Irish writers, do not have the cold, dispassionate brain to join with acute sensibility.

Tenenbaum, Louis. "Two Views of the Modern Italian: D. H. Lawrence and Sean O'Faolain," *Italica*, XXXVII (June, 1960), 118–25. Contrasts both writers' impressions of Italy. Lawrence insists that the Italians have allowed their senses to dominate their lives. O'Faolain asserts that the Italians have united the needs of the flesh and the spirit. Lawrence knows Italy through intuition while O'Faolain knows it through the intellect. Their differing attitudes about Italy can be explained by the disparity between their cultural and moral backgrounds.

Index